ZHIRINOVSKY

Also by Vladimir Solovyov and Elena Klepikova

YURI ANDROPOV: A SECRET PASSAGE INTO THE KREMLIN

BEHIND THE HIGH KREMLIN WALLS

BORIS YELTSIN: A POLITICAL BIOGRAPHY

By Vladimir Solovyov (in Russian)

A NOVEL WITH EPIGRAPHS

OPERATION MAUSOLEUM

THE GHOST WHO IS BEATING HIS HEAD AGAINST A WALL

ZHIRINOVSKY

RUSSIAN FASCISM AND THE MAKING OF A DICTATOR

*Vladimir Solovyov
and Elena Klepikova*

TRANSLATED
by Catherine A. Fitzpatrick
IN COLLABORATION WITH THE AUTHORS

 Addison-Wesley Publishing Company

*Reading, Massachusetts   Menlo Park, California   New York
Don Mills, Ontario   Wokingham, England   Amsterdam   Bonn
Sydney   Singapore   Tokyo   Madrid   San Juan
Paris   Seoul   Milan   Mexico City   Taipei*

Many of the designations used by manufacturers and sellers to distinguish their products are claimed as trademarks. Where those designations appear in this book and Addison-Wesley was aware of a trademark claim, the designations have been printed in initial capital letters.

Library of Congress Cataloging-in-Publication Data

Solov'ev, Vladimir.
    Zhirinovsky : Russian fascism and the making of a dictator / Vladimir Solovyov and Elena Klepikova ; translated from the Russian by Catherine A. Fitzpatrick.
      p.   cm.
    Includes bibliographical references and index.
    ISBN 0-201-40948-8
    1. Zhirinovskiĭ, Vladimir, 1946– .   2. Politicians—Russia (Federation)—Biography.   3. Russia (Federation)—Politics and government—1991– 4. Soviet Union—Politics and government—1985–1991. I. Klepikova, Elena. II. Title.
DK510.766.Z48S65   1995
947.086'092—dc20
[B]
                              94-47148
                              CIP

Cover design by Jean Seal
Text design by Ruth Kolbert
Set in 11-point New Baskerville by Weimer Graphics, Inc.

1 2 3 4 5 6 7 8 9-MA-98979695
First printing, June 1995

CONTENTS

To Eugene Solovyov

PREFACE

PANDORA'S BOX

Of all our books, this is perhaps the most crucial. In contrast to our previous subjects—Andropov, Gorbachev, and Yeltsin—the subject of this book holds no high office, although his fame is worldwide and his influence on the course of events in Russia is enormous. Yet he has managed to impose his vision on an entire nation that even after the collapse of the Soviet empire still possesses enormous military might. Perhaps he could be ignored as a jester and a buffoon, were it not for his political triumph in the December 1993 parliamentary elections and the subsequent realization of his super-patriotic slogans by Yeltsin's Kremlin team. It would be hard to imagine, for example, the Kremlin undertaking its barbarous military adventure in Chechnya in the winter of 1994/95 without Zhirinovsky's victory in these elections the year before. If he is fantasizing his own victory in the next presidential elections, we cannot ignore the public opinion polls in his favor.

In writing about Zhirinovsky, we were unexpectedly faced with the task of sketching a portrait—even if only in profile—of the nation prepared to entrust its fate to him. A nation, like an individual, is defined not so much by statistical data as by its own sense of itself, which is not always objective and does not entirely correspond with reality. Which is more wounding now to Russians: the lowering of their standard of living, or the fall of the empire and the loss of the status of superpower? Perhaps the nation is staking its claims on this man full of complexes because it is full of them itself?

The purpose of our book is to analyze the phenomenon hidden behind the notion of the "Zhirinovsky phenomenon," which is not only Zhirinovsky himself but his electorate, and the powerful connection between them. While we cannot know in advance what new features the Zhirinovsky phenomenon will acquire, nor do we intend to make political predictions, it is enough that we are trying to describe, as J. B. Priestly said, "a bullet in flight." The present too quickly becomes the past and slips away into history—such is the dynamic of current Russian life. How quickly Gorbachev became a historical figure; and now Yeltsin is already looking like a political anachronism, out of step with the times. After several years of the West's (primarily America's) almost complete influence over the course of events in Gorbachev's and Yeltsin's Russia, a time of unpredictability and disorder has once again come. As during the cold war, the West is an observer of what is now a former superpower, but one nonetheless still bristling with nuclear warheads. A wounded beast, as is known, is more dangerous than a healthy one.

One thing we have become convinced of fairly quickly: Zhirinovsky cannot be understood only through comparison. His ideas and behavior are often reminiscent of Hitler, and Russia today is like Weimar Germany, but this analogy leads us away from the object (or rather objects) of our investigation. What kind of "Russian Hitler" is he when he is Zhirinovsky—he has already staked out a place in politics, and perhaps in history, that is unique.

There is a joke about two psychotics screaming at each other in the middle of Deribasovskaya Street, Odessa's main pedestrian boulevard. "I'm Napoleon, I'm Napoleon!" one kept yelling. "I'm Zhirinovsky. I'm Zhirinovsky!" the other screamed back. Soon the police arrived and took Napoleon to a psychiatric hospital. The other, more disoriented man was released. After all, you can't arrest a man for shouting his own name.

This anecdote attests not only to Zhirinovsky's political ego-centrism but also to his sensational fame throughout Russia.

Furthermore, the comparison to Hitler underestimates Zhirinovsky's danger, because if he is to become the leader of Russia in a year or two, he will have at his disposal what Hitler never had—the famous nuclear button he promises to use. There is no greater mistake than underestimating an enemy, even if only a potential one for the time being.

He disassociates himself from analogies and from time to time sues those who compare him to Hitler or call him a fascist. Thus, in the fall of 1994, a Moscow court ruled favorably on his suit and ordered *Izvestia* and former prime minister Gaidar to pay Zhirinovsky one million rubles in damages for the publication in which Gaidar called Zhirinovsky a fascist. He prefers euphemisms, although among his statements are positive and even apologetic characterizations of Hitler. We decided to introduce the word *fascism* into the book's subtitle to imply neither a political label pinned on Zhirinovsky, a person without convictions and principles, by the domestic and foreign press, nor a historical concept connected with a certain time and certain country. There is a difference between the recent participation of postfascists in a right-wing government in the homeland of fascism, nuclear-weapons-free Italy, and neofascists struggling for power in a country with such a mighty nuclear arsenal as Russia. However, there is also a continuity with previous forms of fascism.

"Fascism is a complex phenomenon, multifaceted and, historically speaking, far from extinct," wrote the political historian Ivan Ilyin, in 1948:

> It has healthy and sick aspects, old and new, elements preserving as well as those destroying the state. Therefore in evaluating it, calm and impartiality are needed. . . . Fascism emerged as a reaction to Bolshevism, as a concentration of the state-preservative forces on the right. During the onslaught of leftist chaos and leftist totalitarianism, it was a healthy and inevitable phenomenon. Such a concentration will come again, even in the most democratic states: in the hour of national danger, the healthy forces of the

people will always be concentrated in a conserving and dictatorial direction. So it was in ancient Rome, so it was in the new Europe, and so it will be in the future.

Russia can and should be added to this list, because the barracks socialism of Stalin is undoubtedly the Russian brand of fascism. Now, forty years after the death of the tyrant, the people have freely expressed their will in parliamentary elections in favor of the Liberal Democratic Party of Zhirinovsky, who promises that if he comes to power, he will become a dictator and persecute dissenters, Jews, and other ethnic minorities. He will restore the empire and make a new partitioning of the world (the so-called "last push to the south," Zhirinovsky's geopolitical doctrine). Is this not a paradox, that embryonic Russian democracy is just about to give birth to the next dictatorship? Democracy in Russia is a Pandora's box, and Zhirinovsky is one of the chief misfortunes to be let out.

The *bête noire* of Russian politics, Zhirinovsky could become the same for the world if he is elected president of the country.

Not surprisingly, the last hope of the Moscow democrats is in the Russian people's anti-Semitism. The most popular comic in Russia, Mikhail Zhvanetsky (a Jew himself), said outright that only anti-Semitism could save the country from voting for Zhirinovsky: "I think that anti-Semitism will protect the basic masses from such a tragic mistake." Judging from the 1993 parliamentary elections, however, the anti-Semitism of Russians has been greatly exaggerated. Or else the people prefer the Jew and anti-Semite Zhirinovsky to the Russian non-anti-Semites.

The rapidly changing situation also plays into Zhirinovsky's hands, where unpredictability is the only thing that can be predicted. No matter how difficult it was to imagine the fall of communism in Russia and Eastern Europe and the collapse of the Soviet empire, equally unimaginable was the return of the communists to power in Hungary, Poland, Bulgaria, Lithuania, Ukraine, and Belarus. Only a few years after what seemed to be their final departure from the political stage, they have returned through democratic elections. Local "Zhirinovskys," the new leaders of Ukraine and Belarus, echo Zhirinovsky's slogans about the reintegration of the former Soviet republics into a new union—even if only economic for the time being: "I warn you: out of the ruins of the Soviet Union will arise a new, powerful Russia!" Zhirinovsky's ominous tirade now sounds feasible. Especially in light of Chechnya, which Yeltsin undertook with the prompting and direct support of Zhirinovsky and other extremists in the Parliament. "The 'push to the south' had begun. The first step toward the warm waters of the Indian Ocean has been taken," the *Moskovsky Komsomolets* wrote, parodying Zhirinovsky's slogan. In any event, the "brown factor" can no longer be attributed to Zhirinovsky alone. Yegor Gaidar, former premier and former aide to the once "democratic" Yeltsin, was right in summer 1994 when he warned about the greatest danger of all—"the union of bureaucracy, bourgeoisie, and Nazis." The result of this alliance is the "party of war," which unleashed the conflict in the Caucasus with the aim of throwing a scare into outlying pockets of nationalism and the Moscow opposition, while at the same time bolstering the doddering authority and power of the Kremlin boss. The ensuing paradoxical dilemma has been accurately pinpointed by the liberal economist Nikolai Petrakov thus: "a monarchy with Yeltsin or a republic with Zhirinovsky?"

The "new order" that was established in Europe in the early 1990s to the applause of the West turned out to be fragile and short-lived. Now a new "new order," suspiciously reminiscent of the old one, is coming to take its place. Zhirinovsky must be taken seriously, not only because a nuclear power stands behind him but because he reflects the tendencies of the people. That is in fact the reason for his popularity in confused, desperate Russia, where he is like a storm cloud ready to unload on the country any minute. Much of the population awaits this downpour with hope, like farmers after a long dry spell.

It is not only a question of the demos but of the behind-the-scenes forces that are betting on Zhirinovsky and therefore spending millions—of dollars, not rubles—on his election campaign. Whoever Zhirinovsky's secret sponsors are—whether Iraqi president Saddam Hussein, with whom Zhirinovsky met at the height of the Middle East crisis; ultra-right Germans and Austrians with whom he has close contacts; the KGB, whose ties have dogged Zhirinovsky since his early youth; or Russian millionaires for whom his party is now lobbying—obviously, Zhirinovsky is not acting alone. And in addition to his personal charisma, talent, and energy, a conspiracy of influential forces with a vested interest in his coming to power also exists. Add as well the people in uniform—the army and state security—who overwhelmingly voted for Zhirinovsky in the December 1993 elections, which is why his supporters call him "the virtual commander in chief."

"Vladimir Volfovich is being groomed for the presidency," Alexei Mitrofanov, the foreign minister in Zhirinovsky's shadow cabinet, once blurted while drunk. Mitrofanov has close ties to the nomenklatura, and furthermore is a relative of two former Soviet leaders, Brezhnev and Andropov. "Who's grooming him?" asked Eduard Limonov, another Zhirinovsky associate who soon broke with him (which is how we know about this conversation). "We're grooming him . . . the people who groomed Yeltsin . . . ," explained Mitrofanov.

The creation of this book is the result of a review and analysis of the Russian press and talks with Russians on both sides of the ocean. We were helped in re-creating a psychological portrait of Zhirinovsky by those who know him best—for example, Vladimir Kartsev, former director of Moscow's Mir Press, where Zhirinovsky worked as legal adviser for seven years; Kartsev's account of his former subordinate often seems embellished, however, and does not always tally with parallel testimonies from other acquaintances of Zhirinovsky of that time. Another eyewitness, Vladimir Kozlovsky, attended the Moscow Institute of Oriental Languages at the same time as Zhirinovsky. We are particularly obliged to Kozlovsky because besides giving us information personally, he publishes endless "Zhirinoviana" in *Novoye Russkoye slovo,* the New York Russian-language daily. This is the result not only of his recollections but of his regular talks with his former student acquaintance. Kozlovsky has also graciously provided us with his photographs of Zhirinovsky.

The rest of the photographs are taken from the collection of *Novoye Russkoye slovo,* for which we are grateful to Ludmila Shakov, the editor in chief of that oldest Russian newspaper.

Another New York author, Boris Paramonov, also helped us to assemble materials, and our conversations during walks with him on the current events in our historic and geographic homeland gave us a more subtle understanding.

We were also assisted in our work at various stages by Nikolai Anastasyev, Alexander Mezhirov, Dmitry Radyshevsky, Alexander Trubin (in Moscow), Naci Akkan and Ünal Şengun (in Istanbul), Todd Bludeau, Ilya and Mary Fain, Gregory Polyak, Albert S. Todd, Julia Troll (in New York), and Laura Wolfson (in Philadelphia) who translated the chronology and the footnotes.

Finally, we acknowledge those who directly enabled the writing of this book. First there was our energetic literary agent, Heide Lange of Greenburger Associates. Oh, if only the editors would be as quickly taken with our ideas as was Heide! Although it would be wrong to complain—this is our fourth book to be published in English and in translation in the major European and Asiatic languages (besides our Russian books of prose, for which Heide is still looking for a U.S. publisher). Furthermore, we have been particularly fortunate this time with our editor, Don Fehr of Addison-Wesley, who became interested in the book from a nine-page précis and did much work to adapt the book of two Russian writers on Russian politics for an American audience. And finally, we thank our translator, Catherine Fitzpatrick, who is distinguished for her knowledge of Russian realities.

We are much obliged to everyone. We hope that our joint efforts will not be in vain and that our warning of the dangerous turn of events in Russia will be heeded.

ZHIRINOVSKY CHRONOLOGY

April 25, 1946: In Almaty, the capital of Kazakhstan (then a republic of the USSR, now an independent state), the future leader of the Liberal Democratic Party of Russia, Vladimir Volfovich Zhirinovsky, was born. World War II had ended the year before. According to documents found in Almaty, the authenticity of which Zhirinovsky denies, he was recorded on the birth certificate under the last name Eidelstein, from his father. Volf Isaakovich Eidelstein (1907–1946), a Polish Jew by descent and a lawyer by education, died in an automobile accident the year that Vladimir was born. His mother, Alexandra Pavlovna Zhirinovskaya (1912–1985), née Makarova, was a Russian who did not complete high school. She married Eidelstein when she was five months pregnant, and she had three daughters and two sons from a previous marriage. (Later, sister Lyubov and brother Alexander would work in the Liberal Democratic Party's office as bookkeeper and business manager, respectively). The whole family lived in one room of a communal apartment.

1953: During this year of Stalin's death, Zhirinovsky enters a boys' school. It becomes coeducational the following year, as do all other schools in the country, one of the first signs of the post-Stalin thaw. Volodya's performance in school is below average, but he is active in school affairs. In the lower grades he is elected chairman of the Young Pioneer group; in the higher grades, class Komsomol organizer.

Summer 1964: Khrushchev is overthrown as the result of a palace coup. Zhirinovsky graduates from high school, changes his last name from Eidelstein to Zhirinovsky (his mother's last name), arrives in Moscow, matriculates in the Turkish department at the Institute of Oriental Languages (later renamed the Moscow University Institute of Asian and African Studies). Lives in a dormitory in Lenin Hills, is an A student, active in public affairs (for example, secretary of the class Komsomol organization, secretary of the class trade union organization).

1967: Yuri Andropov is appointed chairman of the KGB to retaliate against dissent and heterodoxy. Zhirinovsky begins, unsuccessfully, his political activity: he writes a letter to the Central Committee of the Communist Party containing a proposal to carry out reforms in agriculture, education, and industry, and gives an outspoken presentation at a student debate titled "Democracy: Theirs and Ours" (that is, in the West and in Russia). As a result Zhirinovsky falls into disgrace, and early the next year he is refused permission to make a monthlong trip to Turkey.

1969: Zhirinovsky undertakes an eight-month internship as an interpreter/translator at Iskenderun Iron and Steel Joint Soviet-Turkish Works. He has high career hopes for this trip, but it ends as a complete fiasco when he is arrested under suspicion of espionage and deported from Turkey. After this he becomes politically unreliable, which prevents him from joining the party, in spite of several attempts, and from making a political or diplomatic career.

1970: Zhirinovsky graduates from college with honors and is drafted into the army, where he serves for two years as an officer at the headquarters of the Transcaucasian Military District.

1971: Zhirinovsky marries a Muscovite, Galina Alexandrovna Lebedeva, whom he met in 1967 at a student youth camp in Pitsunda on the Black Sea. Thanks to his marriage, he can return to Moscow after his army service, where he lives with his wife's parents until 1973, when he, his wife, and his son, Igor, move to a separate cooperative apartment on the outskirts of Moscow.

1972–1975: After his discharge from the army as a reserve captain, Zhirinovsky works for two years at the Soviet Peace Committee (as a foreign liaison); but unable to hold onto the job, he is forced to find employment in the dean's office at the Trade Union Movement Academy (where he is responsible for foreign students). Realizing fully the hopelessness of trying to make a career as a Turkish area studies specialist, given his inability to travel out of the country (after his Turkish disaster), Zhirinovsky enters the evening division of the Moscow University law school and on completion acquires a more promising profession.

1975–1983: Zhirinovsky works as a legal consultant at the Foreign Bar Association, but is forced to leave as a result of conflict with the management.

1983: Zhirinovsky receives an invitation from Israel and plans to emigrate from the USSR, but soon abandons these plans.

1983–1990: Zhirinovsky works as a legal adviser at Mir Press, where he becomes close to Stanislav Zhebrovsky, who subsequently becomes Zhirinovsky's closest comrade in arms in the Liberal Democratic Party.

1988: Zhirinovsky participates in the founding of Shalom, the Jewish anti-Zionist organization.

1988–1990: At the height of Gorbachev's glasnost, Zhirinovsky visits rallies of widely varied political hues at which he speaks, polishing his rhetorical skills.

Spring 1990: On March 16, Article 6 of the Constitution of the USSR, providing for the monopoly of the Communist Party, is repealed. Zhirinovsky is elected chairman of the Liberal Democratic Party (LDP) at its founding session.

Summer 1990: Under the aegis of the Central Committee, the Centrist Moderate-Radical Bloc is formed, of which the LDP, along with other tiny parties, is a member.

April 8, 1991: The LDP is registered with the USSR Ministry of Justice.

April 12, 1991: Vladimir Volfovich Zhirinovsky is nominated candidate for president of the Russian Federation by the Second Congress of the LDP.

June 12, 1991:	Boris Yeltsin scores a victory in the election for the president of Russia, and Zhirinovsky comes in third, slightly behind former prime minister Nikolai Ryzhnov, gathering 6,211,007 votes, about 8 percent.
August 19–21, 1991:	Close comrades of Gorbachev make an unsuccessful attempt at a coup d'état to halt the collapse of the country. Zhirinovsky supports the conspirators.
December 1991:	On December 8, at a meeting in Belovezhsky Forest, on the Polish border, leaders of the three Slavic republics—Boris Yeltsin, Leonid Kravchuk, and Stanislav Shushkevich—announce the creation of the Commonwealth of Independent States to replace the USSR. On December 25, Mikhail Gorbachev, president of a now nonexistent country, gives up authority as supreme commander in chief and passes the "nuclear briefcase" (the control box of the country's nuclear weapons) to Yeltsin.
1992:	During this entire year, due to the intensifying rivalry between Yeltsin and parliament, Zhirinovsky is forced into the background and is, for all intents and purposes, doomed to political inactivity. In addition, in August the LPD's registration is annulled, "having been drafted with egregious violations of the law and based on falsified documents," but in December the party is reregistered.
November 1992:	Zhirinovsky makes a visit to Iraq, during which he has a four-hour meeting with Saddam Hussein.
January 22, 1993:	Volunteers are sent to Iraq "to fight American imperialism" with a ceremonial send-off by Zhirinovsky at Sheremetyevo airport.

May 1993: The Constitutional Convention opens session at the Kremlin, with Zhirinovsky an active participant. He supports Yeltsin's idea of a presidential republic.

Fall 1993: Yeltsin issues a decree to dissolve parliament, with opposition by the deputies, led by speaker Ruslan Khasbulatov and Vice President Alexander Rutskoi. Parliament is dispersed by tanks and special forces (about 150 killed and hundreds injured); leaders of the anti-Yeltsin opposition are arrested. Zhirinovsky doesn't support either side of the conflict, promoting himself as a "third force." Zhirinovsky's autobiographical work *Last Push to the South,* which calls for a geopolitical repartitioning, is published and immediately becomes a scandalous best-seller.

December 12, 1993: The LDP is victorious in parliamentary elections, occupying first place in the party lists (about one-quarter of the votes cast). As a result, reformists led by Yegor Gaidar quit the government and the Kremlin's domestic and international policies undergo a reversal.

January 11, 1994: The State Duma opens session, then henceforth becomes not only a forum for Zhirinovsky but also his main venue for instigating brawls and scuffles.

February 23, 1994: This is the Defenders of the Fatherland Day. On Zhirinovsky's initiative, the Duma announces an amnesty for Yeltsin's political enemies—for the leaders of the August 1991 coup, as well as for the leaders of the October 1993 rebellion. Zhirinovsky appears at this session of the Duma in a lieutenant's uniform. Several days later, he greets General Rutskoi with a bouquet at the gates of Lefortovo prison.

April 2, 1994: The Fifth Congress of the Liberal Democratic Party elects Zhirinovsky as chairman with unlimited powers for a term of ten years (until April 2, 2004).

April 28, 1994: Yeltsin, Zhirinovsky, and other Russian politicians and public figures gather in the Saint George Hall of the Kremlin to sign the Agreement on Civic Accord, a kind of truce between political opponents.

Summer 1994: The writer Eduard Limonov, former secret police chief in Zhirinovsky's shadow cabinet, releases an anti-Semitic brochure in Moscow, *Limonov vs. Zhirinovsky,* and appeals to the Duma to pass a law that only ethnic Russians can be elected president of Russia. "We don't want power to fall into the hands of Rutskoi, much less Eidelstein-Zhirinovsky."

August 1994: The election campaign opens. Yeltsin on the cruise ship *Rossiya* and Zhirinovsky behind him on the cruise ship *Alexander Pushkin* make a campaign tour down the Volga, stopping at major cities and meeting with voters.

September 15, 1994: Moscow District Court rules in favor of Zhirinovsky, who has sued *Izvestia* and former prime minister Yegor Gaidar for slander. Zhirinovsky had been referred to as a fascist in Gaidar's article, and the court orders him and *Izvestia* to pay Zhirinovsky a million rubles in damages for the publication defaming his honor and dignity. The Moscow newspaper *Segodnya* [*Today*] printed a notice of this trial under the ironic headline VLADIMIR ZHIRINOVSKY NO LONGER FASCIST.

October 1994: At rallies and press conferences during his campaign trip through Siberia, Zhirinovsky announces the withdrawal of his party from the Agreement on Civic Accord, which he had signed along with other leaders in the Kremlin only a few months before, and predicts a complete change of leadership in the coming year.

November 1994: Zhirinovsky makes a one-week trip to America, with speeches and press conferences in San Francisco, New York, and Washington.

December 1994: "A new Russian army is being created in the Caucasus," Zhirinovsky warns.

Winter 1994–1995: With Zhirinovsky's ideological prompting and with his direct support, the Kremlin launches its military campaign against Chechnya.

February 16, 1995: During the annual presidential address to both houses of the Russian parliament, Zhirinovsky presents to Yeltsin a memorandum demanding to "close off Russia for 5–10 years" and "restore order." If this is not done Russia will perish, Zhirinovsky warns.

The end of February 1995: Zhirinovsky makes his second visit to Iraq, this time an official one, as the head of a delegation of political, public, religious, business, and military figures, and meets with Saddam Hussein. During his visit Zhirinovsky calls for an end to sanctions against Iraq and for the creation of an anti-Western coalition whose members would be Orthodox Christians and Muslims from all over the world who suffered from the "Western-style slavery."

ZHIRINOVSKY

1

THE MAN FROM NOWHERE

(SUMMER 1991)

No matter what the political destiny of Vladimir Volfovich Zhirinovsky, he is already the most influential, flamboyant, and mysterious politician on the Russian scene. If he comes to power, Zhirinovsky could be as powerful and dangerous a leader as Stalin. No wonder Zhirinovsky's growing popularity and political successes are causing such commotion, even panic, both inside Russia and abroad. Whether we like it or not, we must acknowledge Zhirinovsky and take him seriously. We must learn to distinguish his slapstick antics and shocking behavior from the actual politician—a politician with a well-conceived program of action.

Zhirinovsky has been extraordinarily lucky, as if history has been paving his way to power. In any other time, he would be a marginal figure, a political clown with his maniacal dream of a Great Russia incorporating Poland, Finland, and Alaska; and this is exactly how he was perceived before his sensational triumph in the December 1993 parliamentary elections. Historical circumstances are coming together in his favor, however. The collapse of the Soviet empire; Russia's loss of its superpower status and its political instability; the growth of crime, the economic depression, and the drastic plunge in the standard of living—all have provoked yearning for a leader in an abandoned and panic-stricken people. Zhirinovsky's calls for order and a strong government fit perfectly with the common people's desire to transfer the responsibility for their fate to a father figure. The situation is reminiscent of the one in Weimar Germany that brought Hitler to power, through a free expression of popular will at the ballot box.

Zhirinovsky sprang on the Russian political scene as suddenly as a genie from a bottle. No amount of cursing will push him back in. He cannot be silenced or neutralized, however much some may desire it. Since winning the parliamentary elections and becoming his party's faction leader in the legislature—the State Duma—Zhirinovsky has had a powerful influence over both the Kremlin's domestic and its foreign policy. Under his direct pressure, a return to an imperial-nationalist ideology is under way, along with a rejection of democratic reforms, cabinet shuffles, and amnesty for Boris Yeltsin's political opponents, who only a few months earlier had mounted an armed rebellion. After the December elections, even Yeltsin himself began to speak and act as if he were under Zhirinovsky's thumb. A cartoon in *Le Monde* showed Yeltsin at the podium, glancing backward at Zhirinovsky as if for prompting, while Zhirinovsky says to him, "Make it look like I'm not here." In Moscow, people joke that Zhirinovsky has temporarily taken the pseudonym "Yeltsin."

When Zhirinovsky has been ridiculed and taunted in recent years, it has rolled off him like water off a duck's back. He has been called a political jester, an eccentric, a scandalmonger, buffoon, an upstart, a loudmouth, a demon, a magician, a shaman, a corrupter of the nation, an adventurer, a headless horseman, a populist, a prattler, a demagogue, a fascist, a Nazi, a führer, and a Russian Hitler. Throughout, his principle has been that people can call him whatever they like, as long as they pronounce his name correctly. He appears thick skinned, impervious to name-calling and insults. As the Russian saying goes, you spit in his eye and he thinks it's heavenly dew. The general dislike of the government and its contrived campaigns makes people form their opinions in reverse: if someone is denounced, the people think that must mean he's one of ours; the government curses him because they're afraid of him. This phenomenon was once true of Yeltsin: the more abuse the Kremlin heaped on him, the higher his popularity rose among the people. Now it is the case with Zhirinovsky. He seems so unstoppable that even Russian democrats have contemplated the most extreme solution.

One documentary about Zhirinovsky is a video titled *How to Kill Zhirinovsky*. It is not only a metaphor. Screenwriter Alexander Gordon plays the role of the "murderer." He bypasses the guards and makes his way to Zhirinovsky, ending up face to face with him, but instead of a pistol he takes out a microphone and interviews Zhirinovsky. When Gordon tells a Moscow democrat and former aid to Prime Minister Yegor Gaidar about the would-be assassination, the Gaidar aide seriously bemoans the missed opportunity. Another Moscow liberal, prominent theater director Mark Rozovsky, called Zhirinovsky a mad dog and urged that he be brought to justice immediately: "As a citizen of a country that shed blood during the war in the name of victory, I demand of our president, the army, and the Defense Ministry to destroy this Hitlerite and not debate him." Even the Polish writer Adam Michnik, known for his pacifist views and searches for compromises, noted the diabolical paradox: "Zhirinovsky and his comrades will have the road to power paved for them if extreme measures are not taken."

Zhirinovsky has taken this possibility into account and goes everywhere, including to the beach, surrounded by a horde of professional bodyguards. He also uses doubles. However, if Zhirinovsky were to die today at the hand of a hired assassin, he would immediately become a folk hero; then his place would be taken by people of similar, or even more extreme, beliefs who would struggle for power under the same banners.

Only a few years ago no one had heard of Zhirinovsky. He emerged from political obscurity only in 1990, when he organized his Liberal Democratic Party (LDP). His fame spread throughout all of Russia in the spring of 1991 when he ran for president and came in a spectacular third with six million votes. Finally, when Zhirinovsky beat the democrats in 1993 in the parliamentary elections, he became a pretender to the Russian throne. His phenomenal, fairy-tale-like career took off with dizzying speed, even allowing for the prolonged idleness and artificial restraint of those years known as the Brezhnev stagnation, after which Russian history rushed forward, destroyed the state itself in its wake, and either demolished or elevated the careers of individual citizens. Ever since, Russians have been saying that for them one year is like five, just as during the war.

Zhirinovsky organized his party two weeks after the communists renounced their monopoly over power and removed Article 6 of the Constitution, which had granted the Communist Party the "leading and guiding role" in the country. He gave his party the first name that came to mind. All the Moscow newspapers, starting with *Pravda*, as well as radio and television, reported this unprecedented event; after all, for more than seventy years the Communist Party had been the sole ruler of this gigantic country of eleven time zones—truly an empire on which the sun never set. Every attempt to organize even a far cry from a political party—a little group, an association, even a circle of people who met in their homes—was nipped in the bud and the instigators sent to jail or psychiatric prison. In 1990 came the first sign of spring, an alternative party organized by a complete unknown, Vladimir Volfovich Zhirinovsky.

Zhirinovsky can therefore be considered the pioneer of a multiparty system in Russia. Even his political opponents grant him that much. But the hasty appearance of this party seemed questionable and smacked of provocation. There were real grounds for such suspicions. While forced to retreat from their positions, the communists left behind pegs to pull themselves back up to power, under pseudonyms. Many suspect the Liberal Democratic Party of being such a peg. These suspicions could be attributed to so many years of the KGB's vigilant surveillance. Although its power was noticeably diminished, any new signs of political life were still attributed exclusively to the secret police's manipulations.

Zhirinovsky himself categorically denied any link between his party and the KGB. Moreover, he asserts that his party was conceived well before the abolition of the communist monopoly:

> As far back as January, we were intending to hold
> our constituent congress on March 31. We had no
> way of knowing that the Constitution would be

amended. It just coincided in time that the LDP assembly took place two weeks after Article 6 was removed. And everyone decided—and the press made a particular effort—that our congress was virtually inspired by the KGB or Communist Party, as if to say, here, take Zhirinovsky's party, here's a multiparty system for you. But we never had any ties whatsoever with either the Communist Party or the KGB. You can get this information from the KGB.

In fact, Zhirinovsky acquired the file himself, an act unprecedented in Soviet history. He made an official inquiry to the Committee for State Security (the KGB) concerning his ties with them and received the following reply:

> To Comrade V. V. Zhirinovsky
> Chairman of the Liberal Democratic Party
> In connection with your inquiry, we would like to inform you that no materials providing evidence of your cooperation with state security agencies are contained at the USSR KGB.

That Zhirinovsky can now wave this document at press conferences as proof that he and his party are independent of the powers that be doesn't prove a thing. If Zhirinovsky is really a clandestine creature of the KGB, it is neither in their interests nor hardly in keeping with their practices to divulge their own mysteries. Of all organizations, surely they know how to keep their mouths shut. Zhirinovsky's opponents have no proof to the contrary, however—only rumors and suspicions usually presented as incontestable facts.

Anatoly Sobchak, mayor of St. Petersburg, made an even broader allegation. In early 1994, at a press conference for his new book of memoirs, Sobchak announced:

> At a Politburo meeting, Gorbachev said something to the effect that "a multiparty system is looming on the horizon; we have to overtake events. We have to create the first alternative party ourselves, but a party that can be managed." The then Committee

of State Security was assigned to find a candidate for the role of leader. As usual, it fulfilled the assignment nicely—it found in its "active reserve" (there is such a notion!) a man with the rank of captain and a name now widely known [Zhirinovsky]. The party's name was also conceived at the time—"liberal democratic." It seemed a real find; obviously the word "liberal" has long been compromised in our country. Two weeks later, the new party was officially registered. It was the first political party in the country to obtain such a status.

This quite plausible version of the story was immediately refuted as slander by the person Sobchak implicated—not Zhirinovsky, but Gorbachev. The former president of the country and general secretary of the Communist Party stated that he had a clear recollection of the March 1990 meeting of the Politburo, the ruling body of the country at the time. There was a discussion of party policy under new circumstances after losing its constitutional hegemony, but the idea of creating "manageable alternative parties" never came up. Gorbachev called on Politburo members of the time as witnesses: former prime minister Nikolai Ryzhkov: Alexander Yakovlev, the ideologist of glasnost; and others who could confirm his story. Sobchak hadn't attended that meeting because he was not a Politburo member. Not wanting to ruin his relations with Sobchak, an old acquaintance and former protégé, Gorbachev speculated that someone had deliberately—for reasons not entirely clear—fed false information to Sobchak as he was writing his memoirs. Gorbachev added that he himself was writing his own next volume of memoirs, in which he would tell what actually happened.

Although Gorbachev completely disowns the role of godfather to Zhirinovsky, he does not rule out the possibility that the Zhirinovsky phenomenon was born behind the KGB's walls. "I don't know anything for certain," Gorbachev stated. "Can the KGB create a whole party? Zhirinovsky is unquestionably a remarkable actor. It's very important to figure out who is directing him, who is behind him. Without a doubt his talents were noted and there are plans to go on using them in the future."

We will explore Zhirinovsky's ties with the KGB, but wherever his support comes from, the Liberal Democratic Party itself was conceived by Vladimir Bogachev, a former dissident and political prisoner. He and Zhirinovsky came together in the spring of 1989 in a group known as the Democratic Union, a radical organization that nonetheless promoted the principles of democracy and free enterprise. Both Bogachev and Zhirinovsky soon left the Democratic Union, however—Bogachev freely, whereas Zhirinovsky was expelled "for communist predilections." Bogachev shared his party idea with Zhirinovsky and invited him to be a partner. At the first party congress, attended by thirteen people, Bogachev was so impressed by Zhirinovsky's legal, theatrical, and oratorical brilliance that he nominated Zhirinovsky to be chairman and was himself content to take the office of party coordinator. Actually, the formation of the LDP was so haphazard that the assignment of posts among the devil's dozen members had no real importance.

The same was true of the LDP's eclectic political program, borrowed from parties of the same name in Western Europe and hastily cobbled together to fit the Russian situation. Andrei Zagorodnikov, a teacher of Marxism-Leninism at the Moscow Institute of Transportation, was the author of everything except the section on foreign policy and the party charter. He has gone on record as saying that he regarded his assignment as a joke. Zhirinovsky, however, assured him that Alexander Dzasokhov, at that time the Communist Party's Central Committee member in charge of ideology, would facilitate the publication of the LDP's program. Zagorodnikov now feels like Dr. Frankenstein for having created the Zhirinovsky monster.

In fact, Lenin's and Hitler's parties got their start in the same play-pretend spirit. They began frivolously, amateurishly, in jest. One could suspect virtually anything of their motivations—youthful idealism or homosexuality—but surely not the launching of epochal movements. The twenty-year history of the Russian communists before they came to power in 1917 can easily fit on a half-page of paper, so inconsequential were their theoretical discussions and splits—beginning with the very first one, into Bolsheviks and Mensheviks. Lenin described the dialectic of party life: before uniting, you must

7

determine your differences. The party of Russian Liberal Democrats was constructed along the same principles.

In June 1990, under the aegis of the authorities, the so-called Centrist Moderate-Radical Bloc was formed. Several "dwarf" parties joined it, including the Liberal Democratic Party. This block was encouraged by Boris Oleynik, a member of the Central Committee, who had provided the party's elite hotel, the October, for the press conference to announce the LDP's formation. Ordinarily, only communists are permitted to use this facility. Besides the official meetings, there were also a number of confidential gatherings behind closed doors at one of the Central Committee's residences in the Moscow suburban village of Arkhangelskoye.

Zhirinovsky gained particular sympathy from the LDP's official sponsors for his initial readiness to cooperate with the communists. Even Prime Minister Nikolai Ryzhkov would meet with him. Meanwhile, Zhirinovsky's street rally rhetoric became more populist and imperialist, to the increasing dissatisfaction of his fellow party members. Moreover, he was advocating a coalition government with the communists. (Several months later, in early 1991, when communist influence declined, Zhirinovsky quickly disowned the communists and proposed that parliament declare the Centrist Block a committee of national salvation and transfer full power to him.)

In October 1990, Zhirinovsky traveled to Helsinki to a meeting of the Liberal International. On his return to Moscow, he learned he had been expelled from his own party "for pro-communist activity in the Centrist Bloc," a formulation suspiciously similar to that used a year and a half earlier when he was kicked out of the Democratic Union.

This time Zhirinovsky simply refused to buckle. He accused Bogachev, who had fomented the expulsion, of financial abuses. He convened an emergency party conference that in turn expelled Bogachev and his supporters from the party. It replaced Bogachev with Akhmet Khalitov, an elderly water-tower operator from a collective farm outside of Moscow who also didn't last long in the party's leadership. (On the whole, Zhirinovsky has had bad luck with party personnel. There is a constant turnover in the people closest to him, and only one old hand has stayed with him from the beginning: Stanislav

Zhebrovsky, whom Zhirinovsky met in 1983, at the Mir publishing house where they both worked.)

Bogachev, incidentally, has now left the political stage for good and has called Zhirinovsky a fascist and a Stalin.

The struggle for purity in the LDP coincided with the struggle for a legitimate status for the party. Another year would pass before Zhirinovsky's party was officially registered. The problem was that under the new law, a nationwide party had to have at least five thousand members in at least eight of the Soviet Union's fifteen constituent republics. Party lists had to be submitted to the justice minister. It was not an easy job to turn the LDP's several dozen actual members into five thousand. Zhirinovsky found a way out, however, by falsifying the lists. Later it developed that among the lists Zhirinovsky submitted was one consisting of all 2,714 inhabitants, from babies to the elderly, in the village of Gantiadi on the Black Sea in Abkhazia (a disputed region within the republic of Georgia). Zhirinovsky had once given a lecture there. Another list was made up of people in a Moscow neighborhood who were expecting to receive humanitarian aid. When the lists were entered into a computer, it turned out that the same people appeared two, three, or even four times. A Moscow newspaper said that LDP was carrying "dead souls" on its list, a reference to Nikolai Gogol's *Dead Souls*, a novel about a swindler who devised a scheme to mortgage dead serfs.

The USSR Justice Ministry keeps a file (no. 66), where all the documents about Zhirinovsky's party kept by V. N. Zhbankov, head of the department, are preserved. Attached is a chronology filed by Zhbankov before he was removed from his position:

> 2/4/91: Zhirinovsky submitted lists of 111 people, 21 people, and 14 people.
>
> Zhirinovsky was advised to submit lists of LDP members totaling 5,000 people and to supply documents that the LDP's organizations operate in eight union republics.
>
> 2/12/91: Zhirinovsky submitted in person lists of LDP members: Latvia (14 members), Odessa (18 members), Tadzhikistan (103 members), Belgorod

(27 members), for Moscow and Moscow region (108 members), from Abkhazia (1,120 members). Place of residence, name, and patronymic were not indicated. Also four records of founding organizations from Azerbaidzhan, Georgia, Tadzhikistan, and Latvia.

Zhbankov turned down Zhirinovsky's request to register his party due to the lack of the required documents.

The indefatigable Zhirinovsky then immediately made the following attack on the Justice Ministry, according to Zhbankov's record:

> 3/1/91: Zhirinovsky submitted to the Justice Ministry in person lists of 4,196 persons (without indication of address, dates of birth, or names and patronymics).
>
> 3/14/91: Zhirinovsky was invited to the Justice Ministry, where he was told that out of the 5,462 LDP members on the lists submitted, only 530 names were recorded in accordance with regulations.
>
> Zhirinovsky promised to do everything required, but he could not give a deadline for when he would submit the documents to the Justice Ministry.
>
> 4/3/91: All documents were returned to Zhirinovsky for further work, primarily because of the lists.
>
> 4/8/91: Zhirinovsky submitted all the documents to the Justice Ministry. The lists, especially those from Abkhazia, were not prepared in accordance with the requirements.

But instead of rejecting the LDP once again, officials decided to register the Liberal Democratic Party on April 12. Justice Minister Lushchikov himself notified Zhirinovsky personally of his acceptance that same day and congratulated him. The occasion was indeed an auspicious one, even historic: the LDP was the first party in the country to be registered.

Zhbankov, a stickler for the law, was removed from his position.

Meanwhile, without even waiting for the LDP's registration, an official publishing house—where the works of Marx, Lenin, and Gorbachev were printed—ran off fifty thousand copies of *The Liberal Democratic Party of the Soviet Union: Materials and Documents* with lightning speed.

The remarkable haste with which the LDP was registered was perhaps due to the imminent elections for the Russian presidency. One day after the party was registered, the LDP nominated Zhirinovsky for the office at an emergency congress of the party—its second.

The job vacancy of president appeared for the first time in the history of the Soviet Union, after the citizens of the largest Soviet republic—Russia—decided in a referendum that they would elect a president by popular, direct, and secret ballot. The election was scheduled for June 12, 1991. This decision worked in favor of Yeltsin, then chairman of the Russian Supreme Soviet (or speaker of parliament), who had been elected by the Russian parliament to this largely ceremonial post by a majority of only four votes. With his broad popular support, Yeltsin wanted not only to strengthen his power but to legalize it. His chief political opponent, Soviet president Mikhail Gorbachev, didn't dare to run for election by the people, because of his unpopularity. A struggle between two forms of liberty—one directed from above, measured out and controlled by the authorities; and a second, real, unlimited freedom rising from below—was played out in the personal conflict between Yeltsin and Gorbachev.

Gorbachev regarded Yeltsin as his personal nemesis, which was in fact true. Beginning in the late 1980s, Gorbachev had tried in every way to thwart Yeltsin's political career. Although there was little he could do by 1991, Gorbachev could run anti-Yeltsin candidates in the elections. Gorbachev pressured his former prime minister, Nikolai Ryzhkov, and his former interior minister, Vadim Bakatin—both communist candidates—to put their names on the ballot. Another anti-Yeltsin candidate—General Albert Makashov, commander of the Volga-Ural Military District—surfaced, backed by the army.

It was to this crew that Vladimir Zhirinovsky aspired. Judging from the help he received in registering his party as well as the continuing financial and organization support, his secret patrons were betting heavily on him. Zhirinovsky's campaign leaflets and posters, for example, were done at the same printer the communists used. Many of the LDP's political documents were drafted by two staff members at the Central Committee's Institute for Social Studies. Naturally, none of Zhirinovsky's patrons expected this man from nowhere to be elected the Russian president, but in conjunction with other anti-Yeltsin candidates, they hoped he could take away votes from the public's favorite and ensure that Yeltsin would not prevail in the first round. The anti-Yeltsin forces were hoping to regroup during the runoffs.

Now, however, Zhirinovsky was faced with a new obstacle. To make the list of presidential candidates, Zhirinovsky either had to gather one hundred thousand signatures in support of his candidacy or be approved by the Russian parliament. Perhaps recalling his endless missions to the Justice Ministry with party lists or maybe counting on his gift of persuasion, Zhirinovsky chose the second route. In any case, because the sessions of the Russian parliament were broadcast over radio and television and widely covered in the press, he would have a nationwide grandstand for advertising himself. With only three weeks to go before the presidential elections, Vladimir Zhirinovsky appeared before the Congress of People's Deputies, the national legislature, to plead his case.

"Whom do I represent? The ordinary, common folk," claimed Zhirinovsky in his speech. "Not people at the top, from the elite. And not from the bottom—prison guards, drunkards, and the homeless. No. Our common people are millions of Soviet citizens." One of his simplest formulas for success was "I come from where you do, from below, but I have enough education to understand what's going on!"

Although populist and self-promoting, Zhirinovsky's speech to the Russian parliament was generally restrained. It emphasized economic priorities, was sufficiently democratic and not very aggressive. The novelty of his formulations and the almost hypnotic magic of his speech tempered his arrogance and bragging, his unassailable appraisals, his peremptory, imperious pronunciations, and his imperative gestures. Zhirinovsky deftly avoided the pitfalls in the political battle and offended neither the democrats, nor the communists, who together composed the majority of the parliament. During his speech

Zhirinovsky unexpectedly switched from Russian to Turkish, in a bid for the Turkic-language deputies from the Muslim republics. They were impressed, as were Russian-language listeners, both in the hall and watching television. It was an effective theatrical flourish as well as a sign of the speaker's erudition—it turned out that Zhirinovsky had graduated from two institutes and spoke four foreign languages. Besides Turkish, he knows French, German, and English, which is unusual among Russian politicians.

No one had yet spoken from the parliament's podium so directly, so sincerely, so bluntly, with such aplomb—and in such a fascinating manner. He was a marvel to everyone: for some, he was convincing, for others, he was amusing. Watching him, the audience came to life, as if at the theater rather than the Congress of People's Deputies.

Deputy Father Gleb Yakunin, a former political prisoner and now democratic activist, asked Zhirinovsky about the number of members in his party. "Seventeen thousand founding organizations from Moldova to Kamchatka," the would-be presidential candidate claimed without batting an eye, naming the farthest points west and east in the Soviet Union. "If you need the total membership, we'll calculate it for you." To a direct question from Deputy S. Sheboldayev on ties to the KGB, Zhirinovsky replied in the negative but evasively, adding that "the most talented and very capable people are gathered in the KGB." In denying any KGB links, he managed to emphasize his loyalty to that organization.

The deputies themselves were shocked by the results of the secret ballot. Zhirinovsky needed only 213 votes to confirm his candidacy through parliament; he gathered twice as many (477), more than half of those present.

Of the six registered candidates, Zhirinovsky was the least known, a nobody compared with the universal favorite Yeltsin or Gorbachev's ministers Bakatin and Ryzhkov, who could be glimpsed on television occasionally, or even with Makashov, the war general. Opinion polls at the start of the three-week election campaign gave Zhirinovsky the support of only one-half of 1 percent of the electorate. The establishment press of all political tendencies regarded him as a political clown, a parvenu, and a cheap populist. Central state television allotted

Zhirinovsky two and a half hours—one-tenth of Yeltsin's twenty-four hours. The printing capabilities serving Yeltsin exceeded many times those at Zhirinovsky's disposal; the country was literally awash with posters and leaflets carrying Yeltsin's picture. Zhirinovsky was forced to start from nothing, which gave him impetus. He conducted the entire three-week campaign blitzkrieg with energy and self-assurance, even arrogance. Rarely would he stop by the Hotel Moscow, where LDP headquarters was located in room 748; instead he was driven from one rally to the next throughout the country, appearing everywhere, pleading, coaxing, and collecting votes. Although he was far behind his rivals in recognition, he far outstripped them in enterprising spirit and energy. The campaign was his element. No Russian politician then or since has made use of the opportunities of democracy as skillfully and as cleverly.

For example, in June, Zhirinovsky went to Chelyabinsk, a large industrial center in the southern part of the Ural Mountains region. From the airport he was driven directly to the television studio to speak. The next morning there was a meeting with deputies from the local legislature, then on to students at the Thermal Technology Institute, with a lunch break at a tractor factory.

"I have never been in power, I am not to blame for the disaster Russia now faces," Zhirinovsky claimed to pro-Yeltsin workers.

Finally, there was a rally at a factory square. "We're going to vote for Yeltsin anyway!" shouted the workers. "Go ahead and vote for him," Zhirinovsky replied, seeming to concede. "You want to give him and the others a chance. But they've already proven their helplessness and incompetency in governing you. In five years there will be new elections, and I'll come to see you again. But they won't be coming to see you; they will have nothing to say to you."

An impulsive orator and indefatigable talker, a resourceful polemicist and talented actor, Zhirinovsky turns out to be unusually sensitive to his listeners, especially to a mass audience that prefers simple answers to even the most difficult questions. His populism and simplifications charm the crowd, hypnotizing the people with instant solutions to all the most urgent problems. Once he promised voters that he would feed the country within seventy-two hours. How? "I'll bring troops into former East Germany—a million and a half people, they'll rattle their weapons, including the nuclear ones, and everything will appear."

"If I win, I will raise the monetary compensation for an officer to four thousand rubles," said Zhirinovsky, tossing a bone to the army. Where will he get the funds? From selling Soviet arms abroad, where there is still a demand for them, and using the hard currency that Soviet military people receive for serving in the UN's troops.

His promises are obviously impossible to keep, but the panic-stricken voters are easily led. "Deceiving him is not hard for he is glad to be deceived," as Pushkin said in a famous poem. Freud prescribed the proper dosage: "Whoever wants to influence [the crowd] has no need to prove his argumentation logically; he has merely to depict things with the brightest colors, to exaggerate and keep repeating the same thing." That's exactly what Zhirinovsky did.

Zhirinovsky knows how to sympathize, instill hope, and enchant, and he never overlooks a constituent. For soldiers returning from the army, he promises land. For single women, he promises husbands. For thirsty drunks, he offers vodka: "Vodka is the national drink. It will be cheap when I come to power, and it will be sold at all retail outlets." Of course, all of this was nothing more than a pipe dream, but in Russia's desperate situation, a segment of the public found these assurances more convincing than Yeltsin's harsh program of economic reforms and political freedoms.

Let us consider just the alcoholics, of which there are millions in Russia. Although things were already quite bad for them, Gorbachev turned their lives into a living hell when he launched his antialcohol campaign on entering the Kremlin. The price of vodka skyrocketed, but the drink disappeared from the stores anyway. The police began to pick up drunks like stray dogs and forcibly place them in work/therapy camps. It was virtually a war against the nation, because alcoholism had already long since become the national disease in Russia and had acquired not only epidemic but genetic proportions.

People drink from one generation to another, which inevitably leads to the destruction of the gene type and ethnic degradation. Yeltsin, a storehouse of popular dissatisfaction, disregarded alcoholics. By contrast, Zhirinovsky realized their political potential and lured them with the hope of easy access to cheap vodka.

His success was also due to his response to Russia's downward spiral. He promised to stop the fall of the government and the disintegration of the army; to resolve painful ethnic issues effectively by dividing the country into *gubernii,* areas similar to states, instead of national-territorial regions; to revive the economy; to establish harshly centralized control; to combat crime and corruption ruthlessly—including execution on the spot, without an investigation or trial; and to restore the offended honor and dignity of the Russian people.

Zhirinovsky was particularly aggressive on the question of hurt pride. His chauvinist slogans and statements increasingly recalled fascist ones. He promised to poison neighboring Baltic republics, strident about their independence, with radioactive wastes. He threatened to create an independent state consisting exclusively of blacks on U.S. territory if the United States did not stop supporting separatist movements in the USSR.

An ideological improviser and eclectic, Zhirinovsky would, despite these statements, simultaneously insist on the need for a rapid transition to a "European model of society: free economy, human rights in first place, and civil society."

Yeltsin's victory was inevitable; he deserved it and was destined for it. Zhirinovsky was an outsider, a political parvenu who annoyed the political elite with his cockiness and populism. Not only the pro-Yeltsin press came down hard on him, but even at times the anti-Yeltsin press as well. He was ridiculed, slighted, mocked, called a chauvinist, a Stalinist, a fascist, a brown-shirt, and "possessed." Even direct analogies to Hitler were made. Yet despite all this, in the first free elections for the president of Russia, the political debutante received not the half percent of the vote predicted but 7.81 percent. With more than six million votes (6,211,007), he took third place after Yeltsin, and was only slightly behind Ryzhkov. One in every twelve Russian citizens who came to the polls that day voted for Zhirinovsky.

Zhirinovsky had every reason to consider his defeat in these elections a victory. His success was as much of a surprise to his supporters as to opponents. He had anticipated receiving three million votes but got twice as many. His prediction at the beginning of the campaign that he would come in third might have been rhetoric, but it is also characteristic of him to talk his audiences into believing in his future triumphs. Success made Zhirinovsky independent from his sponsors. He had served in good faith to siphon off the votes of the dissatisfied and to split the anti-Gorbachev opposition. But now Zhirinovsky seemed to trade places with his former patrons, exploiting their services for his own aims. To compare him to Petrushka, the famous puppet character in a ballet who ran away from his puppetmaker, would be an exaggeration, but unquestionably Zhirinovsky was becoming master in the theater, where he was playing the leading role.

No matter who presided at his political birth, no matter who supplied him with advice, plans, and money during the election campaign, he owes his success primarily to himself—to his bubbling energy, his temperament, his talent, his calculations, and his ideas. He understood his voters' numbers exactly: the workers, who had been first hit by inflation and shortages of food and necessities; military officers, humiliated at Russia's loss of status as a superpower and the sharp decline in the army's authority; panicked pensioners and angry lumpen[1] whose cradle-to-grave welfare had been taken away; and young people, for whom Yeltsin was just as much an anachronism as Gorbachev was.

According to statistics from Monitoring, a Russian sociological survey agency, Zhirinovsky didn't have a single social base. By comparison, Yeltsin was supported by advocates of radical reforms; Ryzhkov and Bakatin, by opponents of reform; and General Makashov, by the neo-Stalinists, who turned out to be

---

1. The German word *Lumpen* ("rags") means the underclass of society—vagrants, beggars, and the criminal element. *Lumpen* are people who have hit bottom, who have been pushed to the margins of life. At the turn of the century, Maxim Gorky's play *The Lower Depths* introduced the notion of social depth to the Russian language. Naturally, now at a time of radical disruption of the former foundations of life, an impoverishment and *lumpenization* of large segments of the population is taking place.

few in number. It is impossible to divide Zhirinovsky's electorate into any ideologically defined category. Lumpens and
marginals, people who have been pushed to the periphery of
life as a result of social and political cataclysms, were the largest social group among his voters. Between 50 and 90 percent
of inmates in prisons and labor camps (whose population totals nearly a million in Russia alone) voted for Zhirinovsky, as
did policemen from special riot troops, KGB and Interior Ministry schools, and a large percentage of pensioners. More than
half of his voters either graduated from or at least attended
college; according to sociologist Igor Yakovenko, director of
Monitoring, these people are the potentially unemployed or
forced to give up their profession because of the new socioeconomic situation. In light of subsequent events, Yakovenko's
conclusion seemed prophetic: "There are Zhirinovskys in every country. But they are supported everywhere only by those
segments of society that have nothing to lose. . . . Zhirinovsky's popularity will grow in proportion to how bad the political and economic situation will get."

An essay by the anti-Zhirinovsky Leonid Radzikhovsky in the
weekly *Ogonyok* [Little flame] is perceptive if disdainful.
Rightly supposing that a politician should have some model of
his voter in mind and what kind of leader that voter wants,
Radzikhovsky writes that there are two routes to the voter:
"playing to noble instincts," when a politician, seemingly elevates the voter in his own eyes; and "playing to base instincts,"
which was Zhirinovsky's method.

> "Yes, you're that way, and I'm this way," this kind of
> politician seems to say. "See, we don't tuck napkins
> into our shirts (although we are more educated than
> some others, by the way!). Yes, we're not ashamed—
> our insides are all displayed, we have no reason to
> hide. Relax, don't hold back! We push people in
> lines, we shove aside women, we are rude to one an
> other, we are inherently aggressive and angry—and
> we're proud of it! That's how we are—and there's no
> reason to hide it. And don't kid yourself! 'Up there,'
> 'those people,' those noble politicians are the same

way, exactly the same way! Only they all lie, but I (we) are all honest and open."

The repulsive grimace never leaving his face, the maniacal persistence with which he chants, like a megalomaniac: just vote for me! just vote, relax, and don't think about anything! He and his colleagues read about all this in popular Western advertising brochures on "brainwashing." It remained only to find an actor who would play all of this out, à la Stanislavsky, and everything was all set. . . . To play the most inconvenient, unpleasant, irate crank and troublemaker. And that's what attracts voters?! Apparently so!

Radzikhovsky believes that Zhirinovsky deliberately aims at depravity in people, whipping up the most blind, sado-masochistic instincts, primarily racial hatred, and provoking the most primitive and low feelings of his voters. There is something sadistic in Zhirinovsky's treatment of his audience:

Note how he talks rudely to people, denigrating them, threatening them, promising them the stick (although the carrot as well), shouting at them. Zhirinovsky rages on the screen, and his madness is transferred to the viewer and infects him. Zhirinovsky is not afraid that the madness will turn against him in the end. . . . The main thing is to take them out of their state of equilibrium, their indolent irony, the main thing is to cut them to the quick. If that is achieved, then it works. It's a great opportunity—people are only too happy to strip off the "thin layer of culture" (Hitler) and sensing that "everything is permissible" [Dostoyevsky], "there is nothing to be ashamed of," they gleefully follow after the *vozhd'*, *the great leader* who is not ashamed to lead them.

The idea of the *vozhd'* is key to understanding Zhirinovsky and his successes. It's odd that the word *vozhd'* did not become current in other languages in the 1930s, when the other languages added terms that differed phonetically but not semantically, such as *führer, duce,* and *caudillo.* Why did the names for Hitler, Mussolini, and Franco become international terms, but the Russian analog did not gain wide currency, despite two such Russian *vozhd's* within our century—Lenin and Stalin?

Zhirinovsky is the third pretender to the position of a Russian *vozhd'.*

Instead of the customary pronoun "we" always used in Russian politics, Zhirinovsky uses the unaccustomed declarative "I." His egocentricity is unusual amid Soviet standardization and depersonalization. His conception of *vozhdism* differs little from the fascist or national-socialist notion of a leader, and Zhirinovsky himself believes that Hitler discredited a good idea: "Of course, some of Hitler's ultra-radical statements caused a certain damage, but on the whole, his ideology did not contain anything negative in it."

The plebeians see in Zhirinovsky a boss, a leader, a *vozhd',* for whom they have yearned since Stalin. Opinion polls indicate that the overwhelming majority of Russians consider Margaret Thatcher and former KGB chief Yuri Andropov to be ideal leaders. The *vozhd',* the iron hand, the dictator, even the tyrant, which Zhirinovsky brought to the political scene, fell on fertile ground.

The desire for order has been in the Russian air since the late 1980s, and it grows stronger with each passing year that the empire crumbles and the government's authority dwindles. It is already impossible to stop the chaos and anarchy. The state is disintegrating faster than democratic institutions can become established to give popular sentiment a legitimate outlet, a constitutional safety valve. The ship of state is lurching from side to side, and the crew and passengers, tired from the rocking, are ready to welcome any captain who will remove responsibility from society and take it on himself. It is said that anarchy is the mother of order; it may also be the mother of dictatorship. The right-wingers of the Gorbachev era were the first to speak about dictatorship as a panacea: the chauvinist and anti-Semitic Pamyat [Memory]; popular Leningrad television reporter Alexander Nevzorov's ultra-patriotic group called Nashi [Ours]; and the conservative bloc Soyuz [Union] in the Soviet parliament. Fearing a reactionary coup, liberals demanded that Gorbachev stage a preventative, progressive coup. Many respected figures, from Patriarch Alexei II, Russian Orthodox leader, to actor Nikolai Gubenko, signed the "Letter of the 53," calling on Gorbachev to "impose a state of emergency and direct presidential rule." When Yeltsin reproached Gorbachev for moving to the right, Gorbachev replied for his edification: "I'm not the one who's moving to the right, Boris Nikolayevich. Our society is moving to the right." By mid-1991, according to public opinion surveys, 56 percent of the population believed that only a strong government was capable of leading the country out of the economic and political impasse.

A confused society—from the Kremlin nobility, the party nomenklatura, and generals of the army and KGB, down to the intelligentsia in the arts, the proletarians, and the lumpens—was afraid of democracy before it even got to know it. The first mouthful of freedom stuck in their throats, and they could neither swallow it nor spit it out. As Antonio Gramsci, the Italian Marxist theoretician, once wrote of a similar period: "The old is dying, and the new simply cannot be born. In this interregnum, there arises a great diversity of morbid symptoms."

One of these morbid symptoms was the idea of a powerful leader, although no one had claimed the role. Without beating around the bush or displaying false modesty, Zhirinovsky proposed himself: "When I come to power, I will be a dictator. Russia needs a dictator now." Explains his supporter Sergei Putin: "The LDP is a leader's party. While Zhirinovsky exists, there's a party; if there's no Zhirinovsky, there's no party. . . . And therefore it's quite justified that Zhirinovsky is striving to become the father of the nation."

But meanwhile his closest party colleagues perceive him in one capacity—as father—and some of them call him "Papa." Or *vozhd*: "Put on your bullet-proof vest, *vozhd*!" his closest colleague, Andrei Arkhipov, urges him. Even Eduard Limonov, who is skeptically inclined toward him, uses this word in describing a meeting with Zhirinovsky in his diary: "The *vozhd* sat in the car. The *vozhd* is of course a Jew, and there can't be any doubt about it: a red-haired, cunning, energetic Jew." His numerous portraits—both in the Liberal Democrats' Party press and in their headquarters—testify to Zhirinovsky's personality cult. This is not a superiority complex, but naked, cynical, and precise, almost scientific calculation. That this is all done by Zhirinovsky himself is unlikely; there are reliable reports that he has psychologists and psychoanalysts working with him—a kind of brain trust. Zhirinovsky's advisers seem to have a very close familiarity with theoretical works about mass psychology by Freud, Fromm, and Ortega y Gasset, as well as the practice of Mussolini and Hitler.

In *Mass Psychology and an Analysis of the Human Ego*, Freud maintains that the masses want to be possessed and subjugated, they want to fear their master, and therefore the *vozhd'* "must possess an impressive will, which the weak-willed masses will borrow from him." The crowd forgoes its own ideal "I" and replaces it with a mass ideal, embodied in the *vozhd'*. By what principle does it choose this leader? "Often he has merely to possess the typical qualities of these individuals in a particularly acute and pure form and make the impression of great force and libidinous freedom, and the need for a strong authority figure immediately responds and imbues him with super power. . . . "

As for the Russian experiment with voters conducted by Zhirinovsky and his colleagues in the first free presidential elections, it not only proved the theory but even exceeded the expectations of the experimenters. It showed that even the mechanism of democracy, if one knows how to use it, can be forced to work in the required and predicted direction. In any event, free elections are still not a guarantee that democracy will prevail in a country with a long tradition of totalitarianism.

Here, of course, the question could be raised as to whether Zhirinovsky is a coldly calculating politician or a neurotic hothead, whether he is consciously manipulative or acting instinctively. To understand this man better, we must take a look into his past.

2

THE SUPERMAN COMPLEX

(1946–1991)

The Secret Jew

Like other famous narcissists with dictatorial ambitions—Napoleon, Hitler, Stalin—Zhirinovsky has clambered to power on the steps of his life's failures, seeing the only possibility of overcoming them in the acquisition of personal power. He wears complexes and phobias on his sleeve—in his memoirs and many speeches, interviews, and conversations. He talks about himself constantly, seeming to be sincere, to be a man who knows everything about himself and says everything, throwing off taboos, prejudices, and conventions, baring the most secret, shameful, and base parts of himself. The more attentively we listen to this often contradictory and sometimes disconnected stream of consciousness, however, the more frequently we stumble on reservations, lapses, gaps, and silences. Here, perhaps, we will move closer to the real Zhirinovsky. We begin with the aspect of his life that most troubles him—that he is half Jewish.

On the night of December 13, 1993, immediately after the parliamentary elections, without waiting for the tallies, Moscow television broadcast a show from the Kremlin banquet hall called "Celebrating the Political New Year." The democrats in power at the time had decided to celebrate their victory, of which they apparently had no doubt. As they were celebrating, news began to come in from the electoral districts, and the democrats' festive mood switched to one of gloom. Many hurried to leave the party, but Yuri Karyakin, a well-known democrat famous for having asked Gorbachev pointedly after the August 1991 coup why he had ever appointed the future coup plotters in the first place, couldn't restrain himself. He shouted into the television cameras: "Russia, come to your senses! Have you gone mad?" In all respects this cry came too late, not to mention that it was like threatening your image in a mirror. Like children covering their eyes in fear, the frightened democrats (who had only a few days left in power) imposed a blackout on all information about the election results. For this they were appropriately thrashed by other democrats in the opposition.

The banquet in the Kremlin nevertheless continued, although the television coverage for tens of millions had been cut off. Vladimir Volfovich Zhirinovsky, pleased with the success of his party in the elections, paraded like a victor among the tables, in a cloud of euphoria, magnanimous, festive, in black tuxedo, with a bow tie around his neck, holding a glass of champagne. When he passed by the Moscow public prosecutor Telman Gdlyan, a man of Armenian heritage notorious for the sadistic methods of his investigations, Zhirinovsky clapped him on the back with overfamiliarity and said, "When will you be appointed to command the Armenian army?" Without missing a beat, Gdlyan shot back in the same vein: "When you are appointed to command the Jewish army." Reacting instinctively, Zhirinovsky slammed a roundhouse punch into Gdlyan's ear. Gdlyan was about to hurl himself at Zhirinovsky when he was restrained in the nick of time by Zhirinovsky's bodyguards, who never leave their master, even at the beach or in the bathroom.

It was the first time that Zhirinovsky reacted so furiously to a reference to his Jewish background. The question of his parentage was his Achilles heel, the only sensitive topic for this man, who intended to become not just the next Russian president but the *vozhd'* of the Russian people.

In 1991, when Yeltsin was elected president and the unknown Zhirinovsky came in third, Zhirinovsky was forced by the campaign rules to characterize his parents and mention their ethnic affiliation. He resorted to a subterfuge that instantly became a catchword for all cynical reporters and spread through the public as a joke—Zhirinovsky's mother was Russian, and his father was a lawyer. In the campaign unleashed against him in the democratic press, his ethnic background (known as "nationality" in Russia) was always described this way: "son of a Russian woman and a lawyer." Everyone knew that he was avoiding a crucial aspect of his background. Sometimes it was enough merely to mention Volfovich, a patronymic (father's name) that did not sound Russian. Paradoxically, Jewish journalists opposed to Zhirinovsky made much of his Jewishness as a flaw, in the hope of turning Russian voters away from him. Ethnic Russian journalists from the democratic camp opposed to Zhirinovsky avoided such discussions because they didn't want to seem anti-Semitic. Once, in denying that he was an anti-Semite, Zhirinovsky complained that 90 percent of the journalists writing against him were Jews. "It makes you think," he said.

We should note the special importance of the notion of Jew in the Russian political lexicon. For ultra-right-wingers, not every Jew is an enemy, but every enemy is a Jew. Thus Boris Yeltsin, the only ethnically Russian leader since Peter the Great, is declared "Russia's chief Jew" by hostile propaganda; his real name is Baruch Elkin, and he is an agent of the Mossad and world Zionism, a Judas who has created a kahal (a self-governing council of elders in a Jewish community) in the Kremlin. Because the word *Jew* is so often used and misused as a political curse word, it has become devalued, drained of its ethnic or religious content, its very meaning atrophied. In this looking-glass world, the pure-blooded Russian Yeltsin is a Jew, and the part-Jewish Zhirinovsky is taken for a pure Russian.

Naturally we would not have dwelled on his partial Jewish background if it were not for his own frequent statements on the Jewish question—even anti-Semitic diatribes:

> The only problem is that unfortunately Jews have not been playing the most favorable role as far as all

the misfortunes that are happening in this country are concerned. They are in the mass media and are simply infecting the country. . . . That does not make Russians very happy. . . . They went for the socialist idea, they tried to make a world revolution and have Jews dominate the world. But the world revolution didn't come to pass because they tried to stay here in leadership positions. Now it's become a paradox. Jews, Jews, Jews.

The Russian patronymic (in Zhirinovsky's case, Volfovich), is not like an English middle name. A patronymic is a necessary attribute of an adult Russian, almost as important as his own name. Foreigners know the names of great Russians such as Leo Tolstoy, Fyodor Dostoyevsky, Vladimir Lenin, Joseph Stalin, Nikita Khrushchev, Mikhail Gorbachev, and Boris Yeltsin. But in their own country, these figures are known as Lev Nikolayevich, Fyodor Miklailovich, Vladimir Ilyich, Joseph Vissarionovich, Nikita Sergeyevich, Mikhail Sergeyevich, and Boris Nikolayevich. It is an old folk tradition to call a person not by his first or last name but by his patronymic; thus Lenin, for example, is affectionately called Ilyich.

In the case of assimilated and Russified Jews, the patronymic is often the only sign of their Jewish background. For example, both authors of this book have Russian first and last names, but one is ethnically Russian and the other is ethnically Jewish, a fact given away immediately by his patronymic—Vladimir *Isaakovich* Solovyov. Zhirinovsky's patronymic gives him away even now that he has changed his last name. His father was named Volf, a common Jewish name. Zhirinovsky's first name was in honor of his father, but he uses the Slavic version. Etymologically, by the way, Vladimir is the most ambitious and proud Russian name there is—it translates as nothing less than "possessor of the world" (*vladet' mirom*).

The question of Zhirinovsky's patronymic is so important and painful that he considers it necessary to dwell on it in the very first page of his confused autobiography:

> I am Vladimir Zhirinovsky. I have a Russian name—Vladimir—but my father was called Volf; that was

what was written in his birth certificate and his passport. But Mama simply called him Volodya, and it would have been easier to call me Vladimir Vladimirovich, but because of bureaucracy or paperwork—I don't know why, but one way or another, I became Vladimir Volfovich. I am proud of my name, since it is my father's name, although it is not so familiar to the Russian ear.

To be a Vladimir Vladimirovich, like the writer Nabokov or the poet Mayakovsky, would be an important advantage.

Page after page of Zhirinovsky's autobiography is filled with proof of his Russian ethnicity. He lists legions of relatives on his mother's side and does not mention a single one of his father's relations. Finally, he invokes the laws of orthodox Judaism, whereby a person is considered a Jew only if his mother was Jewish: "I have always considered myself a Russian since I was born of a Russian woman, Alexandra Pavlovna Zhirinovskaya, née Makarova, whose mother, my grandmother, was Fiona Nikiforovna Makarova, née Serguicheva."

Zhirinovsky does not undertake such genealogical research of his father's family tree. Elsewhere he explained this omission by saying: "What can I do? There is nothing left of my father. If I had my father's full genealogy, I would have told it, but what can I do if he's from Western Ukraine, the place the Germans plowed under in the war! They burned everything down and shot everybody! What can I do? He was the only one left."

Once, answering a charge of fascism, Zhirinovsky blurted: "For me, fascism is the most repulsive thing. Almost all of my father's family was shot by the fascists." This detail about Zhirinovsky's father's family is missing from his book, because most such massacres were perpetrated against Jews. Until very recently, Zhirinovsky never said anywhere that his father was a Jew. Only once did his perpetual desire to please his audience betray him. In an interview with the Israeli newspaper *Maariv*, he let slip that he was part Jewish, and continued: "Jews in Russia are in a special situation. Lenin's party was 90 percent Jewish. Therefore many are certain that the democratic revolution in Russia today is also being made largely by Jews.

Russians aren't courageous enough to join this process. And 90 percent of the members of my party are also Jewish." His statement about Lenin's party is an exaggeration, although there were in fact many Jews among the Bolsheviks. There were even more Jews among the Mensheviks. As for the ethnic composition of Zhirinovsky's party, only he is in a position to tell, but we suspect that here, too, he has overstepped the bounds of reality. To be sure, Eduard Limonov, a former Zhirinovsky associate, claims in his anti-Semitic brochure *Limonov Against Zhirinovsky* that many LDP leaders, including Alexei Mitrofanov and Stanislav Zhebrovsky, are Jews.

How can this be juxtaposed with his statement in December 1993, after his parliamentary victory, that he was prepared to form a government that would consist of 99 percent Russians?

While Zhirinovsky was justifying his compromising patronymic (the interview in Israel was, after all, not intended for a Russian audience), his political opponents were not to be caught napping. In the spring of 1994, the Moscow journalist Boris Trushin discovered information in archives in Almaty that certified Zhirinovsky's partial Jewishness far more irrefutably than his patronymic. It turned out that until 1964—at least in official documents—no such Vladimir Zhirinovsky existed. Instead there was only Vladimir Eidelstein, from his father's name, Volf Isaakovich Eidelstein. As for the last name, Zhirinovsky, it had belonged to Vladimir's mother's former husband, the father of her previous five children. It was true that she had managed to register her youngest child in school under the name Zhirinovsky so that he would not encounter anti-Semitism. Immediately after graduation, however, he was forced to apply to the relevant agencies to change his name from his father's to his mother's (by her first husband), so that by the time he came to Moscow he was already Vladimir Zhirinovsky. Under the laws of that time, when a person reached the age of maturity (not earlier!) he had the right to choose his father's or mother's last name, but not to change his patronymic. That is why Vladimir Zhirinovsky-Eidelstein was never able to rid himself of his patronymic, which gave away his Jewishness. We can only sympathize with Vladimir Zhirinovsky-Eidelstein, who from his very childhood was forced to live a double life and conceal his real name from his classmates.

This naturally could not help but influence the formation of his character.

Zhirinovsky himself denied the authenticity of the documents discovered in the Almaty achieves and declared them a secret police forgery. After a careful examination of these documents, however—the marriage certificate of Alexandra Zhirinovskaya and Volf Eidelstein; the birth certificate of Vladimir Eidelstein; his request to change his name from his father's to his mother's, with the signature "Eidelstein"—we concluded that they are authentic.

Of course, to some people, a half-Jew named Eidelstein seems now far more suspicious that a half-Jew named Zhirinovsky; but no matter what he was called previously, those who tried to discredit him in the eyes of voters had only the opposite effect. Voters were not baited by talk of Zhirinovsky's Jewishness on the eve of the parliamentary elections in December 1993. "The Russian common man, who, in the opinion of so many, is infected with anti-Semitism, seems to have passed this test and not even noticed [the issue of Zhirinovsky's Jewishness]," commented Moscow journalist Mikhail Gorelik.

Furthermore, if we take into account that other prominent Russian politicians and likely presidential candidates—former prime minister Yegor Gaidar, the reform economist Grigori Yavlinsky, the stockbroker Konstantin Borovoi, and General Alexander Rutskoi, who led the October 1993 parliamentary rebellion—have some Jewish blood, then it is difficult to imagine how the discoveries in Almaty can be used against Zhirinovsky.

Would the Russian parliament really adopt Eduard Limonov's law, proposed in the fall of 1994, that only a pure-blooded Russian could be elected president of Russia? "We do not want power to fall into the hands of Rutskoi, much less into the hands of Eidelstein-Zhirinovsky," wrote Zhirinovsky's former associate in his appeal to the State Duma. No such law would pass, however; if Russia is politically reminiscent of Germany, at least for the time being it is Weimar, not Hitler's Germany.

Although ashamed of his father's ethnicity, Zhirinovsky insists that he is proud of his father as a person. He asserts that he owes all the best in himself—his morality and culture—to his father. This is a constant refrain in his memoirs: "It was coded, apparently, in the genes from my father's side—high culture." About his shyness with women and his moral purity he writes; "I think that I got this from my father." In one interview he spoke about the high culture he had inherited, and says that his father studied at the Sorbonne. (The Sorbonne is not mentioned in the autobiography.)

Zhirinovsky's idealization of his father is all the more strange because, according to him, Volf died in an automobile accident in 1946, the year his son was born. Little Vladimir could have known about his father only from the stories of his mother or brothers and sisters from a previous marriage.

That Volf Eidelstein, his father, was an unusual man in at least some respects is quite possible. He married a woman at a significantly lower cultural, education, and social level than himself, and what's more, a widow with five children; this was unprecedented by Soviet standards, especially given the living conditions. Alexandra Pavlovna Zhirinovskaya, a remarkable beauty despite her thirty-three years and five children, was five months' pregnant by the time they were married. Vladimir's father could have considered marriage to her an obligation. After Volf's death, Zhirinovsky's mother found herself in one room of a communal apartment. This widow with so many children had never even finished school. She had made a hasty first marriage to an officer, who reached the rank of colonel before he died in 1944 from tuberculosis. She knew, evidently, how to charm men. The one she brought home when Volodya was four years old, and with whom she lived in a virtual marriage for twelve years, was fifteen years younger than she.

This stepfather "brought us many sorrows," in Zhirinovsky's words, and aggravated even further the boy's narcissism and his romantic notions of his real father. To the single room that had to do for the entire family, the stepfather often came home in the evenings, drunk, smoking persistently. From his earliest childhood, Volodya had a persistent allergy to tobacco smoke that remained as an adult. "The little boy would breathe in that foulness and suffer," Zhirinovsky complained forty years later, speaking of himself in the third person. His mother worked as a cleaning lady in the cafeteria of a veterinary science institute, stealing food from her job to feed her children and lover. "It didn't always work out," Zhirinovsky recalled sadly. "When she had to choose between us, she chose him, because he was her lover." It is clear that Zhirinovsky saw the choice as between her lover and himself.

Although he does not reminisce about it (and perhaps does not remember it), in such a one-room arrangement he would have inevitably and repeatedly witnessed his mother making love to her boyfriend, whom she never married. Besides, until the age of seven, when he went to school, he attended a twenty-four-hour day-care center for six days a week; he tried to run away from it several times. Only on Sundays could he stay home overnight. With his mother's love, his home, and his means of survival stolen by a Soviet Claudius, little Vladimir seemed to have become Hamlet.

He was the youngest child by far, and the only one with a different last name, a different patronymic, a different father, a different background, and a different appearance. Zhirinovsky characterizes his looks euphemistically, in almost an anti-Semitic stereotype of a Jewish boy: "I was a restless little fellow, with curly locks and a loud voice—altogether, I made an impression." He was the only one in his family to be so curly-headed. Further, some of his older half-siblings could well remember his father. He knew Volf only secondhand and was therefore doomed to mythologize him.

In crowded, single-room communal living quarters, arguments and fights are inevitable, and the youngest served as a scapegoat: "I was in everybody's way, I was the youngest." Zhirinovsky felt not only alienated but persecuted. In time he fled a hostile reality for a world of fantasy and in which he was unique and special, a chosen one. It was a world in which he could freely exercise his narcissism, his vengeance, and his messianism. The little outsider sensed himself to be a secret prince, believing his day would come. Egocentrically, he became his mother's main child, essentially her only child, and his brothers and sisters were only precursors preparing for his appearance on the earth: "I was the sixth child in my mother's healthy body, where the whole mechanism of childbirth had been tested by my predecessors, three sisters and two brothers."

In that deeply traumatizing situation, in the hostile world of unreal relatives and a traitorous mother, little Volodya's only defense was the dead, forbidden father whom in his heart he had put on a pedestal—also appropriately in secret. There was also his exaggeration of paternal authority—as with Hamlet. Like Hamlet, he turned his father into a myth, an ideal, a mystery, an alter ego, all of which would become for many years the driving force of Zhirinovsky's life.

Neither in school, at university, nor later in life was Zhirinovsky able to avoid discrimination on the basis of his half-Jewish blood. Besides his curly-headedness, and his obvious patronymic and secret last name, the ethnic background of his parents was required information in many situations—whether in entering the language institute, getting a job, or traveling abroad. Teachers' record books of those years indicated the nationalities of both parents. We remember that when a teacher left the room, and this secret dossier lay on her desk, the whole class would run up to find out who was whom—or to be more precise, who was a Jew and who was not. It is unlikely that school morals in Zhirinovsky's Almaty, the capital of Kazakhstan, were different from those in Leningrad, where we studied.

Zhirinovsky himself recalls quite a few Jews in Almaty, in the class and in the city at large, especially among the intelligentsia and teachers. He tells the story of an "exposed" teacher of the English language, Yelena Mikhailovna Blinder, whose real name turned out to be Esterna Moiseyevna. "Apparently, under the influence of anti-Semitism, she Russified her name and patronymic," which Zhirinovsky never succeeded in doing.

Yelena Mikhailovna in fact became his worst enemy in school. At first she welcomed him and even helped him be chosen as head of his Komsomol group (the Young Communist League, his second leading office; for two years previously he had been chairman of his Pioneer council). But then she abandoned her favorite. "I wasn't manageable, I wasn't a 'puppet' Komsomol leader," explained Zhirinovsky. That was a heavy blow to his ambitions to become *vozhd*': "I became an *ordinary* Komsomol member."

"Perhaps that was the moment my opposition began?" Zhirinovsky asks rhetorically. "In those sixteen years I had become defiant. I did not like the authoritarian style of the homeroom teacher, who did not value a student as a person, but wanted to control him, like the steering wheel of his car.

And in that opposition some elements of my future political soul were crystallized."

Meanwhile, Yelena Mikhailovna Blinder continued to persecute Zhirinovsky, taking out her revenge, so he believes. Knowing that he intended to go to a language institute to study, she unfairly, in his view, never gave him an A in English. A few months later, however, when Zhirinovsky was applying to Moscow University's Institute of Oriental Languages, he got a C on both the oral and written entrance exams despite his additional English-language lessons in Moscow. Zhirinovsky has been obsessed with Blinder, and there is a direct line from her to the "90 percent of journalists," supposedly Jewish, who are persecuting, slandering, and defaming Zhirinovsky. Zhirinovsky, hating the Jewishness that reflected his isolation and rejection, constructs an enemy that embodies it—only now that he is the *vozhd'*, the Jew is no longer his personal enemy but the enemy of the people—both at home in Russia and abroad. Zhirinovsky's personal failures and humiliations become those of the entire nation, and his personal enemies are inseparable from the enemies of the whole country.

Zhirinovsky's probing for the Jews extends to other areas— the Kremlin, among business people, writers, composers, in the theater ("What kind of Russian theater is it when 80 percent of the directors are Jews!"), and in television. Zhirinovsky repeatedly expresses the wish to see nice Russian faces, with blond hair and blue eyes, instead of Jews on the television screen. The blue-eyed Zhirinovsky supposes blue eyes to be the epitome of beauty, charm, and charisma.

When Zhirinovsky speaks about the domination of Jews, he primarily cites fields where their great numbers are obvious to the whole country. He believes that Jews themselves provoked anti-Semitism by coming to the forefront as soon as the barriers of discrimination were removed during the Gorbachev-Yeltsin period. Then they began to irritate people with their non-Aryan faces. Although he expresses the wish to replace television anchormen, Zhirinovsky maintains it is not his idea but the wishes of his constituents.

His advice for Russian Jewry has crystallized in the formula "Don't stick out," which apparently reflects his own experience of adapting to a hostile and discriminatory atmosphere.

Zhirinovsky's anti-Jewish statements vary from announcing the inevitable exodus of Jews from Russia to his proposal of a final solution for the Jewish question on an international scale: gathering all the Jews on islands, so that there won't be any land borders between them and other peoples. He even has specific islands in mind: Cyprus, Madagascar, and Mauritius.

Zhirinovsky briefly attempted to legitimize himself as a Jew in the 1980s, during the period known as the Brezhnev stagnation, when not only he, and not only Jews, but many energetic and ambitious citizens felt, in Joseph Brodsky's famous words, at "the end of prospects." In this stalemate a desperate Zhirinovsky was apparently close to emigrating from the country on an Israeli visa; in 1983 he was sent an invitation from Israel (required in order to exit the Soviet Union) but never made use of it. There is nothing strange in any of this; people ordered such invitations to keep in reserve, for a rainy day, and the number of people who received them far exceeded the number of people who actually left. According to Sokhnut, the Jewish Agency, one and a half million such invitations were sent out from the beginning of the 1970s to the beginning of the 1990s, but the majority of them remained unused. In rare cases the invitations were sent to non-Jews, and in even rarer instances, without any request from the recipient. An invitation to Israel served only as a means to get out of the country, not necessarily to Israel. In those years the majority of emigrants went to the United States, and various Zionist organizations sounded the alarm about this trend.

According to one source, Zhirinovsky was denied exit permission for security reasons because of his ties to the KGB, which had begun back in his student years, after his speech at a political debate at his institute. We cannot judge the truth of this explanation, but it is certainly plausible: people who had access to state secrets were not permitted to emigrate, and a link with the KGB, which Zhirinovsky may have had since early 1969, was precisely the kind of secret that would prevent him from leaving the country.

Another hypothesis comes from a former fellow student of Zhirinovsky, Dmitry Prokofyev, now a correspondent for Israeli radio in Moscow. In his version of the story, the KGB intended to plant Zhirinovsky in Israel, but had second thoughts at the last minute.

Five years after his abortive attempt to emigrate, Zhirinovsky had a brief flirtation with a Moscow Jewish organization called Shalom. In a detailed interview with the New York journalist Vladimir Kozlovsky, his friend from his university years, Zhirinovsky is evasive, although he doesn't deny that he attended meetings of Shalom. Zhirinovsky speaks hastily, and sometimes contradictorily:

> I went to various rallies, in 1987, 1988; there were a lot of rallies. Ethnic societies began to be formed in Moscow at the time: Armenian, Kurdish, Greek, Jewish, and others. . . . It was an active life. . . . I went to where the rally was! Where there was a rally, in order to come and talk with people and make a speech . . . before I formed my own party. I went to all the activities; otherwise I wouldn't have been able to form my own party.

Zhirinovsky continued to attend meetings of the ultra-nationalist and anti-Semitic group Pamyat, where he had a difficult time getting the floor. The communists as well made him wait for a year before they would let him speak, and Democratic Russia's leaders never let him speak at all. Lev Shemayev, organizer of most of the Yeltsin rallies, used to chase Zhirinovsky away from democratic assemblies. Others testified that somewhat later, by the end of the 1980s, Zhirinovsky was cunningly working his way into other people's rallies. He would climb up on the back of a truck, take a megaphone in hand, and win some of the audience over to his side. So, in part, Zhirinovsky was telling the truth: for him it didn't matter at whose rallies he was honing his oratorical skills. By the early 1990s, he had polished them to a brilliance not seen in Russia since the time of Trotsky.

Given Zhirinovsky's episodic ties with the KGB, one can easily imagine why he attended rallies in a country awakening from a long political lethargy. Zhirinovsky's double role in Shalom is fairly certain. It was not only a Jewish group, but one with an anti-Zionist agenda, operating under the aegis of the KGB. In fact, Shalom was created to counteract the independent Jewish movement.

In other groups, when Zhirinovsky tried to get the floor, he was not always successful. But in Shalom he was immediately chosen as a founding director and put in charge of four sections: humanitarian and legal aid, philosophy and religion, history, and fund-raising abroad. Moreover, unlike the open mass rallies and assemblies of other organizations, Shalom conducted meetings with a restricted list of participants. Zhirinovsky attended only two meetings. Either he and his masters quickly realized how pointless their provocateur efforts were, or it was true (as he tells it) that he was caught at a meeting of the anti-Semitic Pamyat and was no longer invited to join the "tame" Jews, as they were known by others in Moscow. A third possibility is that people in the KGB had sensed that Zhirinovsky's potential far exceeded his current assignment and he could be prepared for greater things.

Naturally, Zhirinovsky makes no mention in his memoirs of his invitation to Israel or his brief romance with Shalom.

Since that time, Zhirinovsky's attitude toward emigration has changed. At a meeting of citizens of the Russian Federation, Zhirinovsky said to Gennady Khazanov, a famous actor and comic with dual citizenship: "Only traitors to Russia take out second citizenship. You're all running, packing your suitcases, feeling that your time is already up."

Common people widely believe that in these hard times of collapse in Russia, the Jews (not only Jews but everyone who leaves, although mainly Jews are emigrating) are stealing Russia blind and hauling off hard currency, gold, valuables, and artworks. At a rally on the Palace Square in St. Petersburg, Zhirinovsky shouted, "Let them go, but with empty suitcases!" Such accusations against emigrants and would-be emigrants figure in the programs of the majority of Russian right-wingers. However, in an interview in early 1994 with Alexander Gordon, a commentator from the Russian-American television station WMNB, Zhirinovsky offered a more tempered attitude toward emigration: emigrants should not show off or brag about their émigré status or dual citizenship, because the majority of Russians don't have the opportunity to leave their country, no matter how hard it is for them to live there.

Nonetheless, almost all the LDP's statements that can be considered anti-Semitic come from Zhirinovsky. Other LDP leaders prefer to remain silent about this delicate topic or make evasive comments. "I detest people without a homeland, especially those for whom the whole world is their homeland," said Viktor Kobelev, head of the party's staff. (After Kobelev became a deputy of the State Duma, the new parliament formed in January 1994, he broke with Zhirinovsky.) This silence can hardly be explained by the führer principle dominating the party, especially among those of his supporters who are articulate and candid. Alexei Mitrofanov, foreign minister in Zhirinovsky's shadow cabinet, frequently attracted attention with sensational statements, such as "Our line is reasonable selfishness, our goal is world domination." There is no ban on speaking about the Jewish question in the party; it is more a matter of tact, so that the *vozhd'* does not take such comments as referring to himself. The fact that the *vozhd'* is part Jewish is an open secret in the party.

Other nationalist leaders disassociate themselves from Zhirinovsky not only because he is half Jewish, but for what they see as his profanation of nationalism and his insufficient anti-Semitism. Some—for example, the Nazis from the Russian National Unity—consider him an "agent of Zionism" who has penetrated the national-patriotic movement with the aim of destroying it. The ultra-right brethren accuse Jews of engaging in ritual murders and call openly for pogroms. Compared with this, Zhirinovsky's position seems moderate and his slogans restrained and pro forma ("the Israeli trap," "Zionist influence in France," "the Anglo-Saxon model designed by Zionists"). The Jewish question is marginal in Zhirinovsky's party, whereas it is central to the others. Vladimir Kozlovsky, who repeatedly queried Zhirinovsky about this, claims that although Zhirinovsky does not love Jews, he regards them equitably, without the all-consuming, intense passion that distinguishes real anti-Semites. Zhirinovsky's anti-Semitism is not like Hitler's but more like that of Karl Marx; that is, it is not visceral but theoretical. First, he sees the role of Jews in Russian history as negative—blaming them for the Bolshevik revolution, pro-Western sentiment, reformism, and so on. Second, he believes their role has exhausted itself, and they should leave Russia sooner or later. His anti-Semitism is purely utilitarian; for him, it is a way to disassociate himself from his own Jewishness.

We would also be wary of calling him a "self-hating Jew"—like the head of the American Nazis who shot himself on the day that the *New York Times* exposed him as a Jew. In recalling the October 1965 incident, the *New York Times* columnist A. M. Rosenthal pointedly noted, "Mr. Zhirinovsky may not oblige but in a cold winter it is a warming thought." Zhirinovsky is alienated from his own Jewishness, and he has transformed that alienation into more of a state power or imperial ideal than a local, ethnic, parochial, nationalist one. His idea of a superstate—with territorial and not national divisions, with equal rights for all citizens regardless of their nationality or ethnicity, and with the Russian language serving as a kind of Esperanto—is the cosmopolitan idea, although skillfully camouflaged as imperialism. Like most assimilated Jews, Zhirinovsky is a cosmopolitan; cosmopolitanism is for him a form of overcoming his Jewishness. It is no accident, for example, that Zhirinovsky's Liberal Democratic Party has joined (at least formally) the international liberal movement, which has an abbreviation, "Libintern," paraphrasing Comintern, the Communist International. "We are all citizens of our planet," declares Zhirinovsky. "We are earthlings. . . . And a crucial point: a person's nationality should never be used as a factor for discrimination."

His consciousness is planetary; his ideas are geopolitical. Calls to nationalism are no more than a nod to fashion, disposable slogans in the fight for voters. Zhirinovsky is a nationalist regarding the Russian state, but not regarding the Russian people. For him, Russia is a geopolitical concept rather than a national one. His is a state nationalism, and not *patriotisme du clocher*. All of this explains why dyed-in-the-wool Russian nationalists do not recognize Zhirinovsky.

How much the revelations about his heritage affected the vote is hard to estimate. Zhirinovsky has been on television so often that he is perceived on an individual rather than a racial basis. For his supporters who have either guessed about or know his background, it seems to be a minor issue. "I will vote for Zhirinovsky. Even though he is Jewish, he is decent," a young voter was reported as saying in late 1993 by the weekly *Moscow News*. A few months later, the Moscow journalist Mikhail Pronin predicted: "And it can be expected that voters will not be bothered by what turns off other national-radicals—his nationality. . . . The basic mass of voters, enchanted by the LDP leader's passionate sermons in defense of Russians, apparently forgive him for having the 'wrong' nationality. In the final analysis, the half-Georgian, half-Ossetian Stalin ruled Russia, and who dared to recall aloud the nationality of Kaganovich while he was in power?" (Lazar Kaganovich, an influential Politburo member notorious for dynamiting Russian Orthodox cathedrals, was Jewish.)

Zhirinovsky himself is the one who cannot forget about his own nationality. He has endured too much (we can't really say "suffered") because of it. It is a permanent obsession, a mark of Cain, a shame and a secret, but also a sign of a special destiny. It is the essential impulse behind his narcissism and messianism—that is what his Jewishness means to Zhirinovsky, at least on a subconscious level. It makes no difference how this complex is ideologically colored when it bursts from its underground prison, as Jewish nationalism or as Russian jingoism. It operates like a pump, inflating the secret prince doll that little Volodya felt himself to be in childhood, to the proportions of a *vozhd'*, the father figure of which the orphan-nation was deprived, just as Zhirinovsky himself was deprived.

Orphanhood is the main point of similarity between the people left abandoned with the death of Stalin and the chief candidate for their new *vozhd'*, who has been missing a father almost his whole life. Zhirinovsky has transformed the yearning for a father figure into the idea of substituting himself as father, both for himself and for the entire nation. No one after Stalin—neither Khrushchev, Brezhnev, Chernenko, nor especially Gorbachev—could play that role. Only the former KGB chief Yuri Andropov and Boris Yeltsin could. Andropov died prematurely, however, and the people were once again abandoned. Yeltsin did not live up to the people's expectations; instead of taking responsibility on himself, he proposed that the people should bear their part; that is, he stepped out of the father image and lost his former charisma. There is a niche in need of a statue, and a sacred place does not stay empty for long.

Thus, on the one hand, we have a politically inexperienced people, orphaned and yearning for their *vozhd'*-father, and on the other hand, a politician ready to free the people from the burden of responsibility for their fate. He has suffered most of his life without a father, and the only possibility of overcoming his orphanhood and acquiring a father is to become a father himself. Zhirinovsky says as much when he states at rallies that he is ready to become "a papa, a strict papa, because if a father is not strict his children are not obedient.'"

Blaming all his childhood troubles on the absence of a father, Zhirinovsky naturally attributes the social, economic, and political misfortunes of Russia to lack of a fatherlike figure. The orphaned, homeless, and troubled people—or at least a significant portion of them—agree with him. The oft-used phrase "he was the right man in the right place at the right time" suits Zhirinovsky perfectly.

In his book about Hitler, Erich Fromm writes that although Hitler was neither a genius nor a man of superhuman abilities, his fantastic aspirations and a gift for persuasion unexpectedly combined with a unique social and political reality enabled him to rise to dizzying heights. Erich Fromm predicted: "It cannot be ruled out that among us live hundreds of such potential führers who could come to power if their historical hour chimes."

Naturally, any mention to Zhirinovsky of his ethnic origin is a prick in the inflated, balloonlike figure of the Russian *vozhd'*, as when the public prosecutor Telman Gdlyan imprudently reminded him of his Jewishness. According to witnesses of the incident, Zhirinovsky was insanely furious but quickly collected himself and moved forward as if nothing had happened; his bodyguards shoved Gdlyan aside and created a living wall around their *vozhd'*.

Gdlyan was unlucky, of course; he hadn't suspected that he'd struck such a painful nerve in Zhirinovsky. In punching Gdlyan, Zhirinovsky unleased hurt feelings that had been accumulating for many years, offenses that he had never acted on but only endured and swallowed. Now, at the height of his success, he sensed that he finally had the opportunity to settle with impunity all the scores for his past humiliations and insults, for the persecution that had dragged on since childhood even to the present and that was embodied at that moment in the person of a Muscovite Armenian who is definitely not an anti-Semite. From this incident we can in part determine how Zhirinovsky will act if, by the free expression of the will of the people, he ends up in the Kremlin.

An Acquired Complex: Russian as Minority

While he carefully conceals his Jewish obsession, Zhirinovsky trumpets his Russianness. He suffered acutely, in his words, from being an ethnic minority in Almaty, the capital of Kazakhstan, then one of sixteen Soviet republics and now the largest independent state of all the non-Russian republics that split off from Russia in 1991. Zhirinovsky makes constant reference to his Almaty experience when he advocates restoring the Russian state "at least within the boundaries of the former USSR."

"I myself grew up in Central Asia," recounts Zhirinovsky. "We considered it Russia, not Central Asia. At first only Russians lived there. Russians brought in civilization while the Kazakhs were living in *yurts* [huts], without electricity, without anything, just raising animals, sheep, just like the primitive communities of tribes, where there were no states."

Zhirinovsky complained to an interviewer from the Moscow journal *Novy vzglyad* [New view]:

> Where was I born now? In a foreign country, it seems. My native country is Almaty. It's historical name was Verny [Faithful]. That was what the Russians called it who built it. Where were the Kazakhs, why didn't they build the city? And call it something in Kazakh right away. The Russians built it as Russia's outpost in Asia. The Russians built a space center there—why didn't the Kazakhs build one? They built a nuclear testing site, a large number of factories, but the Kazakhs themselves were raising herds.

Zhirinovsky added sarcastically, "This is a very important branch of the economy, very necessary, they are very good at it."

For Zhirinovsky, Kazakhstan is an inexhaustible mine of

evidence for discrimination against Russians in the empire's provinces:

> The lot of Russians everywhere is hard work. Take the Almaty heavy machine-building factory, the automobile repair factory, or any other factory—it's all Russians, there isn't a single Kazakh. All the technology is run by Russians. The engineers are Russians. Only the boss is a Kazakh, but his deputy is, once again, Russian. He does the work, the managing, and carries the load. The Kazakh doesn't do a thing—he comes in, drinks tea, and then goes home. He was dragged out of some little village for the party's political reasons. But he would be a good shepherd if he were in his proper place.

Zhirinovsky is even more frank at rallies, using the *yurt*, a portable hut built by the Central Asian peoples and moved from one pasture to another, as a symbol. "Let them live in *yurts!*" Zhirinovsky exclaimed to laughter and applause in St. Petersburg's Palace Square. His point applies not only to Kazakhs but to all Central Asian peoples without exception. Not surprisingly, Zhirinovsky uses the word inaccurately. The *yurt* is strictly a summer shelter, for temporary use by the nomadic shepherds who make up a significant portion of the rural population of Central Asia. During most of the year, however, they live in permanent houses, made of clay or adobe, a type of construction they mastered long before Russians appeared in the region.

Most important, however, Kazakhstan has long ceased to be a strictly agricultural nation—with the help of Russia, as Zhirinovsky rightly points out. With oil reserves as large as those in Alaska, Kazakhstan may very soon become a major supplier to other countries, this time with the help of Chevron, an American company. Something like 27 million tons of oil are now extracted there every year (with a local demand for 20 million), and by early in the next century, this figure will reach 100 to 120 million tons. "We need to find outlets in the world market," said Kazakh president Nursultan Nazarbayev, whom Zhirinovsky constantly tries to belittle and offend.

Zhirinovsky's mistakes, exaggerations, distortions, and contradictions are the flesh and blood of his public speeches and interviews. He is concerned about the immediate effect of what he says, not about whether the "facts" he cites correspond with reality. We recall how Shakespeare's Lady Macbeth said that she nursed her children at her breast, although in another part of the play it is said that she had no children.

Indifferent to reality and accustomed to ignoring it, Zhirinovsky does not pay much attention to the world around him. He remembers the names of boys who hurt his feelings, or teachers who were, in his judgment, unfair to him. But he has no recollection of how Almaty looked, although he was born there and lived in the city exclusively until the age of eighteen. It is a city awash with greenery, spicy acacia, with tall, motionless poplars like columns, with apple, pear, prune, cherry, and almond trees, with an enormous, unusual Russian Orthodox cathedral of eclectic and impressive architecture, which is as much a tourist site there as the cathedral of Barcelona. And of course there is Almaty's beautiful setting itself, on a mountain plateau a half mile (nine hundred meters) above sea level, at the spurs of the Tien Shan Range. ("The Alatau Mountains—the name doesn't even sound Russian," grumps Zhirinovsky, as if the Kazakhs are to blame for settling in these parts far earlier than the Russians and naming the mountains and rivers in their own language.) These magnificent snowcapped peaks make it seem, in the words of writer Yury Dombrovsky, "as if two mighty, dove-colored wings have spread over the city—holding it up in the air and not letting it fall."

Yet Zhirinovsky remembers none of this. He recalls, for example, how he sneaked into other people's gardens and stole apples, pears, prunes, and cherries, but he doesn't even mention the *aport*, a local type of apple for which Almaty is famous throughout Russia—the very name of the city, translated from the Kazakh, is "father of apples." A neighbor's garden was for him" extra rations," although perhaps it is hard to demand of a half-starved boy any admiration of flowering trees and their scent and fruits. A Russian among Kazakhs, a minority among a native population, Zhirinovsky identifies with the army of "marginal Russians" not living in Russia proper, turned into "skilled service workers of the 'native peoples,' who had concentrated the land and its fruits in their own hands, along with distributive functions and power."

"I experienced this national oppression from early childhood," Zhirinovsky says in his autobiography. "I asked Mama: why do we have such poor living conditions? Why can't we get a separate apartment?" Mama answered: "We aren't Kazakhs. It's hard for us to get an apartment here. They are given to Kazakhs first." Zhirinovsky's mother worked in the cafeteria of an institute, and the teachers often told her about the exams. A Russian student answering a question in class would get a D; a Kazakh giving an identical reply would receive a B. The reason? National cadres—Kazakhs—were needed. Meanwhile, Russian boys were left with bitterness outside higher academic institutions, whereas Kazakhs without enough knowledge were allowed to study because they were Kazakhs. Is this not ethnic discrimination, is this not national oppression? Did this not affect my soul, my consciousness?"

Zhirinovsky speaks about these feelings even more emphatically in rallies:

> We have mutilated our country, we have made her backward. We have forced the Russian nation, the most advanced, to sink down. We have done it with force. Materially, through laws, and psychologically, through pressure. And now we are being told that we can't get along without foreigners, that we cannot rely on ourselves, on the Russian people. That's terrible. I saw how this began as a boy. I developed an internal protest within my soul. I came to Moscow and, what do you think, once again I see ethnic minorities. I live in a dormitory—they make a lot of noise, and show off—money, wine, girls. They don't work. Just to be on the safe side, the teachers give them a C. A national cadre comes, the son of the chairman of the Georgian Council of Ministers—he doesn't do a thing! I graduated with honors—but I was taken into the army. They got all Cs and Ds, but they get posted abroad. What can you do? When I came to Turkey, they complained to me: "Who

among you does any work? Who are these people you are sending here?" The Turks said this to me, the Turks understand what's going on. "Your Turkish language ability," they said to me, "that's the real Turkish language. But theirs. . . . " I saw all this in school, at work, in my job abroad—everywhere. Everywhere I went, I encountered this destructive national policy. And now Russia is called "an empire," we are reproached, that we, Russians, "live at other people's expense," that we suppress their "identity," their "national pride," that we have seized power everywhere. . . . First we let cooks rule the state,[1] then shepherds. And now we have our backwardness as a result.

In the early 1980s, twenty years after graduating from an Almaty school, its former students, including Zhirinovsky, got together for a reunion. By that time Zhirinovsky was working as legal counsel at Mir, the Moscow publishing house, and considering the possibility of emigrating. The others, however, had not made much of a mark in the world—they had become ordinary engineers, doctors, teachers, machinists, electricians, and drivers. (This story is not included in Zhirinovsky's autobiography.) The reunion took place at the height of the stagnation era, when feelings of failure, depression, and hopelessness were fairly widespread in Zhirinovsky's generation. He would later blame the era for this. But in this case he explains the overall inconsequence of the Almaty graduates with a single reason: they were the Russian minority among the native population and were subject to discrimination. Zhirinovsky's official biographer, Sergei Plekhanov, paraphrases his subject's complaint about "reverse colonialism":

If, other things being equal, they were all Kazakhs, the reunion of classmates would have been quite different. There would have been local government leaders, district party secretaries, executives of the

---

1. A paraphrase of Lenin's famous saying, "Every cook should know how to rule the state."

Council of Ministers and the local Central Committee, award-winning scientists, directors of ware-
houses and stores, members of artistic unions.

In fact, however, Zhirinovsky lived in a Russian family, in a
Russian home, in a primarily Russian city, where to this day
more Russians than Kazakhs live. He went to a Russian nursery
school and a Russian kindergarten and studied in a Russian
school, where the Kazakhs could be counted on one hand,
and even those few had been Russified. Still, the Russian children were bothered by them. Zhirinovsky remembered the
only Kazakh girl in the class, Khalimova (he has a rare memory for names), and explained her presence in a Russian class-
room as due to her father being minister of Kazakhstan's
automobile transportation. He then runs him down to boot:
"As was later determined, his education was limited to the
fourth grade, but he was a Kazakh, and therefore became a
minister in that republic." Did it really require such pull to get
the little daughter into not even an elite school but just a good
normal school? If there was only one (Russified) Kazakh girl in
a class of thirty students; what kind of Kazakh discrimination
against Russians are we talking about? In fact, it was likely the
opposite. Zhirinovsky cannot think of a single example of discrimination against him as a Russian. And indeed, how could
there be any, given that Zhirinovsky did not associate at all
with Kazakhs, was not connected with them in any way, and did
not depend on them? Zhirinovsky left Almaty permanently after graduating from a Russian high school; he simply had no
opportunity to encounter discrimination, even if it existed.

In the anti-Zhirinovsky film *The Hawk*, Zhirinovsky is very
passionate, impulsive, and unquestionably sincere in talking
about the persecution since childhood for his nationality.
"From childhood, people said that I was the wrong nationality:
'You're not Rus . . . '" Zhirinovsky started to say, but caught
himself in time and made the correction: " 'You're Russian!' "
So they called him names, teased him and persecuted him
from childhood not as a Jew but as a Russian. Apparently Zhirinovsky wants so much to talk about this subject that his passionate exhibitionism pushes him to the fatal admission,
though at the last moment he exchanges one epithet for

another. It is a typical moment of transference, in the terminology of psychoanalysis. Zhirinovsky renames his Jewishness Russianness.

The only Kazakh with whom he had a brief conflict was a policeman who stopped him for a traffic violation. That was not the first or last time he was brought to a police station, but, when describing the other times, Zhirinovsky does not mention the nationality of the detaining officers, from which it follows that they were Russian. Zhirinovsky rarely encountered a Kazakh, whether a policeman or a classmate; therefore they stuck in his memory because they were such a rarity. If he had experienced a real episode of Kazakhs violating Russians' rights, Zhirinovsky would not shirk from citing it.

In the post-Stalinist years when Zhirinovsky went to school, from 1953 to 1964, relative interethnic harmony existed in the non-Russian republics. Frictions and mutual accusations naturally occurred from time to time, although they were more likely to be at a mundane level than at the level of politics. "I know many Russians born in the Soviet republics—my wife grew up in the Caucasus, and I myself spent my childhood in Central Asia—but I never met, or at least, not during the times Zhirinovsky describes, such a severe imperial attitude," Alexander Yanov, after his interview with Zhirinovsky, noted with surprise. One of the authors of this book, Vladimir Solovyov, was born in the Central Asian republic of Uzbekistan and spent his childhood in neighboring Kyrgystan. The Russians there lived apart from the natives and had virtually no contact with them. This was even more true in Kazakhstan, the republic most heavily populated with Russians where even today there exists an approximate ethnic parity, especially in the capital of Almaty. In Zhirinovsky's time Russians made up 80 percent of the population and felt themselves to be the bosses. An interesting linguistic proof of this numerical, political, economic, and cultural domination is that the percentage of Russians who speak the local native language in the non-Russian republics ranges from 37 percent in Lithuania to a low of 1 percent in Kazakhstan.

Because of the Russian hegemony in Kazakhstan, the Kremlin did not enforce its own rule of appointing a local quisling as a republican leader and in 1954 sent a Slav—Leonid Brezhnev—to Kazakhstan to serve as first party secretary. Naturally,

violations of Russians' rights were unimaginable under Brezhnev or his successors, right down to the current president of
independent Kazakhstan, Nursultan Nazarbayev, accused by
Kazakh nationalists (few in number) of a pro-Russian line.
If such violations were unlikely in other republics during
Khrushchev's Thaw, in Kazakhstan, where Zhirinovsky went to
school, they were simply impossible.

Zhirinovsky's anti-Kazakh diatribes are not mere demagogic
hyperbole but, rather, an anachronism, sometimes at an un-
conscious level, a kind of aberration of memory, or, as Nabokov put it, the contraband of the present in the past.

Zhirinovsky's Russian complex is of course an acquired one.
It arose not in his childhood but in his adult years; not in "the
little boy Vova," as Zhirinovsky loves to call him, but in the
politician Vladimir Volfovich Zhirinovsky. It isn't even a personal complex, but a collective, nationwide one that arose immediately after the collapse of the Soviet Union, when 26
million Russians suddenly found themselves outside of Russia.
In Kazakhstan alone, there are 6.2 million such Russians. That
Zhirinovsky is "our symbol," in the notion of the Russians outside Russia, is not surprising. The question of their plight in
the countries of the "near abroad"—as the Russians call their
former possessions since the USSR collapsed—is an acute and
sensitive one. No matter how demagogic and opportunistic
Zhirinovsky's statements at times sound, in the Russian diaspora they find an emotional resonance:

> Russians are in the way everywhere—they're in the
> way in Latvia, in Central Asia, in Kazakhstan.
> Nazarbayev would be only too happy to repress the
> Russians, because they might get the idea to cele-
> brate the anniversary of the founding of Russian
> cities. Now, after having founded a European me-
> gapolis there, they are supposed to leave, like Bar-
> barians, like Scythians.

For the first time in their millennium-long history, the Russians have found themselves in the position of the Jews, scat-
tered in a dozen non-Russian states and subjected, at least in
some places, to ethnic discrimination—harassed, unable to

speak the local language, with additional difficulties in finding work or higher education, disenfranchised and lacking any hope for the future. Russians are emigrating in large numbers from the non-Russian states of the "near abroad." Two years after the collapse of the USSR, the Russian population of Dushanbe, the capital of Tadzhikistan, has shrunk by half, to 150,000. In Kazakhstan, Russians are sitting on their suitcases. Hundreds of thousands have already left, and according to a January 1994 survey, about one-third of the Russian-speaking population is prepared to do so. By the most conservative estimates, six million Russians from the "near abroad" can be seen as potential refugees, and a figure of two million is viewed as quite realistic for the near future. Even those who remain for the time being in the "near abroad" try to obtain dual citizenship, under which they automatically receive the right to vote in Russia. Add to them the millions of their relatives, friends, and sympathizers in Russia, and it becomes clear that the Russian diaspora is a powerful reservoir of votes for Zhirinovsky. If he had had no Russian complex, he would have had to acquire one for propaganda purposes, given how acutely painful the problem is for the country. In the summer of 1991, immediately after the presidential elections, the historian V. Kuvaldin wrote in *Izvestia* that Zhirinovsky was skillfully appealing "to the offended, wounded pride of the great Russians," and expressed a concern that turned out to be justified: "Within a matter of days, he was transformed from an unknown politician to a first-rate star; he vividly demonstrated what a dangerous potential is hidden in Russian society."

"I will raise Russia from its knees!" Zhirinovsky promises his voters. At the rallies where he speaks, an enormous banner is usually held up behind him with the slogan "We Need a Great Russia!"[2] "Higher, higher!" he cries to his supporters holding the sign. Then, when the banner wavers and droops to the earth, Zhirinovsky shouts to the crowd: "This is what the Russian has been driven to! He can't even hold up a banner about his own greatness."

---

2. The sentence is the second half of the famous appeal of prerevolutionary Prime Minister Pyotr Stolypin to the radicals of his day: "You need great upheavals, but we need a great Russia!"

And the crowd laughs and makes catcalls and builds up its self-esteem. Zhirinovsky knows the people and calculates their reaction precisely. In that sense he is the most professional of Russian politicians.

Zhirinovsky's commitment, however, does not spring from any great pride in Russia and its culture. Unlike real Russophiles, he has no heartfelt attachments to the flat Russian landscape, to the Russian character, to its patriarchal way of life. He has no nostalgia for the vanished features of the pre-revolutionary life—the gentry's estate, the nobility's culture, the Russian Orthodox church, and other national attributes. Zhirinovsky shares their emotional indifference to Russianness with the twenty-six million other Russians who were born or live in the diaspora. What Zhirinovsky yearns for and loves is the empire, the main political achievement of the Russians, an achievement at the same level with *War and Peace*, Mendeleyev's period table of the elements, the ballet, and the sputnik. The empire brought this people, largely backward in other respects, up to par with the most developed countries and even gave it a feeling of superiority. "If we had not sprawled out from the Bering Strait to the Oder, we wouldn't be noticed," joked the nineteenth-century Russian philosopher Pyotr Chaadayev.

The authors of this book studied in school at the same time as Zhirinovsky and recall how the teacher proudly swept her pointer across the political map of the world. In awe, we learned by heart—and remember to this day—that the Soviet Union occupies one-sixth of the earth's land surface and that the United States could be fitted into the USSR 2.3 times over; or France, forty times; or Great Britain, ninety-two times! These thundering statistics filled us with patriotic pride. It was not just official propaganda, it was a national sentiment. The geography of the USSR took the place of history, politics, and ideology. Geographical patriotism turns out, on closer inspection, to be geographic imperialism.

Here Zhirinovsky is on the same wavelength as tens of millions of other Russians. He articulates a nationwide feeling. Yeltsin demonstrated great maturity when he dissolved the empire, but also a complete lack of touch with the people, who loved this empire achieved through great deprivations and sacrifices, chief of which was freedom. The more you pay, the more you value something.

Zhirinovsky is the last poet of the Russian empire; his patriotic slogans combine pathos, nostalgia, pain, hurt, and the desire to obtain immediate revenge for national humiliation. This is unquestionably love, but an abstract love for Russia as an imperial cosmopolis that incorporates the people only as the builder of a great empire. It is a relationship borrowed from the Russian tsars, emperors, and *vozhds*, who, with rare exceptions, all exploited their people. The historian Vasily Klyuchevsky's famous formula for the malignant development of Russia was "The state swelled, the people withered." Zhirinovsky is a political traditionalist, and the Russian empire for him is more important than the Russian people—the empire is the end, the people are the means.

Zhirinovsky insists, however, that the restoration of the empire is the main condition for renewed prosperity, at least in an emotional sense. His promise to raise the Russian people from their knees, to restore their peace of mind and national dignity, to return the empire, is his panacea for all ills that have beset the Russians in recent years.

The main plank of his platform concerns the borders of the state. At a minimum, the borders that existed before the collapse of the Soviet Union must be restored—even better, those of 1913, before the war, the most fortuitous for the Russians, meaning incorporation of Poland and Finland. He calls himself a "map man" and loves to give explanations with a pointer in hand and a map of Russia in the background—not the truncated Russia after the end of the Pax Sovietica, but that longed-for empire including Poland, Finland, and even Alaska. That is the dream of the great Russia that Zhirinovsky instills in the broken hearts of his fellow citizens. He recalls Stalin, who launched the war against the Finns to push the borders back farther away from Leningrad, and then says, "Now this border is five hundred kilometers from Moscow, a few hours' drive, and all our neighbors wish our demise." This artful demagoguery strikes a heartfelt chord in his audience.

For Russians, one of the most tragic features of Russian history is the constant enemy invasion of its territory. Of

Russia's thousand years of history, about three hundred were under the Tatar-Mongolian yoke. Mongols, Swedes, Poles, Lithuanians, French, and Germans made devastating raids on Russia, century after century, right up to the last war, advancing as far as Moscow (like Hitler) or even seizing it (like Napoleon). The memory of these national catastrophes and humiliations is preserved at a folk level in two rudimentary forms: an acute xenophobia, a kind of allergy to invaders; and a Russian state instinct, whereby imperialism seems purely a defensive action.

The aggression stems from sublimated fear. Now, in addition to the former fear of China, Japan, Western Europe, and the United States, there is the no less substantial fear of previously subjugated nations that have now liberated themselves. Together these fears make Russians feel abandoned and vulnerable in the world, even in their own homeland. It is hard to imagine a better climate for Zhirinovsky's appeals for Russia to be a great power. The eighteenth-century German moralist George Christoph Lichtenberg made a comment about the French Revolution that applies to Russia's current upheavals: "It is supposed that the people are governed by a bunch of evil-doers. But perhaps these evil-doers have exploited the mood of the nation?" Thus defensiveness and aggressiveness about being Russian are characteristic of the Russian people. Their new spokesman skillfully exploits and manipulates these traits.

Zhirinovsky himself has a completely different Russian complex—a Russian among Russians, a provincial Russian among Russians native to the capital. That is a social rather than an ethnic complex, and one with a geographical bent. Zhirinovsky has felt the sting of being provincial since his first days living in Moscow, where he arrived on June 3, 1964, several months before the fall of Khrushchev. He had just graduated from his Almaty high school, and he carried a little suitcase with a change of underwear and a basket of strawberries and tomatoes. His mother had advised him to present these southern delicacies to the members of the institute's admissions office, so that they would take a better view of this applicant from afar. In addition, of course, he changed his name.

Consuming Love

Zhirinovsky's isolation and loneliness were exacerbated by another aspect of his personality—his extreme difficulty with sexuality.

Zhirinovsky arrived in Moscow as an eighteen-year-old virgin and remained a virgin throughout his years at the institute. No doubt he suffered for this. With his strong tendency toward exhibitionism, without passion or shame or restraint, he dwells on his sexual failures and complexes in great detail. He seems to take pleasure in the recollections, as if avenging his past repression by analyzing his misfortunes in love and trying to figure out their reasons and consequences—something like public self-psychoanalysis. How frank these revelations really are is questionable, however.

His sexual metaphors, which he made political currency in the election campaign at the end of 1993, are a calculated effort—justified, as it happens—to attract young people. Not long ago sex was a forbidden topic. Followed by a crowd of reporters, Zhirinovsky stops at a Moscow department store, to demonstratively grab D-cup bras off the counter and wave them around, promising to supply women with good-quality cheap underwear. On television he lectures about sexual pathology, comparing periods of Soviet history to sexual perversions: the Bolsheviks' seizure of power in 1917 was rape; Stalin's party purges was a manifestation of homosexuality; Khrushchev's self-satisfaction and smugness were a form of masturbation; Brezhnev and Gorbachev exemplified political impotence. Expanding on the latter metaphor, Zhirinovsky cast his vote on December 12 with the following pronouncement: "Political impotence is over! Today is the beginning of orgasm. The whole nation, I promise you, will have an orgasm next year!"

After winning the elections, Zhirinovsky, now the leader of the largest faction in the Russian parliament, announced at Moscow University that he "challenged all of Russia's other presidential candidates to a sexual competition, claiming that he could keep going for twelve hours while his opponents would be carried away to coronary wards."

In his sexual candor, Zhirinovsky seems to be making up for lost time. Unlike his squeamishness about his Jewishness, there is nothing shameful or compromising for him in his sexual syndromes and phobias—except for his alleged homosexuality. This he denies as vehemently as his Jewishness, even threatening that as president he will reinstate the penal code article abolished by Yeltsin punishing same-sex love. This threat, however, is a smokescreen, made as a response to rumors that the KGB had a dossier on Zhirinovsky's sexual habits. Vladimir Kozlovsky told us that the only person who could know for sure whether Zhirinovsky was gay was their mutual friend, a fellow student at their institute, who, unfortunately, had died of AIDS several years earlier.

Zhirinovsky grew accustomed to all-male groups from childhood. His first school did not introduce coeducation until after the death of Stalin. At summer Pioneer camps, "friendship with the guys" was almost the only bright memory of his childhood. At the university he shared a room with another male student. In the army he lived for two years with a fellow from Ukraine. Finally, in his own party, membership is strictly male. Zhirinovsky equates male friendship with love for a woman, for which he yearns just as much, believing himself shortchanged in his personal life: "Apparently, that's my fate, that I have never really experienced anything in love or in friendship. . . . Perhaps if I had had a girlfriend—perhaps I would have spent my energy or a large portion of it on her, or if I had had a very close friend—I would have spent time on that. . . . The constant sense of dissatisfaction was a stimulus." Prior to the rumors about his homosexuality, his public statements frequently showed proof of his sexual tolerance, even to the point of allowing marriages between men. (He also recognizes polygamy, practiced by Muslims.) Whether or not Zhirinovsky is a homosexual, his direct and indirect rebuttals of these accusations themselves raise questions. He makes a point of going out in public with his wife, then makes demonstrative, coarse, and at times extremely awkward passes at women during public meetings, with a reporter present. Liberal Democratic Party headquarters was decorated early on with a photograph of the *vozhd'*, brazenly pawing a beautiful woman with a plunging neckline. The caption below read: "They say Zhirinovsky is indifferent to women. Is that so?" All of this has a strictly utilitarian purpose: damage control to prevent the rumors from hurting his own or his party's political reputation. The LDP is now being called (by analogy with the campaign bloc called Women of Russia) Men of Russia or, even worse, the "fag party." In fact, unlike any other party, the absolute majority of LDP members are male. Its representatives in the State Duma are all men, and the party ideals are very masculine: drive, energy, will, brutality, sexism, machismo, and *vozhdism.* Even the family values promoted by Zhirinovsky's party involve restoring the patriarchal way of life and taking the women out of society and production and returning them to the family. "We would like to create a system of relations with the man as the head of the family."

The only woman in Zhirinovsky's immediate circle is the seventy-six-year-old Irina Sergeyevna Kulikova—philosopher, aesthete, author of a panegyrical pamphlet about Zhirinovsky, formerly party press secretary, and creator of the "Zhirinovsky image." She is a kind of surrogate mother for Zhirinovsky, and he obeys her unquestioningly, even her fastidious comments on his manners. Thus, for example, Zhirinovsky took her advice "not to stick out your chin" during speeches.

Zhirinovsky fondly remembers the Stalin years when sexual morals were so strict that the country almost eradicated venereal diseases. This government program of moral purity continued after Stalin's death. When Zhirinovsky was in school, from 1953 to 1964, all twenty girls in the class—at least in his version of the story—were virgins: "Of course it was because they were provincial, but there was something positive there as well. At any rate, in the majority of cases, the young people got married, and the girl was still a virgin. The young man, her husband, was her first man, and such a marriage is stronger; it is the best foundation for future family life." For Zhirinovsky, the female ideal is Natasha Rostova in Tolstoy's *War and Peace.*

On the whole, his view of women is summarized by Kaiser Wilhelm II's four K's: Kinder, Küche, Kleider, Kirche. His misogyny, like his anti-Semitism, is a part of his overall misanthropy. Thus his dislike for women and Jews is not all-consuming—he has enough other things to get mad at without them.

We have had many opportunities to observe how uptight

and unnatural Zhirinovsky is with women. In 1992, on the eve of International Women's Day, March 8, Ostankino Television invited him to give an interview after dancing with a TV camerawoman. He agreed, but it was obviously torture for him; he breathed a sigh of relief when it was finished. Once seated, he spoke candidly and tersely, rejecting out of hand the current model of women in business, and even in social work. A woman, he said, should be free from cares outside the home, so that she can be as fresh as a daisy when she greets her husband every evening when he returns from work. As an example of the incompatibility of love and work, Zhirinovsky cited his unsuccessful romance with a woman housepainter, who smelled of a mixture of perfume and plaster. A women member of parliament is just as unacceptable to him as a woman painter, however. No sooner had the State Duma opened session than Zhirinovsky quarreled with the head of the Women of Russia bloc, not for ideological but for personal reasons, publicly calling her a snake.

"In his circle, everyone thinks that he has some sexual problems," Zhirinovsky's former friend Vladislav Savitsky recalls. "For an entire year, I was in his apartment every day, and I never once saw his wife, although the two of us would sit up until late at night. When I asked him why he didn't get himself some secretaries, he replied: 'Girls and women only make me frustrated and angry.' "

Zhirinovsky tells about his first awakening of sexual feelings at a very early age, about four years, when the nannies in the twenty-four-hour day-care center put the children to bed at 9:00 P.M. and then woke them two hours later so they wouldn't wet the bed. The nannies would turn the light on in the room, put two buckets out in the middle of the floor, and line the naked boys up to one and the naked girls to the other. "I did not understand anything, but I already realized that we were boys, and these were girls, and they had different bodies, different organs."

As we speculated earlier, Zhirinovsky must have heard his mother making love with her younger lover in their one room. In fact, Zhirinovsky describes his relations with his mother and stepfather as a love triangle, as if she didn't already have five children from her first husband (whom Zhirinovsky also speaks of as a rival, although he died two years before Zhirinovsky's birth). By contrast, the sexuality of Zhirinovsky's biological father was never at issue. The boy was ready to replace him in his mother's affections, but her rejection left a wound that never healed:

> After all, I grew up without a father, and what's more, with a stepfather who treated me badly. Everything that my child's soul was capable of was directed at my mother; I very much loved her. I could not imagine that she would die or disappear somewhere. Probably this son's love for his mother absorbed the entire potential for love, including the potential of a boy's love for a girl. Because the soul is one, and there is only one love energy, and it was all directed to my mother. I loved her. Very much. It was a double, even triple love. It was double, because it was for my father as well, and it was triple, because I saw her suffering.

In 1993, Zhirinovsky celebrated his birthday with a Cossack delegation, an ambassador from Iraq, and the leader of a German ultra-right party. The Cossack, at Zhirinovsky's behest, sang the sentimental "Mama, Dear Mama, How I Love You," and a softened, benign Zhirinovsky sang along with an utterly sincere expression on his face.

Moreover, he feels that he used up all his capacity for love. "And consequently, for the rest of my whole life, I never met the one beloved woman I so needed," laments Zhirinovsky. About his wife (whose name, like that of their son, Igor, is not once mentioned in the 143-page autobiography), Zhirinovsky writes: "I never had the feeling that I really, truly love my wife; there were normal personal relations, but not self-oblivion in love. Therefore I was able to conserve my efforts for politics." Not surprisingly, Zhirinovsky's wife confirms his statement, at least in part: "While his mother was alive, his mother, of course, took first place with him." Some "evil-sayers" claim that Zhirinovsky married for the sake of a Moscow residence permit, without which he would have been forced to leave the capital after graduating from the institute. Nevertheless, everyone who knows

Zhirinovsky agrees that he attends to his family's well-being and has always been an exemplary husband and father.

His wife, Galina Alexandrovna Zhirinovskaya (née Lebedeva), graduated from Moscow University with a degree in biology the same year that Zhirinovsky graduated from his Institute of Oriental Languages, also at Moscow University. Almost immediately she obtained a job as a scientist at the Academy of Medical Sciences' Institute of Virology. She and Zhirinovsky met in 1967, when they were both vacationing at a students' camp on the Black Sea. Their tents were next to each other. In those days a romantic melodrama was playing in Soviet movie theaters, in which the hero's name was Voitek and the heroine's name was Sibilla. Volodya and Galya gave each other the names of the movie stars: "and that's what my husband calls me ever since, or else Galyenka, and I call him Voitek," Galina Zhirinovskaya admits today.

They married in 1971, when Zhirinovsky had already been drafted into the army after graduating from the institute; and if we believe her and not him, their relationship has been warm and tender ever since. Of Zhirinovsky's relationship with Igor, Galina says: "My son is crazy about his papa, and his papa loves him very much. And even when I try to influence somehow the way he is being raised, and start complaining to my husband about our son, he always tells me, 'We have a wonderful child, don't start, he's a good boy.'"

Now, however, he insistently distances himself from his son: "Somewhere at a very early stage I had more tender feelings toward him, but now that he is already over twenty, it has all practically become quite average, extremely calm." He sometimes drags Igor along with him to his "meetings with the people," but even there he tries to demonstrate his utter indifference to him, a painful, if sincere, lack of concern: "My son is here," he said at a rally in Belgorod. "Igor, stand up. You see, he isn't a wunderkind, just an ordinary fellow."

Zhirinovsky may be demonstrating his dislike of his family as a tactical move, trying to keep them safe from attack if he enters the dangerous struggle for the greatest power in Russia. Zhirinovsky himself is protected by professional bodyguards and has body doubles, one in Moscow and the other in St. Petersburg. His opponents keep open the option of physically removing him from power, but his attitude makes it useless to intimidate his wife and son—if we are to take him at his word.

According to Kozlovsky, Zhirinovsky once referred to Galina as his first and former wife, and called his second wife "Ludmila Nikolayevna," without providing her last name or any explanation. When Lee Hochstader of the *Washington Post* tried to delve deeper into this story, Zhirinovsky exploded and shouted that he only had one wife. Galina confirmed this: "I'm the only wife of Vladimir Volfovich!" When asked about Ludmila Nikolayevna, Galina was startled and replied: "I just wouldn't let it happen. . . . I didn't want to be in the newspapers." It is hard to explain Zhirinovsky's starting this rumor of divorce and remarriage as anything but concern for his family's safety and security.

After his victory in the parliamentary elections in December 1993, however, when Zhirinovsky had a real shot at the highest office in the land, he was forced to change his tactics. Galina began to appear with her husband at official receptions and on television, and even gave several journalists a group interview immediately after the elections. "I was very surprised when I saw him with his first wife again on TV during the recent campaign," says lawyer Nadezhda Kozlovskaya, who worked with Zhirinovsky at the International Bar Association in the late 1970s and early 1980s.

Whatever Zhirinovsky's relations with his wife, he is undoubtedly sincere in complaining about a lack of love in his youth—about loneliness, alienation, and abandonment. He feels cheated out of a personal life: "At the time when we were supposed to be falling head over heels in love and going out with girls, I was sitting at home studying. And later, from the ages of twenty to twenty-four, it wasn't the same, something had burned out, I had somehow missed that special early surge of romantic lyricism; there was no one to get me in the right mood, and that, of course, impoverished my soul in some way, and as a result, I really never fell in love with anyone."

His "first attempt to engage in the sex act" took place in Sochi, on the shore of the Black Sea, where his whole class had gone on vacation. Volodya Zhirinovsky, then seventeen, found himself lying beside a girl with whom he was friendly. She was wearing a bikini bathing suit, and finally he got up enough nerve to ask her to take off its lower half.

> But what kind of girl is going to be the first one to take off her panties? I didn't know that I was supposed to do this myself, to help—I was embarrassed as well. So we just lay there, until someone broke in on us. That embarrassment and shyness prevented me from beginning a sexual life at the time that I was ready.

For every vacancy at Moscow's prestigious Institute of Oriental Languages—one of the training grounds, albeit not the best, of the Soviet elite—three students applied. Although Zhirinovsky did poorly on his entrance exams (one A, one B, and three Cs), he was accepted because of a quota at the time for students from other national republics. In the institute, Zhirinovsky felt like an odd duck. In his Turkish group of six students, for example, Zhirinovsky was the only one from outside Russia and he had the lowest social background.

His loneliness worsened, and the sufferings of a provincial in the capital merged with his social and sexual complexes. Kozlovsky explains it as follows:

> Zhirinovsky sat in his dormitory in the Lenin Hills for six years and from beginning to end was convinced that we sophisticated kids from the capital, "the golden youth," were living it up, having a great time, into all sorts of adventures, partying till all hours in restaurants and driving around in our daddies' cars. Ever since, he has used this to justify himself. It's pointless to try to prove that this picture had very little to do with reality. . . . His impressions as a student stuck with him forever.

Zhirinovsky fantasized about his peers while he alone lived in the Lenin Hills dormitory (a fine place by Soviet standards, but a dorm nevertheless, with two or sometimes three students to a room). He could barely make ends meet, living on a poverty-level stipend of thirty-five rubles, plus the thirty from his mother in Almaty. To this day he remembers how scrupulously he accounted for those sixty-five rubles, paying for his dorm, books, note pads, food, and transportation. Ice cream or a movie was the only luxury he could allow himself, a restriction that cut him off even further from his fellow students. He never attended their get-togethers or group escapades around town. Even if invited, he didn't go to his classmates' birthday parties—he didn't have any money to kick into the kitty or buy a present. Zhirinovsky's poverty, emotional neediness, provincial constraint, shyness, and isolation from the rest of the student group did not help his love life.

"You see, I was young," Zhirinovsky recalls bitterly. "If we were supposed to go to a café, for example, and order something, of course I always had difficulties paying. Especially on a date with a girl, with movie tickets, concert admission, or dances. All my life there has been poverty. I never had money for anything. But to make up for it I savagely attacked my studies."

Zhirinovsky signed up for evening courses at the Institute of Marxism-Leninism. There he received excellent grades, a fact more likely explained by career aspirations than a love for learning. Even in the first year, Zhirinovsky's teachers began commenting that he was an active and disciplined Komsomol member, politically literate and morally sound—undoubtedly true, although it wasn't his wish!

In 1966, Zhirinovsky traveled abroad for the first time, to Hungary, as part of a student construction brigade from Moscow University. In Budapest he fell in love with a girl named Anika, but they never got beyond the kissing stage. Then he took a vacation in a student camp near Anapa on the Black Sea and in a rest home in Krasnovidovo outside Moscow, where he met some girls, had some dances and dates, dreamed of love, but never got any farther than that. "During those student years I didn't have a single girlfriend. . . . Apparently I was to blame for it myself. I was too concerned about social issues, was spending too much effort and energy on my studies," explains Zhirinovsky, confusing the reason with the result. "It cost me a good personal life."

Zhirinovsky distinguished himself as a group leader, and then as Komsomol leader in his class. The only way a poor student from the provinces who had no influential relatives and contacts in the capital could make it in the world was to have a political career. Zhirinovsky had dreamed of this from his school days, when he was first chairman of his Pioneer group, then Komsomol leader. The ambitions of this Russian Rastiniac, of course, were hardly limited to a career as a professional Turkologist, something he was studying to be by force of circumstances at the Institute of Oriental Languages (later renamed the Institute of Asia and Africa). The graduates of this elite institute went on to become translators, philologists, historians, diplomats, and journalists. Among them are Alexander Shalnev, now London correspondent of *Izvestia*, and Vladimir Kozlovsky. The journalist Lev Aleynik claims that the institute was a crucible for KGB cadres. One-quarter of the graduates went on to a higher KGB academy and became officers of the KGB, which was then an omnipotent organization, the country's secret government. Kozlovsky believes Aleynik to be exaggerating, although he confirms that the institute was sponsored by the KGB. Whatever the case, the Institute of Oriental Languages was connected to the secret police, and that means its students were as well—especially those who were politically active, like Zhirinovsky.

Although ties with the KGB were perceived in refined society as secretive, shameful, and disgraceful, they were an inevitable and necessary step on the way up in elite institutions such as the Institute of Oriental Languages. Without the KGB's assistance, Zhirinovsky could never have achieved the heights he now enjoys. According to our sources, Zhirinovsky was not a full-time KGB officer or informer during his student years (at least, not before the trip to Turkey in the spring of 1969). His ties to the KGB were haphazard, consisting of episodic meetings and inconsequential assignments.

An important caveat must be made here. Komsomol activity and relations with the KGB on a regular or episodic basis were not just an inevitable precondition for a political career at the time. They were the only opportunity to have any political effect, except for dissent, which at that time only a handful of people dared. "Zhir," as his classmates called him, would not have become involved in the dissident movement. Rather than rebel outside the system, he preferred to reform it from within. Although not a dissident, he was freethinking and out-spoken, says Kozlovsky, who became friendly with him in their first years at the institute through their common interest in politics.

Zhirinovsky's late sexual development (in his first year, the dean commented that he was unshaven, but he had not even started to use a razor), his shyness, his virginity, all fostered the early development of political instincts in Zhir. Politics allowed him to sublimate his needs:

> Apparently that was my destiny, that I would never really experience any love or friendship. . . . Apparently, it's fate. . . . So that I would better and more deeply understand the political processes in society, I suffered a feeling of deprivation in all other regards. . . . Perhaps this is really an objective process.
>
> I had to have all my energy concentrated on one thing. If I had had a girlfriend, perhaps I would have spent half my energy or a large part of it on her, if I had had a close friend, that would have taken up time . . . I had a constant concern for society, I thought about the community and its problems, about social issues, about relationships among people. The constant feeling of dissatisfaction was a stimulus.

In his high-school years in Almaty, Zhirinovsky bought popular books on economics, politics, and philosophy in search of answers to the social questions troubling him. At first he dreamed of becoming a career in the military, like his two elder brothers. Then, after watching his fill of detective movies, he wanted to be an investigator. Finally, when he was a senior in high school, he decided to become a diplomat—which led him to the Institute of Oriental Languages.

Zhirinovsky was the type of Russian boy described by Dostoyevsky: if you gave him a map of the stars overnight, he would return it the next morning with corrections. In his second year at the institute, Zhirinovsky went to the dean with a plan to reorganize the whole system of oriental studies in the country. A year later, on April 15, 1967, he sent a long memorandum to the Kremlin leaders, calling on them to begin reforms in agriculture, industry, and education. That date marks the beginning of Zhirinovsky's conscious political activity.

In December 1967 he gave a pointed and rather unusual speech at a student debate, titled "Democracy: Theirs and Ours" (referring to the West and the USSR). In such pseudo-free discussions, naive and politically minded young people loosened their tongues. Inevitably, such speakers were summoned to the KGB. These bull sessions might even have been provocations, to flush out disgruntled young people. One of us spoke at such a debate during approximately this same time period. Vladimir Solovyov was summoned for interrogation during a university lecture, and the KGB threatened and attempted to blackmail him. Zhirinovsky found himself in a similar situation; the first blow fell immediately after his speech at the debate. As a politically unreliable person, he was not recommended to accompany a sports delegation on a trip to Turkey.

At the time Russian dissent was a kind of underground extension of the Thaw, which was officially brought to an end by the overthrow of Khrushchev in October 1964. The writers Yuli Daniel and Andrei Sinyavsky were tried for "anti-Soviet propaganda" in 1966 and sentenced to five and seven years, respectively. The academician Andrei Sakharov and Alexander Solzhenitsyn openly criticized the very foundations of the totalitarian state. In 1967, the year Zhirinovsky sent his letter to the Central Committee and spoke at the debate, Yuri Andropov was appointed chairman of the KGB, with a mandate from the Kremlin to crush dissent. Having successfully completed that assignment, a decade and a half later Andropov ascended to the Kremlin as the fifth Soviet leader.

In toughening the country's police regime, the KGB interpreted dissent rather broadly. Any politically independent activity could be so construed and punished. Unrealized rebellion, still at the fantasy stage, or ill-conceived, naive, impulsive protest was also persecuted. Apart from prison and exile, forensic psychiatry was also employed and the disobedient were thrown in madhouses, a practice of prerevolutionary times. Diagnoses were invented—"truth-seeking mania" or "reform urge"—which could apply to any person with a heightened sense of civic indignation. Thus, in the 1970s, such brave human rights activists as Vladimir Bukovsky, General Petro Grigorenko, and Vladimir Khlebanov, the "Russian Walesa," founder of the first independent trade union in the USSR, were all jailed in psychiatric prisons. If Zhirinovsky, with his "reform urge," was able to avoid such a fate, it was because in the 1970s, instinctively sensing the frigid weather replacing Khrushchev's Thaw, he went into hiding in time and vanished into the deep underground. Only about fifteen years later, when Gorbachev was in the Kremlin and glasnost was declared, did he burrow up to the surface of politics. He was still being watched by the KGB. A report in the Moscow newspaper *Argumenty i fakty*, with the characteristic title "Diagnosis: Political Activist," ran as follows:

> From the perspective of psychiatric specialists who have been observing Zhirinovsky's career from the very beginning, [he] is in need of "minimal psychiatric help or consultations with a psychoanalyst. With a large degree of certainty we can assume that his difficult childhood and the absence of a father has further resulted, as the personality was developed, in megalomania and reform delusion."

That this is published in the Yeltsin era, years after the government renounced the use of psychiatry as a means of persecution, is amazing. Surely any of the Russian reformers—even Yeltsin and Gorbachev—could have fallen under the definition of "reform delusion."

There is no question that Zhirinovsky has psychological complexes, and his *vozhdism* is a means of compensating for these complexes—from his Jewish to his sexual obsessions. Eduard Limonov calls Zhirinovsky *meshugenah* and compares him to the characters of the Russian-Jewish writers Sholom-Aleichem and Isaac Babel. Nevertheless, no clinical deviations can be observed in his psyche, and when he says that "inside, I am a calm and ordinary person," there is good reason to believe him. His oratorical zealousness, his emotional agitation, his extravagant capers and extremist slogans, all are elements of the theater. If "all the world's a stage / and all the men and women merely players on it," then politicians are in the leading roles—especially populist politicians, and there can be no doubt that Zhirinovsky is one of them. He is acting a part on the Russian political stage, and it is precisely as an actor that he is gaining success; he is better than his rivals at the art of theatrical metamorphosis and affecting an audience. Kozlovsky talks about a completely different Zhir at get-togethers of old classmates—easygoing, relaxed, even loose. Reminded of some of his crazier political statements—for example, the one about dumping radioactive waste along the borders of the Baltic republics and turning on powerful fans at night to blow the radioactive dust over to their side—he waves his hand dismissively and laughs, admitting that it was nothing more than propaganda. "Close up, he gives the impression of a rather smart person—his speech is logically constructed, packed with arguments and facts," says Vladimir Isakov, a fellow parliamentarian. "But as soon as some reporter aims a TV camera at him, he goes into his 'circus act.'"

Other evidence of Zhirinovsky's psychiatric stability is his amazing proficiency at assuming a role and then just as quickly shrugging it off. This trait is noted by everyone who has "been fortunate enough" to observe Zhirinovsky "going crazy," whether it is the mentioned scuffle with Gdlyan or his fistfights in the Duma with other deputies. "His hysterias are well planned," says democrat Galina Starovoitova, a former Yeltsin adviser and psychologist by her original profession. "He [Zhirinovsky] knows when to stop, when to start, how to keep the public attention on his person." The journalist Mikhail Pronin shares a similar observation about Zhirinovsky: "He plunges into excitement swiftly and abruptly, but just as quickly, without a transition, he comes out of it. Undoubtedly he has a gift for acting."

Finally, we find a close analysis of Zhirinovsky's "artistic" nature, the complex combination in him of rationalism and impulsiveness, calculation and inspiration, from the leading Moscow theater director and actress Galina Volchek:

> I think that he is a fairly good actor in the hands of a brilliant director. The highest art of an actor is shown at the level of meditation, when a transmigra-

tion of the soul takes place, total reincarnation. I think that when he is lying with someone under a blanket, he exists in another rhythm, thinks differently, speaks differently. But by day, when he enters the image he has chosen for himself, he fulfills the assigned role with the highest mastery of an actor. Even so, if you were to tear off his mask, I think he is hardly a fool and is really a terrible person. . . . I saw his eyes up close. I dare to think that I myself am not a bad actress, but he is a better actor than I. In fact you cannot act such an "eye," you have to have it. You have to "be" and not "seem."

To claim Zhirinovsky is insane is like accusing the actor who plays Othello of murder. The attempt by Zhirinovsky's political rivals to label him deranged is a weapon of the previous Soviet era, when people were forcibly sent to madhouses after the authorities diagnosed them as politically insane.

Zhirinovsky's intense political activity does not indicate that he is unbalanced although he undoubtedly belongs to a certain Russian type with an excessive social activist bent. Even that type is not enough to explain the reference to Dostoyevsky's boy, who, without the slightest clue about astronomy, overnight makes corrections to a map of the universe. Although the human is a "social animal," clearly Aristotle's characterization can be applied to people to varying degrees, depending on their political temperament. In Zhirinovsky, certainly this political sense has been overactive since his youth and has been reinforced by his isolation and prolonged virginity. In a democratic country, such a passion for politics would have easily found expression in political or social activism. Under totalitarianism, a person with a political temperament is forced to make use of any loopholes—a speech at a debate or a letter to the Kremlin. Against the general background of the society, in contrast with his silent fellow citizens, such an activist may look a bit weird, and the government's diagnoses of reform urge, truth-seeking mania, and megalomania seem apt to an intimidated public. No wonder a relict of this diagnosis has been preserved to this day, although no repressive measures are being taken against the supposedly insane person.

Vasili Shukshin, a popular writer of the Soviet period, depicts such a politicized type in his 1973 story "Brush-strokes to a Portrait." His hero lives in a district settlement and repairs television sets. By night, though, whenever he gets the chance, he writes in secret, filling up eight notebooks with his criticisms of the government. No matter where he goes with his notebooks, everyone views his project as a dangerous eccentricity, and see his quite reasonable proposals as an unattainable utopia. Some take him for a crazy man, others for a provocateur. "Give it up! They'll figure things out without us," a friend tells him. Even his wife regards his political eccentricity with sorrow and fear. Finally, despairing of finding understanding among his fellow citizens, the hero of the story decides to send his notebooks to the Kremlin. Unfortunately, some farsighted citizens intercept him at the post office and turn him in to the police along with his writings.

This story captures an important feature of the reality of the time—homegrown Russian reformism, a certain explosive mixture of political amateurishness and moralizing. It is also notable that the hero's political odyssey is cut short not by the authorities but by his fellow citizens, who turn him in to the authorities, believing him to be a dangerous maniac.

If Zhirinovsky had continued his independent political action, he probably would have met the same fate as the real heroes of dissent or the fictional character from Shukshin's story. However, a summons to the KGB and punishment—disallowing his trip to Turkey—not only brought Zhirinovsky to his senses but angered him, spurring him to revenge. Without giving any more details, he recalls in his book that he "applied the utmost efforts" to be allowed to make his first trip to a capitalist country—again, Turkey—this time, for an eight-month internship. "I practically sent myself to Turkey on a foreign internship," he says.

Zhirinovsky exaggerates his independence somewhat, however. In fact, his "utmost efforts" coincided exactly with the KGB's tactics, which, in eradicating dissent, involved both the carrot and the stick. Turkey was used in both capacities—at first as a stick (not letting him go) and later as a carrot (letting him go). The trip to Turkey was almost certainly accompanied by a special assignment from the KGB. If even a tourist going on a ten-day tour of a capitalist country was given such tasks, Zhirinovsky could not have escaped them. In the late 1960s, Turkey was the chief battlefield between the espionage agencies of the West and East. It was in Turkey—and in 1969 as well—that Aldrich Ames, an American, began his spy career. He eventually began working for Russia and was finally exposed twenty-five years later as a double agent. The Moscow journalist Yevgenia Albats, author of a book published in 1994 about the KGB (*The State Within a State*), cites an unnamed source in the KGB who claims that Zhirinovsky has long been an agent of that organization. A former KGB general, Oleg Kalugin, who broke with the KGB in the Gorbachev years, agrees. Although Kalugin himself did not see the documents, his colleagues presumably told Kalugin that Zhirinovsky was in fact recruited by military counterintelligence in his student years and was called "our Volodya" at the KGB.

When he set off for Turkey in 1969, Zhirinovsky must have been in a wonderful mood. The anathema for his outspokenness at the debate had been lifted, and it was clear sailing ahead with nothing to prevent his career. Although it meant a career in espionage rather than diplomacy, spying probably more suited Zhirinovsky's adventurist nature, and no doubt there was a better future in it.

He could not have imagined how badly mistaken he was in looking so optimistically into the future.

The Underground Man

Failure has dogged Zhirinovsky literally from the day he was born, when the ambulance was late arriving to pick up his mother in labor. His uncle, who rented the room with his family next door in their communal apartment, had to cut Zhirinovsky's umbilical cord with a kitchen knife. "Life itself seems to have forced me to suffer from the very day, from the very moment, from the very second of my birth." To hear him tell it, his life has been one long trail of mishaps, without a glimmer of light in his gloomy childhood—no father, constant hunger, and cold when the winter temperature fell to twenty degrees below zero. Volodya had no warm, felt boot liners, or warm clothes, just somebody's hand-me-downs. Then his step-father moved into their already crowded room, a man hostile toward Volodya in battling him for this mother, for food, and for living space. It was a battle Zhirinovsky lost on all fronts. In their filthy communal apartment there were constant squab-bles, lines to the toilet, the stink of excrement and cheap ciga-rettes, and a lifelong allergy to noxious odors. Volodya didn't have a corner of his own in the communal room—not even a bed. At first he slept on top of a trunk, then on the same couch that everyone sat on during the day, falling asleep un-der the electric light, with the radio blaring, and waking up repeatedly because of the noise. No matter how humble, it was nonetheless home, yet Zhirinovsky was kicked out. Initially, he was placed in a twenty-four-hour nursery, then later a twenty-four-hour day-care center, and taken home only once a week, on Sundays. Next came the constant insults—at home, at day care, in school, on the street. He has not a single bright mem-ory from his babyhood, childhood, or adolescence. Thus were spent his first eighteen years of life in Almaty, and he dreamed of breaking away from the provincial city. Finally he fulfilled his dream—flew to Moscow and entered a prestigious institute. "You'll see, I'll become the pride of Kazakhstan!" he ex-claimed when he left his native republic, perceived by him as an evil stepmother. On beginning his studies at the institute, he once again suffered deprivations, harassment, and slights, and dreamed of revenge. "Someday I will be prime minister or foreign minister," he claimed to his classmates.

Thus, from childhood, Zhirinovsky accumulated a great deal of unused, unspent negative energy, sitting in the pitch-dark loneliness of his dorm room, without male or female friends, building castles in his imagination. By contrast, Turkey seemed not merely a ray of hope but the long-awaited begin-ning of his ascent to glorious heights.

"A little incident occurred; they tried to accuse me of con-ducting communist propaganda when I gave away Soviet pins to the local Turkish guys." This is the only fragment in his memoirs about his trip to Turkey, anticipated as the first step of a brilliant career, which in fact buried that promise and doomed the ambi-tious provincial, harebrained schemer and adventurer to an-other two decades of vegetation and obscurity.

Turkey is perhaps the darkest patch in our hero's biography. Ever since his stay there, he has vehemently despised the country. Under his geopolitical program (if he ever gets to implement it), an unenviable fate awaits Turkey. Its territory will be divided up among Russians, Armenians, Greeks, and Kurds. "Nothing will become of the world even if the entire Turkish nation dies, although I don't wish that for them," says Zhirinovsky, who does not speak of any other people so severely, although many of them have it in for him. Zhirinovsky sees Russia's main threat as Turkey and pan-Turkism, since the republic of Russia has a large Turkic-language and Islamic population that can easily be swayed by religious and nationalist slogans. But his notions are so extreme, even in the context of his geopolitical fantasies, that his anti-Turkish diatribes can be explained only as an objectification of his disappointment. Zhirinovsky's Turkish obsession remains with him a quarter of a century later. He blames all his languishing and despair during the endless Brezhnev stagnation on his brief spell in a Turkish prison.

Zhirinovsky traveled to Turkey for an eight-month assignment in April 1969, but was arrested before the end of his stay. Only after intervention by the Soviet Embassy was he released and immediately (within twenty-four hours) expelled from the country. Lev Aleynik, Mikhail Pronin, and other Russian journalists report that the Soviet Embassy in Ankara was even forced to pay a bribe in dollars to spring Zhirinovsky and prevent an international scandal. In countless interviews, he embellishes the innocent story of the souvenir buttons. To hear him tell it, before departing for Turkey, he bought the pins with his last three rubles. Later he handed them out in a coffee shop. The buttons had a portrait of Pushkin, but the ignorant Turks mistook the Russian poet for Karl Marx. The secret police appeared on the scene and hauled Zhirinovsky away, but eventually released him and even apologized for their mistake.

In fact, no one apologized to him, and the buttons (regardless of whether they had Pushkin's or Marx's picture) were a diversion. Zhirinovsky is not lying when he claims that he was detained while passing out the buttons. He merely is forgetting to mention that he was really caught for something else, and the buttons were just camouflage, an old trick used by Soviet intelligence. In this case Zhirinovsky is not voluntarily concealing the truth. At the KGB he signed a statement swearing not to divulge secrets and does not have the legal right to provide details about his Turkish adventure.

The incident took place in Iskenderun, at the construction site of an iron and steel works, a joint Soviet-Turkish project. Zhirinovsky's official functions were limited to serving as translator for the Soviet engineers and technicians. His unofficial assignments were more vague and depended on the circumstances. The Stambul newspaper *Milliet* wrote at the time that the Soviet translator was jailed for communist propagandizing despite repeated warnings, after he distributed buttons with pictures of Lenin and Marx among workers and engineers at the Iskenderun works. Both the buttons and the communist propagandizing were a cover.

As it happened, not far from the Iskenderun iron works was an American military base, about which the Russians were legitimately curious. Just getting his feet wet as a spy, Zhirinovsky decided to satisfy his supervisors' curiosity about the base and wound up getting caught. He read the situation inaccurately, however, overestimated his opportunities, exceeded his authority, violated instructions, and displayed unnecessary improvisation and zeal.

The scandal was successfully hushed up in a complicated diplomatic maneuver, quite possibly even involving money, although there is no direct or indirect evidence concerning a payment. The incident became a sensation, and rumors flew that the Soviet Embassy had hired a retired Turkish general to defend Zhirinovsky. Ambassador Nuzkhet Kandemir, Turkish envoy of the United States, cites his government's claim that Zhirinovsky was arrested as a KGB agent, and confirms that Zhirinovsky was held for several days in prison and, under a mutual agreement with the Soviet Embassy, was put on an Aeroflot plane back to Moscow.

Vladimir Kozlovsky recalls, "I was totally surprised that it wasn't the KGB who got Zhirinovsky for dissidence, but the Turks who caught him, supposedly for espionage." In fact, it was a double blow—a scolding at the KGB followed Zhirinovsky's arrest in Turkey. Russian journalists researching Zhirinovsky are surprised that for such a significant misdeed, officially considered an "egregious violation of the rules of conduct of a Soviet person abroad," Zhirinovsky was not taken by the scruff of his neck and booted out of the institute. He had no high-placed relatives to protect him, yet he was not even expelled from the Komsomol. The reporters ascribe the mildness of his punishment to his rapprochement with the KGB. Whatever the case, after that incident, Zhirinovsky was prohibited from traveling abroad, becoming a "nontraveler," in Soviet parlance. The KGB lost interest in this unreliable and ungovernable person. No matter what assignment he undertook, he would screw it up because he didn't follow instructions, displaying independence and unpredictability in his behavior. These features were to crop up again in his future relations with the KGB as well. Even when they would try to employ him in the role of a provocateur, like a puppet, he would finally break the strings connecting him to his puppeteer. This obstinace has been present ever since Zhirinovsky was a tot: "I was an unmanageable child, always getting up to some pranks, never listening to my teachers."

The slip-up in Turkey at the end of the 1960s was the end of Zhirinovsky's career. His classmates recall that Zhirinovsky was unrecognizable when he returned from Turkey. The aggressive, outspoken, self-assured young fellow had crumpled, become depressed, looked beaten and psychologically broken. He withdrew into himself and his former acquaintances shunned him like the plague. Everyone's healthy instinct for self-preservation kicked in—especially since at this time people's careers and futures were being decided, and assignments for work were being handed out. (Under the Soviet system, in return for a free education, students were obliged to accept the state's job assignments after graduation.)

Despite graduating with honors (the Red Diploma), unlike the others, Zhirinovsky had no bright prospects at all.

> I graduated from Moscow State University with honors in the Lenin Hills assembly hall and received my Red Diploma. But there was no one with me, there was no one to be happy for me, to share my joy. I brought that Red Diploma back to the dormitory, to

> my room, and there wasn't even anyone to drink a
> glass of champagne with. I was completely alone.

On graduation from the institute, he was drafted into the
army, where he was supposed to do penance for his sins in
Turkey.

Twenty-five years later, Zhirinovsky believes that the two
years he served in the army (1970–1972) as an officer of the
Transcaucasian Military District headquarters were very useful
to him. He learned what the army was all about, with its political work, special propaganda, and intelligence. He gave lectures, wrote flyers, and traveled a great deal around Georgia
and Armenia. He was broadening his knowledge of the Russian "underbelly," to use Solzhenitsyn's word. He had known
the Central Asian part of the Soviet Union since childhood
and now became more closely acquainted with the Caucasian
part. Of course, Zhirinovsky flaunts his military experience to
the army and the militaristically minded crowd, even showing
up unexpectedly at the State Duma on a military holiday wearing his lieutenant's uniform.

In the early 1970s, however, Zhirinovsky viewed military service as meaning only exile, punishment, and the utter collapse
of his career. After attendance at such a prestigious institute,
the army was as low as he could go. Few people fell so far; his
fellow student Kozlovsky could not recall for us a single prece-
dent of drafting into the army after graduation from the institute. Although a graduate of a prestigious foreign-language
institute, the twenty-four-year-old Zhirinovsky was now like Joseph of the Bible, thrown in the bottom of a well, his coat of
many colors stolen.

Although officers in military service almost automatically became communist, Zhirinovsky was still unable to get into the
party, membership in which would have been a first step out of
this circle of hell. Zhirinovsky's path to the party, where he certainly wanted to be, was closed for him forever because of the
mishap on his Turkish mission. Those were the days when the
KGB's new chief, Yuri Andropov, was restoring the organization's former political might, weakened after Khrushchev's de-
Stalinization, and was extensively promoting both covert and
overt KGB agents in other spheres of Soviet life. Zhirinovsky was

neither an overt nor a covert agent, which partially explains why he was left to rot in the 1970s and the first half of the 1980s.

After the army, Zhirinovsky returned to Moscow, thanks only to his wife, Galina, who was a Moscow resident. The couple lived for more than a year at her parents' house, where their son, Igor, was born. In the spring of 1973, they moved to a cooperative, three-room apartment on the outskirts of Moscow, in a district called Tyoply Stan. Zhirinovsky continues to be proud that he made the first payment himself on their home, although Galina's parents kicked in to buy the furniture, bedroom, and kitchen sets.

For two years Zhirinovsky worked as a researcher in the international liaison sector of the Soviet Peace Committee, another organization affiliated with the KGB. In his official capacity, he often met with delegations from Western countries, taking part in the Congress of Peace Advocates in the fall of 1973 in Moscow and striking up close acquaintances with the World Federalists, who preach the idea of a common European home, that is, Europe without ideological borders. Max Habbit, a Swiss attorney and politician, invited him to visit his country. Unfortunately, Zhirinovsky remained a "nontraveler," an odd situation given his official position and the nature of his work. Of course, he reported to the KGB about all meetings with foreigners, but that was a routine practice, and his relations with the KGB probably did not go beyond these official communications. In any event, they were not sufficient either to get him into the party or to secure permission for a trip abroad—or even to keep his sinecure. Zhirinovsky was forced to turn over his position to the niece of then Central Committee secretary Boris Ponomaryov, who immediately began traveling abroad widely.

Meanwhile, Zhirinovsky's career continued to regress. He studied foreign languages and graduated from Moscow University's evening law school. For a time he had a very inconsequential job in the dean's office of the Trade Union Movement Academy, once again dealing with foreign students under the KGB's watchful eye. Thanks to the law degree, however, in 1975 he was able to join the International Bar Association, where for the most part he defended the rights of Soviet citizens with property inherited abroad. He also volunteered service as a trade union leader, which under the conditions of the time was a strictly formal position.

His former colleagues describe him as energetic and competent. His only shortcoming, in their view, was his passion for talk about politics and his harsh judgments, which placed Zhirinovsky's cautious colleagues in a difficult position. His immediate superior, Yevgeny Kulichev, recalls how Zhirinovsky constantly entered his office to strike up controversial conversations, for example, making a point of denouncing Turkey as Russia's chief enemy. In 1981, Zhirinovsky decided to apply to the Communist Party, for which he needed the approval of the International Bar Association's leadership. They refused him on the grounds that he was emotionally unstable, hypercritical for no reason, and politically unreliable. Their rejection was virtually a denial of promotion in his job. Since the International Bar Association is a quasi-official organization, and one directly associated with foreign countries, a non–party member could not advance in it.

Zhirinovsky's reaction was abrupt, stormy, and desperate. According to Kulichev, Zhirinovsky drafted one complaint after another to the district party committee. Not restricting himself to official letters, he sent several anonymous notes accusing his bosses of poor leadership and indecent intoxication, according to Kulichev, whose dislike of Zhirinovsky has not waned over the years. Kulichev claims that five anonymous letters were sent back to the International Bar Association. Zhirinovsky was identified as the author by style and content, and by the fact that he was the only troublemaker of his kind at work. He himself denies that he wanted to join the party and that he asked for a recommendation from his supervisors at the bar. As for the complaints, he admits that he wrote one letter with justified criticism, and that was it.

Whatever the case, by the early 1980s, quarrelsome, peevish, eternally disatisfied, and constantly critical Zhirinovsky found his position at the bar quite shaky. All that was needed was a formal pretext to fire him from his job, and it was soon found. A client of Zhirinovsky received an inheritance from a relative who had died in West Germany, which included vouchers to stay at a privileged resort. As a sign of gratitude, the client had shared these vouchers with his lawyer. Although not a bribe in the strictest sense of the word, such "presents" were strictly prohibited. As soon as Zhirinovsky's bosses learned of the gift, they hastened to exploit the incident to rid themselves of this squealer and disturber of the peace. Kulichev now admits that Zhirinovsky returned the vouchers unused to his client, but insists that this was done only after the story surfaced.

In mid-1983, the thirty-seven-year-old lawyer and Turkologist was once again on the skids, now with a damaged reputation. It was at this point that he received an Israeli invitation and was prepared to emigrate from Russia. Soon afterward, however, he found a new job as legal counsel at one of the largest state publishing houses, Mir, specializing in the books of foreign authors.

Viktor Dashevsky, who knew him then, claims that Zhirinovsky "somehow figured out how to lose all the arbitrage cases assigned to him." Vladimir Kartsev, then director of Mir, rejects Dashevsky's statement, recalling only one case Zhirinovsky lost. On the whole, Kartsev spoke well of his former subordinate as an inventive person who "knew how to find subtle solutions to ordinary, everyday problems." Judging from his rapid advance in salary—from 140 to 180 rubles, quite decent for those days—Zhirinovsky was successful at his new job.

Mir hired Zhirinovsky to work on copyright issues, but he soon was transferred to doing legal support for employee benefits. In his seven years at the publishing house, Zhirinovsky was able to obtain certain benefits for his colleagues, including free lunches and free rides on public transportation. He demanded even more—that editors be allowed to work at home and that the publishing house pay their apartment rents. Perhaps Zhirinovsky was under the influence of communist propaganda, which he accepted on faith, or perhaps he was recalling his childhood, when, no matter how bad things were, he was completely subsidized by the government, in twenty-four-hour nurseries and day-care centers, in Pioneer and youth camps, with even a free lunch from the cafeteria where his mother worked. The dream of a socialist paradise had entered his flesh and blood, forever shaping his political ideals. "This gentleman tried to create what was essentially a socialist society in our publishing house," Kartsev believes.

Perhaps that is why Zhirinovsky was not accepted into the Communist Party—he took the party slogans too literally and blindly, although they had long since lost their original content and had become merely decorative. It was a paradox in the spirit of Orwell: the party rejected a novitiate because he was faithful to its ideological principles.

After this latest rejection, Zhirinovsky made no further attempts to become a party member and his remarks about communists became even more vehement, but not about communist ideology.

"The communists should be hung according to their territorial affiliation—the Dzerzhinsky District communists should be hung on Peace Prospect, and Lenin District communists should be hung on Lenin Prospect," Zhirinovsky once declared at a meeting.

"But if there are any good communists?" a voice cried from the audience.

Never at a loss for words, Zhirinovsky replied, "We'll bury the good communists in good coffins!"

After acquiring some popularity for his defense of the rights of the workers at Mir, Zhirinovsky decided to run for office in the local legislature from his publishing house. The district party leadership immediately rewrote the campaign regulations to prevent the unreliable Zhirinovsky from taking a seat in the local government body. Zhirinovsky protested the new rules, but in vain.

Kartsev recalls Zhirinovsky as a bull in a China shop and a troublemaker, but also noted that as director of a state publishing house, he had to defend the interests of the state, whereas Zhirinovsky defended the employees' interests.

> We were opponents. Without him, of course, there would have been much more peace and quiet. He caused me a lot of headaches. He was branded with the mark of unreliability. He was a nontraveler, and the district party committee had not approved his application as a member. He and a few others were always in the opposition. We even called them "enemies of the people" as a joke. He was our publishing house's pioneer of glasnost, rousing our sleeping

collective. He addressed meetings, said unthinkable things, spoke searing truths, made a terrible furor. And no sooner would I get back from a meeting than they would be calling me from the KGB: "Why are you letting him get away with this!" They demanded that I kick him out. I didn't go along with them, because there was no law by which you could fire people for political reasons. But I did battle him at work. When there were elections for the new employees' council, I opposed his candidacy because he was unreasonable and unpredictable and would create more problems that he solved. Then there was a secret ballot and he lost. After the meeting he stopped by my office: "All the democratic procedures have been observed, I have no complaints."

Zhirinovsky's last attempt to make a career at the publishing house by democratic means took place in 1990, shortly before he left Mir, when he offered his nomination in elections for the director of the publishing house. He lost, winning only 5 percent of his colleagues' votes.

We are not detailing here the rumors disseminated by Zhirinovsky's political opponents that he was allegedly involved in bribes and foreign-currency speculation but that the KGB got him out of trouble and had the charges dropped. We did not find any confirmation of these rumors, other than the story of the vouchers at the International Bar Association, and those who spread them cite no evidence, just as for rumors that he was jailed in Turkey for foreign-currency speculation (or for homosexual acts, according to another story).

The only significant post that Zhirinovsky managed to obtain during these years had nothing to do with his career but did improve his family's living conditions. He was unhappy with his apartment—on the very outskirts of town, next to the Ring Highway, with no telephone, subway stop, movie theaters, or stores. Worse, the apartment was on the first floor. "It was fearsome," notes Zhirinovsky, although the amount of crime in Moscow was quite modest at that time compared with now. It was in this apartment building that Zhirinovsky became chairman of the building cooperative, thanks to which a year and a half later he managed to pull off a complicated apartment exchange. As a result, the Zhirinovskys moved to another district of Moscow, Sokolniki, to a good apartment on the eighth floor of the building. Now Zhirinovsky recalls his apartment odyssey almost with disgust.

Zhirinovsky was dissatisfied not only because of his usual tendency to grumble, but also because he felt doomed to restrict his activity to his family circle and domestic cares. The desperation of his situation was aggravated by his blocked party membership. "I was in a kind of different caste," he whines. He was chased out of general party meetings as soon as the closed, members-only part began. In Kafka's *The Castle*, the land surveyor K. tries to gain entrance to the longed-for castle but is always barred. Exchange "party" for "castle," and "land surveyor K." for "Vladimir Zhirinovsky," and our hero's plight is explained.

The complex over not being a party member was yet another complex for a man already overburdened with them. But being nonparty would serve Zhirinovsky well during the later election campaigns. In the postcommunist era, he would brandish his nonparty status as an advantage over the other candidates, who, unlike him, were without exception communists: Yeltsin, Rutskoi, Gaidar, Yavlinsky, Sobchak, Popov, and Travkin. Zhirinovsky is the only one who does not have this blot on his record, now shameful by the new standards of the day.

In this dark, dead-end period of his life, Zhirinovsky finally, in desperation, recalled his Jewish roots. In 1983 he thought seriously of emigration, but at the last moment, having already received an Israeli invitation, he rejected this option, perhaps because of his nontraveler status at the KGB. At the end of 1988, at the height of Gorbachev's glasnost, he once again played his Jewish card, but this time with the knowledge and support of the KGB, when he joined Shalom.

Zhirinovsky's flirtation with Shalom was limited to two meetings. Either Zhirinovsky himself decided that, in the new climate of openness, he was capable of more than just infiltrating this group, or the KGB finally became aware that they had underestimated him and recalled him from Shalom. Whatever the case, Zhirinovsky clearly had bigger fish to fry.

Earlier, Zhirinovsky attended rallies and made radical

speeches, at first supporting Gorbachev and then sharply criticizing him and demanding an end to the war in Afghanistan. He also initially sympathized with Yeltsin and, in his words, "was very upset when he [Yeltsin] was not elected to the Supreme Soviet at the first Congress of People's Deputies." In the spring of 1989, Zhirinovsky joined the coordinating council of an extremist group called the Democratic Union. According to Viktor Dashevsky, Mir director Kartsev informed the KGB officer in charge of the Dzerzhinsky District in Moscow (where the publishing house was located) about his behavior, and Zhirinovsky was subsequently summoned for a chat. Kartsev has a different version of the story—the KGB would call him practically every time Zhirinovsky made a public speech and demand that he be fired.

After the meeting with the KGB, however, Zhirinovsky behaved even more boldly and began to take greater risks. He had been accepted into the Democratic Union for his speech-making ability but was almost immediately expelled "for communist predilections." Even that, however, did not deter his political career. Zhirinovsky spent the second half of 1989 and the spring of 1990 at street rallies, honing his oratorical talent and distancing himself further from both the Kremlin and his opponents from the democratic camp. With his van and megaphone, he wedged his way into crowds of demonstrators, primarily Yeltsin supporters, finding a crack that grew wider as the political and economic crisis in the country worsened. He had been kept back for too long and was raring to go. Zhirinovsky came out of the underground, where he had spent nearly two decades, having accumulated an enormous supply of unspent energy and having reflected on several political ideas, chief of which for him personally was the idea of *vozhdism.*

His political and personal life underground further aggravated his psychological underground, that distorted, dreamlike world that since childhood had taken the place of hostile reality. Even he believes that "the constant feeling of dissatisfaction was a stimulus." His entire life was an accumulation of complexes—real or imagined—which, taken together, are very powerful stimuli for his overweening ambition. A Jew among Russians, a Russian among Kazakhs, a provincial among Muscovites, a non–party member among party members, and a perpetual loser—in his family, in love, in friendship, at his studies, at his job.

Over his buried Jewish complex was erected the sturdy monument of anti-Semitism; his Russian complex took the form of great-power chauvinism. The sexual inadequacies of his childhood and adolescence poured out in open preaching of sexism, misogyny, and male chauvinism. The provincial complex mutated into geographical egalitarianism and political anti-elitism. Finally, the failures that had dogged him since childhood, socially and professionally, hardened his desire for revenge and inured him to humiliation and hurt. He had been kicked when he was down. Politics became the means of his revenge in the early 1990s, a way to lift himself above the constant failures, the despair, the depressing horizon of his life. His is not an ordinary ambitious struggle for power, but an idée fixe, an obsession, a mania consuming the soul. The miracle was that the obsession materialized into reality, the perennial loser became a superstar. In one fell swoop, he became *vozhd'*, a political superman, or to use a language undoubtedly more proximate to Zhirinovsky, *Übermensch*. As Nietzsche said, long and great suffering unleashes the tyrant in man.

In mid-March 1990, Article 6 of the Constitution was abolished, ending the Communist Party's hegemony over the government. On the last day of that month, Zhirinovsky founded his Liberal Democratic Party, and a year after that he announced his candidacy for the presidency of Russia. To universal amazement, he came in third, with more than six million votes. Thus began the Zhirinovsky phenomenon, the underground man, the dreamer of revenge, the schemer, the political romantic, the cynic, and the adventurer. *Nezavisimaya gazeta* prophetically headlined its postelection article THE ZHIRINOVSKY PHENOMENON: WE HAVE SEEN ONLY THE FIRST INSTALLMENT.

3

THE UNEMPLOYED POLITICIAN

(AUGUST 1991–EARLY 1993)

After snapping up more than six million votes and winning third place in Russia's first presidential elections, Zhirinovsky proclaimed that he would have won first place if the campaign were three months long instead of one. At a press conference after the elections, Zhirinovsky remarked confidently to a foreign correspondent that in the next elections he and his party would get not six, but sixty, million votes. The democratic newspapers were furious. But this time Zhirinovsky was sincere in bandying about figures like sixty million (typical of his demagogic rhetoric). He said it on impulse, revealing how exhilarated he was from his dizzying success as a presidential candidate.

Zhirinovsky is so used to failure that the tiniest bit of success is an extraordinary boost for him. He believes himself destined to be a perpetual loser, and his officious self-promotion and his self-assurance are attempts to charm away this destiny. That is why he overreacts when success comes—always unexpected by him—even to the point of temper tantrums, paroxysms, and hysterical self-intoxication (as happened after he won the parliamentary elections in December 1993).

June 12, 1991, was a lucky day in Zhirinovsky's political career. From an unknown presidential hopeful he was transformed into a nationally known figure. Although his election campaign was impressive, it had been hastily cobbled together and he was unhappy with it, expecting at best three million votes. He was stunned and shaken when twice that many people voted for him. Only a year before he couldn't get himself elected as director of Mir Press, scraping up a pathetic 5 percent of six hundred votes.

Perhaps more important was Zhirinovsky's discovery of the electoral process. In the odyssey of a campaign battle, it seemed possible to scale the shining peaks of power on the horizon. Except for Boris Yeltsin, Zhirinovsky was unrivaled among Russian politicians in the art of populism and was tremendously skillful in estimating mass psychology and fighting for votes.

Zhirinovsky's main job after the election festivities was to build on his success and not allow his victory to wither on the vine. But, like a gambler staking his winnings on a larger bet, he rushed headlong from one campaign to another, this time to the highest rank—the president of the USSR. Gorbachev, still formally president of the USSR, had been forced by public opinion to accede to elections for the Soviet presidency, an opportunity Zhirinovsky immediately exploited. Without waiting for the official announcement of the elections, he launched a new campaign on the momentum of the previous one.

He immediately headed to the empire's hottest spot, to the front line: the Baltic republics, whose very allegiance to Moscow was increasingly in question as local peoples struggled for their independence. Both sides were adamant. Lithuania, Latvia, and Estonia declared their sovereignty, and Moscow retaliated with a trade embargo, rattling its weapons and even deploying them against peaceful demonstrators. From the perspective of international law, the question of Baltic state sovereignty was indisputable. But if their independence was to be recognized, a rather complicated and sensitive issue arose involving the Russian-language population, which had reached 40 percent in Estonia and Latvia. In some regions where heavy industry was concentrated, Russian speakers now constituted the overwhelming majority (in Narva, for example, a city in northeastern Estonia, where 95 percent of the population is Russian). The Kremlin's imperialist and colonialist policy was responsible for this demographic shift, and we can understand the Baltic separatist leaders who sought a return to a monoethnic state, where the rights of Russian-speaking aliens would inevitably have to be curtailed, making them into second-class citizens. Heine's famous metaphor is applicable to this interethnic clash: the crevice of the world runs through the human heart.

Zhirinovsky exploited this explosive situation when he went to Estonia in early August at the invitation of local pro-Moscow organizations. He gave speeches at the large centrally run factories serving the entire Soviet Union, where the majority of workers were Russian. Here Zhirinovsky was acting as an agent of Moscow, and if not actually provoking passions and grievances, was helping to stir them up in a republic split into "Russian-speaking" and native populations. His oratory was at its best and audiences listened to him in sympathy and agreement. He correctly calculated that these people were his primary constituents. No one defended the interests of the Russian minority in the non-Russian republics so passionately and persistently as Zhirinovsky. He promised that if he won the presidential elections, which he tentatively predicted for "the spring of next year," he would preserve Russia within the borders of a "united and indivisible USSR." Instead of the flawed division into national, ethnic-based territories introduced by the Bolsheviks, he would move to a system of *gubernii* (as provinces were designated in prerevolutionary Russia). Thus Estonia, Latvia, and Lithuania would be merged into one Baltic *guberniya*—one of many in the future Russian state à la Zhirinovsky. He further announced to thunderous applause that "Viktor Alksnis has agreed to be governor of this Baltic *guberniya*." Colonel Alksnis, was a Latvian who, along with Yevgeny Kogan, an Estonian Jew, and Nikolai Petrushenko, a Ukrainian, formed the conservative bloc Soyuz [Union] in the Soviet parliament, which advocated the preservation of the empire by any means. "Call me a reactionary—I have no objection," this Baltic governor "appointed" by Zhirinovsky told journalists point-blank.

Zhirinovsky concluded his propaganda workover of the Russian-speaking residents of Estonia with a paternalistic parting promise: "all nations, large and small" under his rule would be happy. His farewell revealed his formula for ridding Russia of obstinate aliens: "I promise that if I become president, the Estonians will be happy. Those who are not satisfied will leave for Sweden and Finland."

In advocating the preservation—or, ideally, the expansion—of the empire, Zhirinovsky was enlisting a powerful reserve of voters in his favor: the twenty-six million Russian speakers in the non-Russian republics! He planned to visit them all in a preelection marathon. Even the abuse hurled on him by the Estonian nationalist and Moscow liberal press worked in his favor; while criticizing and lampooning him, they were informing a growing number of his future supporters of his imperialist position.

Zhirinovsky intended to travel to Lithuania in the latter half of August, at the invitation of pro-Moscow communists there. Zhirinovsky and the Lithuanian quislings had a common goal—to keep the Soviet Union united and intact—as well as sponsors in common who had a vested interest in a political alliance among the conservative forces in the country regardless of their location or national affiliation. The Kremlin placed particular emphasis on Lithuania at the time, since that Soviet republic had gone farther than all the others in the struggle for independence. In January 1991, Soviet special-assignment troops, the OMON, had waged a bloody retaliation against peaceful, separatist demonstrators in Lithuania. Fifteen people died in one night. Then in early August, the OMON attacked a Lithuanian border post, shooting six Lithuanian customs agents at close range with assault rifles.

Two weeks after the border massacre, the pro-Moscow communists of Lithuania and the local OMON division began to organize a trip for Zhirinovsky and his bodyguards. Miraculously, some official documents have survived:

August 14, 1991 To the Commander of the OMON of the USSR MVD[1] in Vilnius, Police Major B. Makutynovich.

Please assist in the organization of security for representatives of the Liberal Democratic Party of

---

1. MVD is the Russian acronym for the Ministry of Internal Affairs, which is in charge of the police.

the USSR during their stay in the cities of Klaipeda, Vilnius, and Snechcius during the period starting at 15:00 hours on August 20 to 8:00 hours on August 23. . . .

The procedure for security will be determined by agreement. . . .

Yu. Galtsev, executive secretary of the Vilnius City Committee of the Lithuanian SSR

The trip fell through, however. Zhirinovsky couldn't take advantage of the hospitality of the Lithuanian communists on August 20–23, because a national emergency interfered with his plans. On the day before his intended departure with his party cohorts, a coup d'état was attempted in Moscow. While Gorbachev was at his dacha in the resort town of Foros on the Black Sea, he was removed as leader of the country, and power passed into the hands of his closest comrades in arms—the vice president, the prime minister, the defense minister, the KGB chairman, and the chief of police—who had declared a state of emergency.

Although it's easy to think of the coup plotters as a bunch of villains, it is perhaps equally true that they had harkened to the mood of the society. In August 1991 the Soviet empire was crumbling before everyone's eyes, and the dream of order emerged as a panacea for its fatal disease. The August coup was a last-ditch attempt, in some eyes, to save the empire from collapse.

Gorbachev himself sat out the coup in his Black Sea dacha. Later it was determined that he knew about the plans for the coup in advance, but had decided simply to see how things turned out. In fact, the coup was not aimed against him personally, but against his liberal line, which was not paying off. Besides ideological considerations, Gorbachev also had personal reasons to treat the coup plotters condescendingly or even to encourage them. As the empire crumbled, power slipped from his hands. Only the putschists could return it to him and put a halt to this political avalanche. If the anti-Gorbachev coup had lasted longer than three days, Gorbachev most likely would have joined it himself and returned to the Kremlin.

Yeltsin, however, had a personal stake in the dissolution of the Soviet Union's fifteen constituent republics into independent states because then he would become the leader of an independent Russia. He condemned the putsch, led the resistance, and in the end prevailed.

Throughout those three days of political and personal resistance by the main heroes of the drama—the decisive Yeltsin and the temporizing Gorbachev—Zhirinovsky, the self-styled Soviet presidential candidate, was in a kind of frenzied ecstasy. He dashed around Moscow with his party retinue, agitating for the new GKChP[2] government and for renewed law and order. The coup plotters' slogans were his own—a firm hand and an indivisible Russia. On the morning of August 19, the first day of the coup, he hurried to release a statement in the name of his party in support of the coup plotters: "The Supreme Council of the Liberal Democratic Party of the Soviet Union expresses its support for the transfer of all governmental authority in the USSR to the USSR GKChP." And this at a time when even communists were staying on the sidelines and keeping their mouths shut.

The anti-Yeltsin coup culminated in Yeltsin's triumph. Gorbachev returned to Moscow from his fake confinement in Foros. The Justice Ministry gave the Liberal Democratic Party an official warning for supporting the coup plotters and demanded the punishment of the guilty. Zhirinovsky's party instantly caved in:

> The Supreme Council of the USSR LDP has discussed the above-mentioned statement, has indicated to the chairman of the USSR LDP that the statement was approved hastily, and has demanded of V. V. Zhirinovsky, chairman of the USSR LDP, not to permit such statements in the future. Signed, Members of the USSR LDP Supreme Council, V. V. Zhirinovsky, S. M. Zhebrovsky, A. Kh. Khalitov

Curiously, the Justice Ministry considered this pro forma reply sufficient. The Communist Party, which had kept mum during the three days, was immediately banned after the failed coup.

---

2. GKChP is the Russian acronym for the State Committee on the State of Emergency, which arrogated full authority to itself on August 19, 1991.

Zhirinovsky not only refused to recant his pro-coup views and actions, he even displayed a certain courage in continuing to defend his authoritarian principles under the new democratic regime. In street encounters in Moscow after the August coup, he promised voters: "I will impose harsh order. A harsh regime. Whoever is for democracy, buy your tickets. Sheremetyevo [airport] will be open."

"A new GKChP will be formed," he went on to say. "I will immediately impose a state of emergency, close down all the newspapers, and disband all the parties."

Several months after their arrest, Zhirinovsky held a rally calling for the plotters' release in front of the prison building. Paradoxically, this support of politicians condemned by the liberal press redounded to Zhirinovsky's credit. It was taken as an indisputable sign of principle in a figure widely believed to be unprincipled and opportunistic. In speaking out for the politically bankrupt coup plotters, he exposed himself to political, if not physical, danger. The triumphant democrats were ready to tear any dissident to pieces. Evidently Zhirinovsky had one or two stubborn convictions for the sake of which he was willing to take a risk and ostracism. He is used to it; in Russian politics he is an outsider, an alien, a Lone Ranger.

Zhirinovsky returned repeatedly to these three ill-fated August days, when, in his opinion, a real opportunity was missed to halt the dissolution of the Russian empire. Putting himself in Gorbachev's shoes, he saw only one appropriate political option: decisive support of the coup. In *The Last Push to the South*, released on the eve of the 1993 parliamentary elections, Zhirinovsky reflected:

> In politics, situations sometimes emerge when you must save the country, to make a decision at that level. . . . Foros, August 1991, Gorbachev. Surely he could have acted differently. Everything depended on him. And events would have turned out completely differently.

In a videotaped discussion after the collapse of the coup, Zhirinovsky imagined himself at the head of the conspiracy, making use of the great lost opportunity. As chief plotter, with the fate of great Russia riding on him alone, he made appeals directly to the wavering generals, giving orders that they had to obey under fear of execution. For the Russian journalists and politicians speculating on his aims, Zhirinovsky the strategist proposed a straightforward answer:

> Whoever was engaged in sabotage shouldn't have been called on the telephone, but should have been shot. If Barannikov, Russia's minister of internal affairs, did not obey orders—he should have been shot! Officers should have come in within five minutes and shot him! If they had shot five or six generals, they would have pulled off a good GKChP. Like Pinochet did. . . . Hey, [General] Makashov, move out, you have 24,000 tanks, move on to Moscow, it's only 400 kilometers, 24,000 tanks should have been in Moscow that evening! Then it would have worked out for sure! Helicopters should have razed the White House. And that whole gang should have been arrested back in Arkhangelskoye [the presidential dacha]. . . . Those generals have decayed and rotted. You know, it's all rotten, they can't do anything. It's their own fault they lost. What of it? Everything was planned down to the last detail, there hadn't been any problems, on August 22 there could have been another country, a powerful USSR!

But faceless, indecisive bureaucrats were running the coup; they had no real *vozhd'*, no charismatic leader who could take charge of a team and save the empire from demise. Caesarism without Caesar no longer worked. The failure of the August coup was yet more negative proof of the correctness of Zhirinovsky's political and psychological aim to become *vozhd'*.

Election Campaign Zhirinovsky-Style: The Nonelection

After the August disorders, Zhirinovsky holed up with his bodyguards for several days in a town outside Moscow called

Sofrin, and then plunged into his interrupted campaign for the presidency of the USSR. He traveled to Krasnodar, Leningrad, Minsk, and collective farms outside Moscow, but for the most part staged rallies in Moscow, appearing almost daily on the streets, in movie theaters empty by day, at markets, at factories, at students' auditoriums. To anyone willing to listen he told his sorrowful tale of the democrats' ruin of the country and the coming collapse of Great Russia, which could be avoided only through an authoritarian government. Off the top of his head, he chose a date for the elections, in April 1992. He tried to impress that date in the memories of the Russian and foreign journalists who interviewed him, and on the masses on the street—his future voters. These unannounced elections, which made less and less sense after the Baltic and Caucasian states' revolt, became Zhirinovsky's personal fixation. Seemingly through an effort of will, emotional pressure, and ominous incantations, Zhirinovsky tried to impose, on a Russia indifferent to its own demise, the presidential elections that were to save it.

Day after day Zhirinovsky screamed furiously in the foyer of the Kremlin Palace of Congresses, gradually attracting onlookers, establishment politicians, people's deputies, and foreign reporters:

> No autonomous republics, no Union republics! There will be one united Russian republic. The Bolsheviks made their experiment—and it flopped! Now the democrats will experiment: everyone will get freedom, democracy, and independence. They will experiment. Then, when they flop, I'll come along. We won't seize Hungary. We'll take just what was in Russia before the October coup. I'll impose order, I'm telling you! I will restore the borders of the Russia state as they were on September 1, 1917. Including Finland. It won't be seizing, but emancipating!

Another time Zhirinovsky screeched at a Moscow journalist: "I must win the presidential elections, and I will win them! Otherwise it will mean civil war and dictatorship, of the kind no scholar has ever described."

These mythical elections became for Zhirinovsky a dual salvation—of himself from his dead-end career, and of the country from collapse. The personal and the political were closely intertwined in his tragic vision of the fall of 1991, when the Soviet empire had suffered a severe crisis but a fatal outcome did not yet seem inevitable. The elections to the Soviet presidency gave him a chance, albeit small (he was realistic about it), to replace Gorbachev, who had grown ineffectual after his return from Foros, and to halt the process of disintegration that the democrats had initiated under the guise of fighting the empire. Since Russia had known only an imperial government for centuries, the "empire" and the "state" have historically been synonymous. This is how Zhirinovsky saw a future Russia, crushed by the democrats:

> Iran and Afghanistan can drag Central Asia over to its side, Turkey is settling scores with the Transcaucasus; Poland and Romania will take care of Ukraine and Moldova. That leaves an embittered Russia, which will torment itself with China and Japan, with the Yakuts and Buriats, with the Volga Region, in an eternal knot of insoluble problems. There are nuclear weapons, and the military factories, and the tanks, and the disgruntled army, returning home from all over: from Germany, the Baltics, Transcaucasia. And all of them are going to Russia, to Russia, to Russia. And now there's rationing of bread, only three hundred grams. It's already only a half a glass of milk for a child in Moscow and then it will only be a swallow. A swallow. And the democrats will say: "That's just what we wanted. Now the country is free. Hungry, but free! The country is half lost, the population is half lost! The power and might are lost! But even so, we're sitting in the Kremlin."

At the same time, Zhirinovsky saw these elections as his entré into power politics, and perhaps his last. Under the democrats, he would be pushed from the political high road to the shoulder. While newspapers howled, in November he publicly urged the Red Army to "defend our motherland, save the country, Great Russia," and called on military people to support his candidacy. Moscow's journalists had a field day over Zhirinovsky's brazen promises that the army would receive heaps of gifts in exchange for its support.

The possibility of this breakthrough, however, was snatched away from Zhirinovsky when, a few months after the beginning of his campaign, the post itself disappeared—along with the empire. In the latter months of 1991, Yeltsin was ensconced at the White House while Gorbachev had dug himself into the Kremlin. In Moscow there were two centers of power, two presidents, two courts, two apparatuses of state. Gorbachev was clinging to power with his last remnants of strength, but there was no legitimate means of getting rid of him except for eliminating the post of Soviet president itself. That in turn was possible only if the Soviet Union itself were dismantled.

By the end of 1991, the struggle between the two presidents entered a critical phase. At the dacha in the Belovezhsky Forest of Belarus, the leaders of three Slavic nations (at Yeltsin's initiative, naturally) announced ex prompto the dissolution of the USSR. With one stroke of the pen, the USSR was dead and Soviet history came to an end. Overnight, Russians residing in the other Soviet republics found themselves in foreign countries. The Commonwealth of Independent States, an ephemeral and fictitious bloc, was created in place of the USSR. In the words of the celebrated nineteenth-century Russian poet Tyutchev, it was "a shroud over an abyss."

The red hammer-and-sickle flag over the Kremlin was lowered. Even without a country, Gorbachev resisted for several days, although he was now lord only of the Kremlin complex itself. He was literally thrown out on New Year's Eve. Yeltsin lost no time in moving into the Kremlin and getting on with political and economic reform, with his accustomed iconoclasm. He banned the Communist Party, hoping to knock the support out from under Russian conservatism and its nomenklatura. His reformist government set about methodically breaking up the old power structures in order to move from a centralized economy to a free market.

These political cataclysms forced Zhirinovsky to halt his campaign and launch a new crusade against the Kremlin, now synonymous with democracy and reform. Thus, by force of circumstances, he was unable to make the most of his political capital—the six-million-plus votes garnered in the Russian presidential elections—nor did he manage to break into the political establishment. During this period Zhirinovsky was gloomily bitter at fate, which had once again dealt him a bad hand, although he had fought it mightily. Before going into opposition to the new democratic regime, Zhirinovsky looked around at the changed political landscape, trying to find his place. All the doors were slammed shut to him, however—there was no crack open into big politics. It was exactly during this black period for Zhirinovsky and the empire that Zhirinovsky began to spout militarist clichés and to preach a nuclear endgame at press conferences, on television, and at student meetings. Impulsively sublimating his fury against "external enemies," he proposed this solution to the problem of Soviet prisoners of war held in Pakistan: "I will summon the ambassador of Pakistan and give him 72 hours. If within 72 hours our Russian fellows are not back at Sheremetyevo, I will send the Pacific Fleet to the shores of Pakistan, and for starters it will wipe Karachi off the face of the earth." Asked how he would handle the controversy with Japan over the Kurile islands, seized by Stalin after World War II as war reparations, Zhirinovsky proclaimed: "If I am in charge, the Japanese will not ask me for the Kurile Islands. Because my ships will be sailing around Hokkaido. Let the Japanese save Hokkaido. They'll forget about the Kurile islands forever." Finally, there was this ominous blast: "I will not stop at using nuclear weapons outside the borders of the USSR."

Political extremism growing out of a temper tantrum is a typical behavior trait of tyrants in general and is true of Zhirinovsky in particular. Indeed, the appearance of a populist politician with a nimble mind and presidential aspirations in a country with twenty-seven thousand nuclear warheads would seem to constitute a threat to global security. But Zhirinovsky has been perceived by Russian society as a "comic character," an opportunist, a monster, a paranoic, or a demon—in any case, beyond politics. If establishment figures spoke of him at all, it was with unconcealed scorn and contempt. This was an opportunity to neutralize Zhirinovsky, to clip his wings, defang him, and defuse his negative potential. Nor did his rivals in the opposition consider him either a worthy opponent or an ally in the struggle for power.

Zhirinovsky was clearly weighed down by his outsider status, frankly yearning for legitimacy, for the establishment. Although he was bluffing out of desperation, as was his wont, he had set his sights on the highest office in the land. He dreamed of attaining the "castle" of power, but could not find a way in through the front or back door. The reason was that one exclusive Kremlin elite (Gorbachev's) had been replaced by another (Yeltsin's) no less exclusive, and there was no place under the sun of Russian democracy for Zhirinovsky. If Yeltsin had taken Zhirinovsky in and found him a spot in the government, he would have rendered harmless Zhirinovsky's destructive potential. Attached to the establishment, perhaps as head of a ministerial directorate or a consultant to the Council of Ministers (or something higher up—he was shooting for something higher at the time), Zhirinovsky might have made his peace with the reformers. Yeltsin should have incorporated him into the state structure, wooed him by power, rank, and status, and for that matter, simply brought him into government management as a new source of energy. Zhirinovsky should not have been left to harangue, seduce, and corrupt the people on democracy's square. It was dangerous to goad him to embittered and angry explosions, to a delusion of grandeur and a cult of personality, to revanchist frenzy and ranting about the bomb. On the whole, considering Zhirinovsky's enormous energy, his *vozhd'*-like charisma, his gift for populism, and, most important, the outrageous villainy of his call to nuclear arms—and much more—the question of how to neutralize Zhirinovsky should have been at the top of the Russian government's agenda.

To neutralize Zhirinovsky in this manner would have required a cunning leader with tactical agility and a foxlike sense of people—all qualities that Yeltsin does not possess. The moment was lost; not terribly perceptive about people, Yeltsin did not heed the warnings of history.

Still not cooled off from the election campaign he had stage-managed, Zhirinovsky was once again at a political crossroads. He was essentially an unemployed politician, even a homeless one—his suite at the prestigious Hotel Moscow, where the LDP had been headquartered during the Russian presidential campaign, was taken away from him. Some observers opined with relief that the Zhirinovsky phenomenon was a nine-day wonder, and that he himself was only king for a day and would remain a small-print footnote in a chapter about Yeltsin in the annals of Russian history.

In fact, however, Zhirinovsky had already shown himself to be a figure of national prominence, affecting the minds of millions of his fellow citizens. The local authorities knew this all too well in the Russian provinces, where people were becoming more and more responsive to Zhirinovsky at rallies. On learning of Zhirinovsky's plans to come to his city in December, St. Petersburg mayor Anatoly Sobchak launched a number of measures to prevent disorder during meetings with the city's workers.

Shouting angrily, "Any future politics in this country is impossible without my participation!" Zhirinovsky left the political stage for the great expanses of Russia and the opposition.

What does this mean? After ending up politically isolated under the democrats and without any electoral prospects, Zhirinovsky suddenly recalled his miniature Liberal Democratic Party, whose ranks had thinned even further after a split in 1991 over the coup. Dubbed a "pseudo-party" or a "joke-party" by the democratic press, the LDP was in fact no real party at all, lacking an ideology or a program of its own. In his two presidential campaign blitzes within eight months, Zhirinovsky had exploited the LDP merely as a vehicle to promote himself.

Now he turned to an ancient form of political life, long forgotten in Russia: leader of the opposition. Although he continued to view his party as a personal promotion machine, Zhirinovsky set about raising the LDP's prestige and popularity to his own level. He extracted some immediate advantage from the failure of the August coup:

> For the current democratic forces have ultimately banned the Communist Party and have destroyed the old, established structures. But they have not managed to build new ones and will never succeed in doing that. Thus there will be a vacuum of power.

> We, the LDP, can go into the vacuum . . . the new
> democratic forces are weak and amorphous, they
> don't pose any political threat to us. It will be easy
> for us to run in the election in opposition to them
> because the democrats are not capable of running
> the country.

Now, for the first time, Zhirinovsky was defining a platform
for his party—as the opposition. A month or two later, after
the sudden demise of the USSR, he redefined the LDP's oppo-
sitional direction and targeted Yeltsin's Kremlin and the reformist government.

He found offices for his party, which had been without any
fixed address and as much as a vagrant as he, in two floors of
an old residential building in Rybnikov Lane in the Sretenka
District in the center of Moscow. This dilapidated building,
with its sagging doorway and broken stairway, soon became a
local landmark. The LDP's enormous emblem, an eagle flying
over a map of a Russia that includes Alaska and Finland, hangs
in Zhirinovsky's office above his armchair, near a huge map of
the world on which the borders of prerevolutionary Russia
have been crudely drawn with a thick, vermilion line. No foreign journalist visiting Zhirinovsky has failed to note Zhirinovsky's best routine: "Zhirinovsky stands in front of a map of the
world with a pointer in his hand, expounding his geopolitical
notions." "He is a comic opera dictator, more Charlie Chaplin
than Adolf Hitler, But that does not make him any less dangerous," said a foreign reporter about Zhirinovsky. In fact,
between elections and without any clear career prospects,
Zhirinovsky had cooled somewhat from his campaign frenzy
and fury. Some of Zhirinovsky's stock slogans and expansionist
calls, taken out of the context of a public meeting, suddenly
sounded almost ridiculous. For a time he seemed to be trying
to fit his radical image into a more acceptable centrist framework—until a new surge of political extremism at the end of
1992. Zhirinovsky was evidently anticipating a long stay in the
opposition camp:

> You see, in order for our party to become the ruling
> party, we need parliamentary elections, but there

won't be any. Not in the near future, at any rate. . . .
I have no rivals. But we aren't in a hurry; the fruit
must ripen. For what reason are the Democratic Russians losing now? They had not expected to come to
power on August 21. They thought they had another
five to ten years of being in the opposition, fighting
with the Communist Party. The unexpected victory
caught them flat-footed. We will not repeat their
mistake.

Despite such statements, Zhirinovsky has not seriously
worked on party-building; rather, he has used the party for
endless campaigning. Finally, in December 1993, emergency
elections for a parliament to replace the one dispersed by Yeltsin were called. At last Zhirinovsky's long preparation came in
handy.

Unlike other parties, blocs, and groupings united by ideological affiliation, the LDP is strictly a political party, with
changeable slogans and a moving platform oriented toward
taking power. For Zhirinovsky, a party is not an end in itself
but a means of attaining power. Accordingly, if he were elected
president, he would immediately halt the activity of all political
parties, including his own. A party is not only created by its
vozhd', but to suit its *vozhd'*, in his image and likeness, oriented
toward the cult of his personality. A party apparatchik charac-
terized the LDP as a "leader's party": "If Zhirinovsky is there,
there's a party. If there's no Zhirinovsky, there's no party." The
Italian fascists founded their parties on the same principle, as
did the German National Socialists and, for that matter, the
Bolsheviks: "When we say party, we mean Lenin," as Vladimir
Mayakovsky, in his poem "Vladimir Ilyich Lenin," said, sum-
marizing the *vozhd'* principle.

Zhirinovsky's party still seems more like a game or a parody
than a real party. Instead of ideological coherence, the extravagant personality of its *vozhd'* is distinctly and indelibly im-
printed on it. His campaign slogans are the party program, his
geopolitical doctrine and imperialist revanchism generate the
party emblem, his strategy and tactics for the achievement of
ultimate power are the party catechism.

The LDP's leader doesn't need ideological supporters so much as a team of workers to operate his campaign machine. Zhirinovsky selected his staff for their ability to work, not for their ideological affinity. One current LDP staff worker recalls how he came to the party in early 1992: "Democratic Russia wasn't accepting members. Only the LDP's doors were open. Zhirinovsky himself personally interviewed everyone. He even advertised through the Manpower Office in order to expand his staff."

Zhirinovsky's main strategic effort at that time was to stay afloat; to keep the press, both domestic and foreign, focused on him; and to remain in the public eye. He portrayed this unmitigated self-promotion as party activity, justifying his political egocentrism as in the party interest. One of a series of such sensations was the announcement in the summer of 1992 of the creation of Zhirinovsky's shadow cabinet, naturally billed as a party activity. With all the imperiousness of an heir to the Kremlin, Zhirinovsky presented his alternative power structure, a startling act in a country where there was still a functioning president, although it was in the form of a parody, "Zhirinovsky's government":

> Our cabinet has about twenty ministers. Some of them are quite active, others are only on the list, knowing that their services may be required at any moment. We are preparing to take responsibility for governing the affairs of the country, and are now working on the formation of structures of power. One leader cannot cope with everything.

Within only a few months, however, a good half of Zhirinovsky's shadow cabinet left the LDP, including the security minister, the foreign minister, and the ministers of culture and information. Tired of working at Zhirinovsky's whim, they have organized their own party on an ideological—national-radical—basis. But the "shadow cabinet" of 1992 was another effective gimmick in Zhirinovsky's campaign.

Zhirinovsky is the dominant topic in the LDP's press, which is largely named for him—the young journal *Zhirinovsky's*

Falcon; the organ of the center *Zhirinovsky's Word* (St. Petersburg); *Zhirinovsky's Truth*; *At Home with Zhirinovsky*; and so on. Although in 1991 a rather dry and factual *Judicial Gazette* had been published, the publications really began coming out thick and fast starting in 1992, when the party's coffers were noticeably bulging with the latest anonymous contribution. Zhirinovsky's face looms up from the front pages of all these newspapers and the covers of the blandly titled magazine *The Liberal*; and each issue of each publication features several articles by and about Zhirinovsky along with his photos. The front pages of the party newspapers also carry hard-hitting quotes from Zhirinovsky, such as "Russian, once you have started a job, do it well. Then you will be master of the world. The moment someone thinks bad things about Russians, he had better get out money for his funeral. Farewell, America!"

One article was titled "Zhirinovsky's Noble Liberalism"; another claimed that "it will be very good for Russia if Zhirinovsky becomes its president instead of Yeltsin." In still other newspapers, fellow LDP party members aggrandize their leader in the Stalin manner: "Our *vozhd'*, Vladimir Zhirinovsky."

These LDP publications, however, are memorable not merely for Zhirinovsky. In *Zhirinovsky's Falcon*, for example, in a column titled "Theory," the "theoretical foundation of national-socialism" as applied to Russia were analyzed. Articles by the famous rock Nazis Andrei Arkhipov and Sergei Zharikov (who were also ministers in Zhirinovsky's shadow cabinet) discussed plans to establish a new racial order in the world. Arkhipov announced ominously: "The bearers of white civilization are disappearing. The world is turning yellow, red, and black. There is no room left on the planet for the white man." He proposes the following program to save the white race:

> Only from Russians can Germans find real support in their struggle against the decaying North Atlantic Civilization. Together with Russians, they can take revenge on the U.S. for its "fervent internationalism" . . . Russia and Germany together can support

the rapid downfall of the U.S. and establish a more healthy racial balance on the European continent.

In an article called "The Superior Race," Zharikov moves from global issues to specifically Russian problems:

> But there is one people in Russia . . . a master people. It is the Russian people. . . .
>
> One thing always has been and will always be certain: when a few representatives of the so-called minority peoples remain living . . . —these insects will finally realize the reason they were born on this earth and that things are turning bad for them— and they will fall down before those whom they have offended and accused of every sin for so long and with such impunity. They will fall down before the Russian master. And we will not seek revenge. We will simply impose order.

Alexei Mitrofanov, Zhirinovsky's shadow-cabinet foreign minister, gives ultimate expression to this great-power notion: "Our line is reasonable egotism; our goal is world domination."

Zhirinovsky's "ministers" are extremist ideologues, unlike their *vozhd'*, who is an opportunistic politician. In speeches before May 1992, Zhirinovsky used the slogans of the ultra-right wing of the LDP. But then, Zhirinovsky, with his instantaneous sensing of the pulse of society, switched from right-wing extremism to left-wing extremism: from May 1992 to the end of summer 1993, he borrowed communist slogans for his rhetoric at rallies. On November 7, 1992, in honor of the seventy-fifth anniversary of the 1917 Bolshevik revolution, Zhirinovsky's Liberal Democrats staged a joint demonstration with communists and socialists on Red Square.

For understandable reasons, the ultra-right ideologues Zharikov and Arkhipov ultimately could not bear the political zigzags of their leader and quit the LDP. Another departee was the Russian writer Eduard Limonov, who had lived in the West for many years and was known for his sexually explicit novels.

Limonov, who had been chief of the secret police in Zhirinovsky's shadow cabinet, left Zhirinovsky when he became convinced of the LDP leader's total ideological insolvency. As he explained:

> Why did I leave Zhirinovsky? The LDP is merely Vladimir Volfovich, and the members of the party are his silent servants. I gradually realized that along with indisputable political talent, utter lack of principle and political opportunism coexist in Zhirinovsky. For example, at a rally in a Cossack community club, he loudly promised the Cossacks that he would rid them of the Armenian mafia. Then, on the next day, in my presence, he swore to a representative of the Armenian mafia to protect Armenian interests in exchange for financial transactions favorable to the party. After hundreds of such incidents, I understood that Zhirinovsky is an opportunist.

Zhirinovsky himself later admitted that people of firm ideological principles did not get along in his party. "In 1991, there was a split over the coup; in the fall of 1992, the extreme right wing split off, then the extreme leftists quit." Now Zhirinovsky was free to change his views, slogans, ideas, and even ideology whenever it suited him.

Although the party would seem orphaned without its leader, Zhirinovsky had so thoroughly imbued his image with party spirit that he is no longer imaginable as an independent politician. Thus the repeated attempts by political opponents, most frequently by the democrats, to discredit the LDP have struck at Zhirinovsky's personal reputation. In August 1992, the Russian justice minister withdrew the LDP's registration, "since it had been performed with gross violations of the law and falsified documents." Zhirinovsky perceived it as a personal tragedy, his banishment from the establishment. His party was virtually banned for five months, until December 1992, when Zhirinovsky submitted new lists and a second registration was made. As a lawyer and a passionate advocate of law and order in his calls at rallies, Zhirinovsky suffered terribly from the LDP's outlaw status. The familiar specter of failure haunted him, though; in public he assumed his wonted facade of arrogance and bravado. When, on November 7, as head of a small LDP phalanx he linked up with a column of communists and socialists in the Red Square march, he was acting under the umbrella of the establishment opposition, secretly acquiring the legitimacy and prestige of which his party had been stripped at that time.

The pace of Russian politics slowed in 1992. Yeltsin, the previous year's hero, was still at the Kremlin center stage, with a new entourage of young reformist ministers headed by Yegor Gaidar. But out of the political crowd scene waiting in the wings, some characters were eager to come to the fore, honing their craft and gaining authority from their criticism of the new government's very first steps. It can be said that Zhirinovsky made his political career on the mistakes of Yeltsin and Gaidar.

The year 1992 was the first and, alas, last year of economic reform. The government lifted price controls and allowed a free market, attempting to move as rapidly as possible from the artificial socialist economy to a natural capitalist economy. But this experiment (later dubbed the Great Liberal Illusion) was hastily and harshly introduced, like a laboratory test without feedback between experimenters and the guinea-pig population, who never received a clear explanation as to why reform was needed or why people had to suffer. The first rounds of shock therapy, compounded by the fall of the Soviet empire, caused such conspicuous material loss and mental trauma that it would have been odd if public grumbling did not seek an outlet. Zhirinovsky was not the only opponent of the government and not even its chief one, although his opposition was the most reckless, brazen, and demagogic.

Having expended his energy destroying the empire, Yeltsin froze in uncertainty, passive and confused in the face of the growing mountain of unsolvable problems. The free market was leading to impoverishment and desperation in a significant part of the population. Freedom was causing a growth in crime. The collapse of the empire was disrupting vitally important economic ties and unleashing discrimination against Russians in the new states. Yeltsin's fear of making an irreparable mistake led to inaction and a paralysis of power. Barely begun, reform was first reined in and then halted, which whipped up the conservative fury—they saw the president's indecisiveness as a political weakness.

The parliament became the president's chief enemy; the crisis of power degenerated into a diarchy, with the parliament on the offensive. Yeltsin made compromises and concessions and finally, in search of a political cease-fire and civic peace, he betrayed his chief economic-reform architect, Gaidar, and in his place appointed as prime minister the economic manager and practitioner Viktor Chernomyrdin, who immediately announced that a great power like Russia "should not turn into a nation of shopkeepers." The divisiveness and confusion in society found its political reflection in the diarchy, or in fact, the lack of authority. On this soil Zhirinovsky's ambitions soared.

Zhirinovsky's greatest anomaly was that he acted not only against the times but instead of the times by arranging a series of desirable events. First it seemed as if the democrats had come to power. Once Yeltsin had squeezed Gorbachev out of the Kremlin, he firmly held his seat, guaranteed to stay in power for five years. Yet Zhirinovsky was already running a campaign for the Russian presidency, confidently predicting that by April 1992, the Yeltsin government would be overthrown either by a popular rebellion or a military coup. ("Nineteen ninety-two is the crucial year!" he said.) Recall that April 1992 was also the date Zhirinovsky himself announced in the fall of 1991 for the hypothetical elections for Soviet president. Consequently, this date was in no way related to the real array of political forces in the country or to Zhirinovsky's prophetic interpretation of them. It was an arbitrary date, imposed by Zhirinovsky on reality and on the crowds at rallies in the course of his self-styled campaign. When April came and went and Yeltsin was still firmly ensconced in the Kremlin, Zhirinovsky moved the date of the presidential elections to the fall, saying that "Yeltsin will not last in the presidential seat through the fall." Then he moved the date yet again from the fall to February 1993, and so on, until emergency elections finally *did* take place in December 1993. This time, there was no question that the government had officially set the date.

Curiously, in both 1992 and 1993, Zhirinovsky made identical predictions for the fall of the democratic government: "The situation will grow worse. If not in October 1992, then in March, Russia will have another political regime. Patriots will come to power, democrats will be removed"; "Nineteen ninety-three will be a turning point. The democrats are running out of steam. A change of government is inevitable."

Zhirinovsky seriously worked the entire country, heading first to the boundless Russian provinces with his zealous propaganda. His two preceding campaigns—the first an actual election, the second an imaginary one—were run too hastily and abruptly to give him nationwide recognition. Therefore he began a scrupulous redesign of his new campaign, methodically pursuing popularity bit by bit, appearing on local TV and radio shows and before any audience willing to hear him—students, workers, military people, rural folks, people on the street. His main theme was the restoration of the USSR, the renewal of Russian statehood in the form of a federation of *gubernii* and republics, protection of Russians in other states, an end to aid to former "fraternal republics," and the return of Russia's national dignity and superpower status. To ordinary people, numb from the insurmountable difficulty of their growing daily problems, he proposed simple solutions and extremely simplified explanations. He proposed, for example, to restore order in Russia within twenty-four hours with the help of military divisions and to shoot criminals at the scene of their crimes. He blamed Russia's poverty and shame on the "criminal clique" of democrats, who were acting at the behest of the Western countries with a vested interest in the collapse of the "great, powerful, and strong Russia."

To his stock slogans such as "The attempt to build capitalism is just another trick!" Zhirinovsky added more up-to-date phrases in keeping with Russian and world developments. There was the "Anglo-Saxon-Israeli plot" against Russia, for example, the nonrecognition of the sovereignty of the Baltic and Central Asia nations ("they belong to the Russian empire"), and the return of the Crimea to Russia.

Zhirinovsky was the first (as early as May 1991) to take up the cause of the Crimea. Khrushchev, in a grand tsarlike gesture, had arbitrarily split off the Crimean Peninsula from

Russia in 1954 and presented it to Ukraine, not even sus-
pecting what a time bomb he had placed under the two countries' relations. Within the boundaries of the USSR, such a gift
was of a strictly formal nature—the Crimea merely changed
from being a subject of the Russian republic to a subject of the
Ukrainian republic, but they were all parts of a single and indivisible country and equally subordinate to the Kremlin. When
the USSR collapsed, the Crimea, with its 70 percent Russian
population and powerful naval bases, became a bone of con-
tention between Russia and Ukraine. Taking up the battle cry
for the Crimea, Zhirinovsky proved to the country once again
that he was the chief patriot of all the politicians.

By the summer of 1992, Zhirinovsky had traveled to campaign events in Siberia, northern Russia, Krasnodar Territory,
and out to the sticks of middle Russia (Vladimir and Murom).
Everywhere he went he set up electoral commissions in the
event of sudden elections ("anything could happen to the
president, he's mortal like all of us"). Zhirinovsky did not for a
minute lose sight of his rival in this one-sided battle—Yeltsin.
On learning that Yeltsin was planning a visit to Arkhangelsk,
Zhirinovsky beat him there by three weeks, wresting from Yeltsin the initiative and the publicity. "Yeltsin's economic program is a good beginning; you just have to do exactly the
opposite of what he is proposing. You have to freeze prices and
stop privatization." That was Zhirinovsky's economic model—
an upside-down version of Yeltsin's program.

Zhirinovsky even copied in full Yeltsin's opposition style. At
the end of the 1980s, Yeltsin had taken politics out of the
Kremlin's back rooms to the popular masses, and had been
the first to introduce "rally democracy" into the country's politics. Yeltsin's mass meetings and encounters with many thousands of people on streets, squares, stadiums, and shop floors
were a triumph of grassroots, spontaneous street democracy in
the face of the nondemocratic Kremlin. Zhirinovsky even tried
to duplicate such a typical scene of the late 1980s in a new
historical context—"the masses' appeal to the popular
leader," at a time when Yeltsin was desperate for popular support, and the popular opposition needed an influential, au-
thoritative, charismatic leader. Only now it was Zhirinovsky
who was proclaiming at public meetings his role of national
leader, savior of the fatherland, and charismatic dictator.

Alone among Russian politicians, Zhirinovsky traveled around the country, indefatigably waging a premature and seemingly pointless election campaign. In the process he learned the moods of the people, how to influence them, and how to recruit adherents to his cause. Meanwhile, the reformers in Moscow were not able to establish a dialogue with the Russian provinces. The common people were ready instead for Zhirinovsky's sharply critical monologues against the authorities. His popularity grew and he saw himself as a victor riding a white steed—once even by appearing on a Moscow street in a white suit riding a piebald horse (because of the shortage of everything in Russia, he was unable to find a white one).

Using Yeltsin's own method of rally propaganda, Zhirinovsky gradually eroded Yeltsin's base. Now comfortable in his Kremlin seat, Yeltsin had almost ceased his public walkabouts, and he was losing his close, almost romantic relations with the popular masses. By contrast, Zhirinovsky escalated his paternalistic tone in his campaign speeches, promising to defend Russia and Russians. Everywhere he filled the vacuum remaining from Yeltsin's mistakes.

Both domestic and foreign reporters who followed his campaign trail were thrown off balance. At that time the foreigners watched Zhirinovsky more intently and wrote about him more frequently than domestic reporters, who unanimously believed that Zhirinovsky had taken himself out of the game politically after the failed August coup. Foreigners paid attention to the LDP leader because he fanned their interest in him—a subject to which we will return. The British journalist Peter Conradi wrote in amazement of Zhirinovsky's campaign trips to the remote corners of Russia:

> The Russian president has given no hint that he will not serve out his five-year term, but that does not dampen Zhirinovsky's electioneering. "Seventy or 80 percent of the people will vote for me next time," he said recently. "Mr. Yeltsin is not ready. He's afraid of the Russian people. I am not afraid. I am ready for the next election."

Independent of each other, two Moscow journalists came up with the same joke regarding Zhirinovsky's fake campaign for the presidency: "Vladimir Volfovich Zhirinovsky is not president yet, it's true, but he will inevitably become president as soon as he can find himself the right country."

Yeltsin, however, did not realize that he had a copycat rival, although everyone but him and the ruling democrats could see it. Former Ukrainian president Leonid Kravchuk hinted at the possibility of a Yeltsin-Zhirinovsky succession, exploding at his maximalist-minded parliamentarians: "We must clearly understand that after the Russia of Yeltsin may come the Russia of Zhirinovsky."

Zhirinovsky himself bragged about his as yet imaginary campaign rivalry with President Yeltsin:

> Today I am the only one who is traveling around the country and the only one whose name is being talked about. If you ask ten Russians, eight will give my name and two Yeltsin's. They'll say, yes, there's Zhirinovsky and Yeltsin, and that's it. We don't want Yeltsin. Then you'll ask who they do want. And they'll say Zhirinovsky.

Mass spontaneous activism against the authoritarian Kremlin yielded a democratic version of leadership in the late 1980s, but in 1992, and even more in 1993, the same spark of grassroots democracy, skillfully wielded by Zhirinovsky against the Yeltsin Kremlin, was producing an authoritarian model of power. Yeltsin failed to notice that Zhirinovsky, with his crude strategy of "doing everything the opposite of Yeltsin," was gradually building himself a massive base right among recent Yeltsin enthusiasts and admirers. It is a pity that Yeltsin ruled so fearlessly, without watching his back. Otherwise he could have quite legally removed his dangerous rival: Zhirinovsky remained available for a post in government service until the very end of 1992.

In December 1992, Zhirinovsky officially announced his intention to run for mayor of Moscow in the local elections Yeltsin had long delayed. He rapidly adapted his presidential campaign program to a mayoral one. To Muscovites startled at his change of direction, he promised "to improve life quickly, to stamp out crime at last and to bring order to Moscow and then all of Russia." Muscovites were in fact thrown off balance when he called them to a street rally, winning them over in the ward heeler's manner with tea and cakes, and asking them to vote for him as mayor. "And in the future, president of Russia," Zhirinovsky felt obliged to add, to tie together the loose ends between the two campaigns. Subsequently the local elections were again postponed, delayed, and finally canceled altogether, leaving Zhirinovsky to continue his campaign for mayor until the end of the summer of 1993, simultaneously keeping an eye—just in case—on the presidential seat.

In running for mayor of Moscow, Zhirinovsky was perhaps trying the following model. Zhirinovsky's obsessiveness with the electoral process matches Yeltsin's, whose election to the USSR Supreme Soviet he watched intently. Yeltsin's iconoclastic style fascinated Zhirinovsky to the point of frenzy. Zhirinovsky adopted Yeltsin's methods, in particular his unending plebiscite as a means of achieving power. When the local elections were canceled, Zhirinovsky anxiously cried out in public, "We need parliamentary elections!"—and went on campaigning for the presidency at rallies, naming a new fictitious date for the next presidential elections.

At the same time Zhirinovsky was terribly fearful of "illegal," forceful methods to seize power without him. In particular, he was obsessed with the idea of a military coup, which could happen at any time in Russia. At the end of 1991, he said, "Either I will stand at the head of the country by next April or military people will come to power in order to prevent complete destruction of everything. And then they will have to resort to my services, in order to lend their rule a legal cover." At the end of 1993, however, when he had reevaluated the potential success of a coup by the army, which had grown remarkably after the crushing of the October parliamentary rebellion, he led the cheers: "If a situation occurs in which a military government will be formed—as a result of a military coup—we, the LDP, will support it."

Zhirinovsky kept running his "election" campaign even while on vacation, at the beach, where he lay tanning himself surrounded by bodyguards. Here is his own account:

> I was vacationing near Sudak in the Crimea. Once when a heavy thunderstorm broke out I went to the

beach to watch the waves. Suddenly I saw a little boy drowning. I happened to be nearby. Well, I dove right in without a second thought. It was up to my neck out there, but for the child it was well above his head. I dragged him out. There was no special heroism here, I'm that kind of person, ready to come to help. I could have said the hell with that kid, but I didn't, I rescued him. After that the boy's father came up to me and said that he was breaking with the democrats and joining the LDP. Many of the people on the beach came to me with the same request. . . . We gave them the contact information for our headquarters, and explained how to fill out a membership application. On the whole, my fellow citizens gave me no peace while I was on vacation. For example, the people of Sudak demanded a meeting with me. Of course I would have rather spent an extra hour on the beach, but duty is duty. I went out to the people and explained my position. I didn't shirk from any controversial questions. The Crimeans were very concerned about the fate of their peninsula. And I assured them the territory was Russia's and would remain so.

Minus the spleen-filled comment that always circumvents Zhirinovsky's humanitarian impulses ("I could have said the hell with that kid, but I didn't"), this boastful tale, chock-full of self-promotion and tailored to the Moscow press, also became part and parcel of Zhirinovsky's campaign.

Zhirinovsky the politician placed his stakes on the elections like an inexperienced but eager gambler, putting everything on a card that had once been lucky for him. A tactical virtuoso, he is unusually weak in strategy; moreover, he is goaded into action by a political inferiority complex and a fear that his luck will suddenly run out. The LDP's ideological eclecticism and opportunism have doomed Zhirinovsky and his party to isolation among both the nationalist parties and similar groups and the other opposition groups. By mid-1992, besides Yeltsin's Democratic Russia, there were numerous opposition parties and blocs, including right-wing and even ultra-right nationalist groupings such as the Russian National Congress, headed by former KGB general Alexander Sterligov (famous for having arrested his boss, KGB chairman Gennady Kryuchkov, during the August coup); the National Republican Party, led by Nikolai Lysenko; the completely rabid Russian National Unity—the Nazi storm troopers under the command of Alexander Barkashov; or even an organization known as REKS, an acronym for the Russian words for "Slash the Jews like dogs." In addition Pamyat [Memory], the first to resurrect great-power nationalism in the post-Stalinist era, had split into several groups hostile to one another. Any of these right-wingers exceed the LDP many times over in ideological extremism. By comparison with Barkashov's storm troopers or the REKS pogromers, Zhirinovsky's "falcons" seem like doves.

As the united opposition of "nationalists" and "patriots" became an independent force in Russian society, it began to take away potential voters from the self-seeking Zhirinovsky and undermine his future electorate. His task was to increase his popularity in the country by stepping up the effect and effectiveness of his political propaganda. Here Zhirinovsky was helped by his ideological cynicism, which, among other things, makes him more inventive and resourceful than the true adepts of the nationalist philosophy. He also surpasses them in rhetoric and extremism, not investing his whole heart and soul in either, but only his political ambitions.

For Lysenko, Sterligov, Barkashov, or Dmitri Vasilyev, the founder of Pamyat, extremism is an abnormal, pathological, but sincere passion. For Zhirinovsky, however, political convictions are only devices to help him get elected. Even the late former U.S. president Richard Nixon noticed this during a visit with Zhirinovsky in Moscow in 1994: "For Hitler, anti-Semitism was a faith; for Mr. Zhirinovsky, it is a tactic, a cynical attempt to exploit popular biases." Understandably, the authentic chauvinists are annoyed by Zhirinovsky—he cheapens, compromises, and profanes ideas that they hold sacred by taking them to the point of farce and, finally, absurdity.

Zhirinovsky, however, began stealing their supporters, winning on their ideological battleground, attaining a popularity they haven't dreamed of, using ideas he lifted from them. A typical example was his political improvisation in the summer of 1992 during the Kurile Islands controversy. With the fall of the Soviet empire, Japan once again hoped to resolve in its favor this old territorial dispute. The Kuriles (their Japanese name is Tsisima, which means "a thousand islands") are a chain of volcanic islands in the Pacific Ocean between the Russian Kamchatka Peninsula and the Japanese island of Hokkaido, about twelve hundred miles in length. These uninhabited islands, covered with sparse tundra and lacking any useful minerals, were transferred back and forth between the two countries for centuries. After the defeat of Japan by the Allies in 1945, they were seized by Russia. The issue revolved specifically around the Southern Kuriles, which had always been Japanese—until treacherously seized by Stalin after Japan's capitulation, in violation of the Soviet-Japanese Neutrality Pact signed in 1941. With the fall of the Soviet empire, the Kremlin could have been expected to make concessions to the Japanese on the Kuriles, returning perhaps some of the islands, or selling or renting them on a long-term lease.

Any option could have been mutually advantageous, and that was understood in Tokyo and Moscow alike. The Kuriles had lost their strategic importance with the development of intercontinental missiles. Their territorial significance was far greater for Japan than for the USSR, the largest country in the world. Moreover, the Kuriles were at the remotest point of the Soviet Union, virtually at the end of the world, far from major metropolitan areas. By surrendering these four islands for temporary or permanent use by the Japanese, Moscow would have received far more financial and economic benefit than it had extracted from them in the past fifty years of its possession or could ever extract in the foreseeable future.

Thus Yeltsin made up his mind to go to Tokyo in September and make a deal commercially advantageous to both sides, announcing in advance that he was taking with him several options for negotiations involving the Southern Kuriles. No one doubted that the territorial dispute would be resolved simply, swiftly, and to the mutual satisfaction of both sides.

A day before his departure, it was announced that the visit was canceled. The Kuriles had transformed from a bargaining chip between the two neighboring countries to a political firestorm within Russia itself. The patriotic press launched a raucous campaign in opposition to the return to the Japanese of "lands that were Russian from time immemorial" and in support of the Russian population of the islands. Starting that summer, Russian nationalists began to call Yeltsin an "enemy of the people," a "traitor," a "Judas," and a "CIA agent."

Of course, nationalism—any nationalism—is irrational. Even such a true patriot as Vice President Alexander Rutskoi noted the paradox in national priorities: "They're hanging on to four rocks in the Pacific Ocean, but what about the Crimea!" The Kuriles were the last straw for Russians, whose national pride was already wounded. With the Kuriles, they were compensating for what they had lost in the Caucasus, Central Asia, the Baltic, and Ukraine—getting their emotional revenge for their national humiliation.

Naturally the "patriot" Zhirinovsky, ever fast on his feet, immediately joined the anti-Yeltsin campaign for the Kurile Islands. No matter how high national passions heated up, he contrived to exceed all of them in both argumentation and extremism. First, he abruptly switched the target of his criticism. While all the other nationalists aimed their diatribes at the Kremlin, Zhirinovsky directed his right back at Japan. He arrogantly expanded his authority and simultaneously restricted the Kremlin's prerogatives. Acting on the principle that "the best defense is a good offense," and abandoning diplomatic etiquette, he leveled direct threats at Japan. "The Japanese won't get the Kuriles!" said Zhirinovsky in a typical broadside. "If they demand the Kuriles, I will send the navy up the shores of Hokkaido. We will demand the annexation of Hokkaido!" (the second largest island of Japan).

"The Japanese already have the experience of Hiroshima and Nagasaki," continued Zhirinovsky. "But fifty years have passed and perhaps they've forgotten what it means. I'll remind them."

This was outright nuclear terrorism, of course—Zhirinovsky promised to "fix the Japanese a second Hiroshima." No less startling and shocking in these threats was his *vozhd'*-like use of the pronoun "I": "I'll remind them," "I'll send the navy,"

"I'll fix them." Zhirinovsky's direct and personal ultimatums, as if he, not Yeltsin, were president of the country, strongly impressed nationalist Russians and assuaged their hurt national pride.

Along with other "patriots," Zhirinovsky whipped up public opinion and got what he wanted by using crude intrigue and brutish bravado in international politics: the very question of returning the Southern Kuriles to Japan was removed from the agenda, and Yeltsin was forced to cancel his visit to Japan at the last minute.

"Obviously, this was done for political motivations," Zhirinovsky immediately commented on Yeltsin's turnaround.

> Perhaps he remembered how the Argentine government was forced to step down upon popular demand after the Falkland Islands were given back to the British. Yeltsin fears raising a wave of popular unrest. Patriotism is something more serious than hunger. People can bear poverty, but insult to their national dignity cannot be tolerated. Yeltsin had the sense to stop. . . . The country was ready to explode over the Kuriles. But it blew over. We'll see what will happen next.

Zhirinovsky was the first to speak in support of the imperialist claims of the Serbs on Bosnia. He was also the first and apparently the only Russian politician to defend Iraq against the United States "with sharp condemnation of the pressure on this sovereign nation." On his own initiative, he personally warned Iran not to spread Islamic fundamentalism to the republics of Central Asia. Zhirinovsky evidently believed his stridency had been successful and did not hide his smugness:

> People who have stopped believing in Democratic Russia, in Yeltsin, will come to us. The names that have grown out of date, for example, the Soyuz group, Alksnis, Makashov, don't get the same rating they used to in public opinion polls. Sterligov is also tied with the previous regime—a Communist, a general. Who's left? Me.

The Strategy of Negative Publicity

The first time Zhirinovsky wheeled out his anti-Japanese invective had been in December 1991, when the Japanese first broached their claims for the Southern Kuriles. He would shout at rallies: "The Japanese won't get the Kuriles! But we will demand the annexation of Hokkaido!"

The potentially scandalous threats involving foreign policy were heard for the first time inside the Moscow University's lecture hall and had no international repercussions at all. But when he joined the fray with the Russian patriots for the Kurile Islands, his nuclear threats were splashed over the world's press the next morning. Zhirinovsky discovered a source of negative international publicity that he has been tapping tirelessly ever since. Japan has remained Zhirinovsky's favorite target for nuclear threats, but gradually he has added other countries, including the United States and Germany.

Zhirinovsky's anti-Western rhetoric sharply intensified at the end of 1992, for a variety of reasons. It was not only for internal consumption, another trump card in his interparty rivalry, but, more important, for the international publicity. Inevitably, analogies are made with Yeltsin's tactics of 1989, gathering extra political points abroad. The way Yeltsin, the first Soviet democratic politician, tried to gain official recognition and status from the West may serve as a lesson to any novice politician. Zhirinovsky, an opposition politician with the official title of "ex-candidate for Russian president," was following in Yeltsin's footsteps, but in the opposite direction. His style was not so much imitation as parody, or rather somber farce. Whereas Yeltsin persisted, persuaded, and eventually won people over, Zhirinovsky intimidates, threatens, blackmails, and terrorizes the West, out of self-promotion. But only the novice politician Zhirinovsky, unknown to anyone even in Russia, who had just officially registered his party, was able to get this kind of publicity in the West.

Zhirinovsky's escapades in foreign policy started with Finland. In May 1991, during the Russian presidential race, he promised to return Finland to Russia as soon as he attained power. He did not become president, but retained the slogan "a Russian Finland" in his speeches at rallies. Finland became one of Zhirinovsky's most effective images, and his famous map of Russia, in the west extending through Finland and in the east through Alaska, became a permanent fixture in his public speeches, official statements, news conferences, and interviews.

The West continued to consider Zhirinovsky a marginal, albeit extravagant, populist politician, but he increasingly exploited his Finnish card as an attention-getting device on the world scene. By threatening Finland's independence, Zhirinovsky hoped to provoke, if not a worldwide scandal, then at least an international incident on a European scale. In May 1992, for example, apropos of nothing, Zhirinovsky suddenly declared to a Finnish correspondent that he considered Finland part of the Russian empire and saw the future of Finland "only as a component of a renewed, powerful Russia." This caused outrage in Helsinki. "Zhirinovsky is regarded in Finland as being something of a harmless loudmouth, but that he is not," said Finnish defense minister Elisabeth Rein. "I see the national chauvinism stirred up by Zhirinovsky as a threat to Finland." Zhirinovsky was very happy that officially, at the government level, a response was made to his strictly unofficial threats. As he summarized his party's reputation abroad at the end of 1992:

> We took the correct position, we are doing well, according to all the opinion polls, our party today holds second or first place. And the party leader is known throughout the USSR. Iraq knows—it can identify my name, the name of the party, and my photograph. Finland knows, but from the other side. It is afraid. Finland is frightened. The defense minister is a woman, and they picked out some kind of thesis "on the possibility of restoring the borders of the Russian empire as they were before October 1917." And they drew their own conclusion that Finland should be a part of Russia.

Throughout his entire nonelection campaign, for many months Zhirinovsky did not tire of frightening and offending

Finland with the inevitability of its return to the bosom of the Russian empire, to which it legally belonged until 1917. In threatening Finland, or to be more precise, in hinting at every convenient opportunity that the role of a stray cat did not suit Finland, Zhirinovsky was proceeding from the legitimacy of Russia's claims to its historical property. On that same basis he considered all republics recently split off from Russia, and even Alaska—a possession of tsarist Russia before 1867—as Russia's possessions from time immemorial. In exploiting the idea of Russian Alaska, Zhirinovsky was trying to provoke an American response. He introduced it into his regular repertoire of speeches almost simultaneously with its Finnish counterpart. When he saw that "Alaska back to Russia!" was being dismissed in America—and far from the desired top level—as a bad joke, he refrained from any further elaboration on this topic, but nevertheless continued to mention the propaganda cliché about a Russian Alaska among the lands subject to imperial requisition. For example, in an interview with the Long Island *Newsday* in November 1992, Zhirinovsky declared that "Russia should be restored to its historical borders, including the Baltics, Poland, Finland and Alaska." At his forty-seventh birthday, celebrated with pomp and circumstance with the Iraqi ambassador and leader of the German ultra-right-wingers, Gerhard Frey, Zhirinovsky raised a toast "to German Prussia and Russian Alaska."

Then Zhirinovsky began to develop the theme of Russian Finland tirelessly, each time striking at the vulnerable point of Finland's imaginary—as he believed—independence from her superpower neighbor. A Moscow journalist even likened Zhirinovsky's playful baiting of Russia's northern neighbor to a cobra lazily hypnotizing a doomed rabbit before inevitably swallowing it. In the spring of 1992, *Zhirinovsky's Falcon* repeated one of the variations on the theme under the heading "Getting Rid of Fear":

> In order to rid themselves of a perpetual fear for the fate of their state, the residents of Finland should make a determined plea to return to the bosom of Russia, which it unlawfully left. All international law and historical justice is on the side of Russia. Russia

needs a permanent border in the West. That will be
the border with Sweden and Germany. Finland will
become a northern resort for Russian pensioners
and kids looking for Father Frost in Lapland.

Despite the threats against Finland, Japan, and America,
Zhirinovsky didn't get the scandalous publicity from the West
he desired, but attracted only the attention of foreign corre-
spondents in Moscow. The West, however, was not alarmed
that an unknown Russian presidential candidate invoked nuclear blackmail in his campaign speeches. So Zhirinovsky was
left no choice but to threaten the West directly with nuclear
weapons.

At the end of 1992, Zhirinovsky acquired international notoriety when he announced openly that he "would not stop at
using atomic and chemical weapons," threatened America
with "nuclear weapons based on special platforms in space,"
and reminded Japan of Hiroshima and Nagasaki. At the end of
1993, by then leader of the largest faction in parliament, Zhirinovsky created a worldwide sensation when he promised to
launch a nuclear strike at Japan and Germany if they interfered in Russia's internal affairs.

Zhirinovsky sought such notoriety not only because he was
incapable of gaining recognition in the West any other way in
such a short time; he was also convinced that ill repute would
last longer than the renown of a decent political figure. Undoubtedly Zhirinovsky's rhetorical terrorism brought him
political dividends. In a short span of time, he acquired approximately the same level of international recognition that Yeltsin
fought long and hard to get from the American president in
1989. By contrast, Zhirinovsky, within a year, had achieved the
title of "popular and dangerous politician," unquestionably a
promotion from his previous descriptions such as "political opportunist." Even the domestic liberal press, repulsed by the
Zhirinovsky phenomenon, was forced at accept the facts: "Criticism (any criticism) . . . helps him gain notoriety."

At a meeting of the LDP's parliamentary faction in February 1994, Zhirinovsky shared with his inexperienced fellow
party members his tried-and-true methods of dealing with the
press:

There is enormous attention to us in the world. If
they sometimes distort things, that's also a plus. Negative propaganda also has a positive effect. Just think
of what would be if the opposite happened? If they
began to praise us? It would be a catastrophe! Then
it will be the end of the party, the end of our faction!
If they begin to praise us, we will lose any future elections! So God forbid that they start applauding us!

It has still not come to that, either in the foreign or Russian
press.

The Ultra-Rightist League

At the end of 1992, still only halfway to his scandalous foreign notoriety, Zhirinovsky decided to define himself ideologically. Above all, this meant rejection of the mask of a
liberal democrat, which had compelled him to show up at
meetings with his fellow party people in Finland, Italy, Slovenia, and elsewhere. At these meetings Zhirinovsky chafed
at the role he had assumed of leader of the Russian liberal
democrats, a decent but absolutely hopeless role for his political career, and frequently shocked his foreign sponsors with
his views. He decided to refrain from meeting with his osten-
sible fellows in other countries, although he kept the name
of his party as a fig leaf. He quickly set about establishing ties
with his real fellows, the nationalist leaders of France, Germany, and Austria.

In August 1992, Zhirinovsky visited Germany at the invitation of his friend Gerhard Frey. He tried so hard to please his
hosts that when asked in an interview with *Deutsche Nazion-
alzeitung* whether any of his family members had suffered during the German-Russian conflicts of this century, he replied
without batting an eye: "Relatively few. One of my thirty relatives—an uncle—was killed in 1941 outside Moscow." This,
despite his earlier statement that his father's entire family had
been executed by the fascists. To deflect accusations of fascism
in his own country, he had talked about Jewish relatives in
western Ukraine who were massacred by the Germans, but

with the German ultra-rightists he could just as easily sacrifice those martyrs.

In another interview Zhirinovsky said that he was "disturbed by the obvious weakness of German national sentiment and will for self-preservation, most likely as a psychological consequence of the two world wars lost by the German people." He was ready to meet them halfway, however, and offered compensation for their territorial losses: "I will go even further: I advocate a common German-Russian border," which would automatically mean the partitioning of Poland. In fact, Zhirinovsky soon clarified what a "common German-Russian border" would mean: "Let Germany move eastward. We need a common border with the Germans. Germany is our natural ally. Let Germany take Poland, and Russia will extend its influence southward."

After he returned home from his German trip, a Moscow journalist tried to get Zhirinovsky to give him his opinion of Hitler. Although with some reservations, Zhirinovsky exonerated the führer: "This is a political figure of Germany that we have seen in a slightly distorted form. Of course some of the deeds and actions of Hitler brought harm to Germany. Some ultra-radical statements worked against him, but on the whole, his ideology does not contain anything negative in it."

Germanophilia is a trait Zhirinovsky shares with other Russian nationalists. Solzhenitsyn, for example, believes that Russia was artificially dragged into conflicts with Germany by other countries. However, Zhirinovsky's extremism annoys people who are undoubtedly his ideological confrères—Solzhenitsyn, for example, who speaks of Zhirinovsky with unconcealed uneasiness and disgust. Solzhenitsyn tries to observe international propriety (although he does not always succeed), whereas Zhirinovsky violates the international rules of the game. Zhirinovsky discredits the Russian idea in the eyes of the world. As the Russian proverb has it, "What a sober man thinks, a drunken man speaks." Zhirinovsky is playing the role of the "drunk" here, exonerating Hitler and redrawing the map of Europe in the interests of Russia and Germany, at the expense of the Central European states.

In September 1992, Zhirinovsky traveled to Paris. Eduard Limonov, then director of the political police in Zhirinovsky's shadow cabinet, took him around the red-light districts of the French capital. On rue St. Denis he viewed a sex show, after which the outraged Zhirinovsky put up a fuss and demanded the money back: "Where is the [sex] act? The act was promised, and we didn't see the act."

As for the political side of the visit, Limonov arranged a meeting for him with Jean-Marie Le Pen, president of the ultra-right Front Nationale. The two leaders naturally found a common language, although more respectable right-wingers refused to meet with Zhirinovsky—Jacque Chirac, the mayor of Paris, for example, who made the excuse that he usually schedules such meetings a half a year in advance. Nevertheless, the Russian political eccentric attracted attention in France, and prominent Sovietologist Michel Tatu introduced him to the French public in *Le Monde*:

> Vladimir Zhirinovsky speaks in a categorical tone, a tone that has grown even harsher since his campaign race against Boris Yeltsin for the presidency of Russia. He has not forgotten that he received 8 percent of the votes then, and believes that today he would get 52 percent. During his visit to Paris, he outlined his "program" to journalists, which provoked troubled anxiety in his audience.
>
> Monsieur Zhirinovsky informed Monsieur Le Pen, with whom he spoke for two hours on September 25, and whom he invited to the next congress of the LDP, about his intention to turn Moscow into a "center of right-wing parties."

Zhirinovsky's unification idea bears watching, given the increasing number of radical rightists in Europe: Le Pen in France, Gianfranco Fini in Italy, Jorg Haider in Austria, Franz Schenhuber, and Gerhard Frey in Germany, and the Serbians Slobodan Milosevich in former Yugoslavia and Radavan Karadzic in Bosnia. Zhirinovsky's name is used to characterize local neofascists: the "Italian Zhirinovsky," the "Austrian Zhirinovsky," and so on.

Despite the ideological similarity among the ultra-rightists of various countries, the idea of an international association of

revealed that he had lectured the Iraqi leader for nearly four hours on the need to unite against "the American-Israeli plot" to dominate the world.

"I was the first Russian he received after the war," bragged Zhirinovsky. "For two years, he did not receive anyone, not a single diplomat. There was neither hide nor hair of a Russian in the Iraqi Presidential Palace. But Saddam received me because I was a friend, a person whose position was well known." He added: "We exchanged presents."

Zhirinovsky was modestly silent about his presents to the Iraqi leader, but Saddam's presents to him are known: a portrait of Saddam himself in a frame; a painting of Arabian horses in the desert, the Iraqi flag, a uniform of a colonel in the Iraqi army, and a paisley silk cummerbund stitched with gold, which Zhirinovsky has donned on especially ceremonial occasions ever since.

Zhirinovsky returned from Baghdad in an ideological frenzy and organized one of his most militant press conferences right at Sheremetyevo airport: "You destroyed Iraq, and now you want to destroy Russia!" he shouted indignantly at an American correspondent. "You Americans want to be the sole superpower and rule the world. . . . You, however, will have to exclude Russia from your plans. . . . If you will continue to interfere in our affairs, we will install nuclear missiles on space platforms targeted on America. . . . You are more afraid of war than we. You have something to lose, and we have nothing. We're hungry, and you're full," concluded Zhirinovsky dramatically.

A month after the meeting with Saddam Hussein, Zhirinovsky published a programmatic article in *Liberal*, the LDP's theoretical journal, titled "On Prospects for 1993." He declared "the last historical role of Russia is to save the world from American expansion"—by means of nuclear blackmail. Blinded with rage, hysterical with fury and an almost maniacal aggressiveness, Zhirinovsky escalated his anti-American rhetoric to suicidal proportions:

> We have to light a match in one place, and the whole planet will explode. We have such a quantity of weapons, of any type, that all anyone has to do is to explode something one time in one place, and if

something explodes on the territory of Russia, the entire planet will be infected and will perish. In our country alone—we don't have to attack anyone—in our country alone. If we explode everything in our country, the planet will perish. So in that sense there's no risk to us. People say that America is interfering. America will not interfere anywhere, they'll clear off to their own country, to Washington and New York, they'll keep silent and will never interfere in the conducting of Russia's independent foreign policy. The Turks will shut up, the Persians will shut up, the Afghanis will shut up. They will keep quiet and write down what the President of Russia says. They will write it down and obey it.

Of course, Zhirinovsky supplies an image of such a Russian president, a "tough new strong president of Russia" who will dictate his terms to an obedient humankind.

So greatly was Zhirinovsky moved by his meeting with the Iraqi president that he agitated Muscovites at rallies "to root for Saddam." Hanging from a balcony bedecked with the flags of prerevolutionary Russia and modern Iraq, pitching his street orator's voice to its highest register, Zhirinovsky shouted to the crowd in the square below that Saddam Hussein was their natural ally: "We have the same enemies as Iraq— America, Israel, and Turkey. . . . America and Israel are both waging wars against Russia and Iraq. This country [Iraq] is our faithful ally who will never betray us."

Caught up with international problems, Zhirinovsky had been neglecting pressing Russian problems, including issues in Moscow, which is why the rally on the freezing streets was being held—mayoral elections would be held soon. A woman reminded him of this from the square. She wanted to know when they would get rid of the "Caucasian mafia" (peddlers from the Caucasian mountain states) that had invaded Moscow. Immediately switching gears from the role of a world strategist to a candidate for mayor of Moscow, Zhirinovsky shouted in reply: "When I become mayor of Moscow. Within two weeks, not a single one of them will remain in Moscow. Crime and robbery will end."

Thereafter Zhirinovsky included Iraq in his well-honed collection of stock slogans. He called for the "restoration of ties with our reliable partner, Iraq," and in his geopolitical doctrine included "Iraq, forever friendly with us, our strategic ally." In January 1993 he sent his "falcons" to Iraq as volunteers "to fight American imperialism" and solemnly accompanied them to Sheremetyevo airport himself. He even involved Iraq in his panacea for the economic salvation of Russia:

> Iraq owes us eight billion dollars.[3] They cannot repay it immediately. One billion a year. For that billion we could take all their dates and their oil. . . . In the South, there is an abundance of produce, in the North there isn't enough. But in the North there is enormous heavy industry, and Iraq doesn't have enough. Iraq doesn't have weapons, and we do. We could give them tanks, and they could give us dates, clothing, shoes, meat, wool, cotton, and everything else. . . . Therefore, when you are told that there is a crisis, you are being deceived. There's no crisis in the country, it's the incompetent leadership in our country. Because they go into debt, and they do not take back from those who are willing to return their debts. Iraq says "take it," and we aren't taking it.

On another occasion Zhirinovsky cited Saddam Hussein directly: "Hussein even said to me: 'I am amazed at your [country's] diplomacy. I say to them: take it, it's your money, and they don't take it.'" In other words, Iraq is ready to pay its debts to Russia, in exchange for a renewed flow of arms. Unquestionably, Zhirinovsky really did receive such a proposal from Saddam during his visit to Baghdad and he now tirelessly agitates for Saddam.

For Saddam Hussein, Zhirinovsky provides not only an opportunity to restore the Iraqi lobby in Moscow, but a personal stake in the Russian political struggle, no matter how paltry

---

3. Zhirinovsky plays fast and loose with the numbers; on other occasions he has given the figure of ten billion.

Zhirinovsky's chances were. Arabs know how to wait and watch, looking far into the future. But what did Saddam mean to Zhirinovsky?

Zhirinovsky has made intensive use of the Baghdad meeting ever since for substantiating himself politically and raising the prestige of his buffoonish party. But we also can't rule out Zhirinovsky's genuine attraction for Saddam—if he is capable of such a feeling at all (which people close to him deny). Zhirinovsky obviously feels something for Saddam Hussein. There are numerous reasons for this, from the commonality of political ideas to the reverence that Zhirinovsky feels before the powerful, whether Saddam Hussein, Rothschild, or Yeltsin. (His invective against Yeltsin is merely an effort to overcome this reverence, which he always displays during his rare meetings with Yeltsin. Yeltsin himself felt something similar for Gorbachev. As it is said, hate is only a step away from love.) We cannot disregard the charisma of the *vozhd'*, which the Iraqi dictator obviously possesses. In any event, ever since meeting with him, Zhirinovsky has held up Saddam Hussein as his standard— more as his human and even male ideal than as a political model. When Zhirinovsky returned from a trip to Chechnya, a small Caucasian republic that had split off from Russia, he commented: "I like the way Dzhokhor Dudayev looks." The Chechen leader has male charisma, a general's epaulets, and a combat pilot's glory. "He looks like Saddam Hussein in some ways," Zhirinovsky added, bestowing his highest compliment. This personal evaluation of Dzhokhor Dudayev did not prevent Zhirinovsky from later throwing his full support behind the Kremlin and its campaign against Chechnya.

Besides the romantic emotions and political prestige, the Baghdad meeting seemed to bring Zhirinovsky something more tangible: money.

The sources of the funding for Zhirinovsky's party have always been shrouded in mystery. One thing is obvious: neither Zhirinovsky himself nor his party has the money for the publication of promotional literature, television appearances, the party staff payroll, rent of the party's office space, the salaries of bodyguards, the organization of party congresses and grandiose banquets in honor of Zhirinovsky's birthdays, or the numerous trips around the country and abroad. (On the stair landing in front of the entrance to LDP headquarters on Rybnikov Lane, there is a little plywood box, with a slot in the top like a piggy bank, and the sign "Party Fund.") Zhirinovsky says that, besides party dues, certain commercial organizations yearn for a strong authority and order and therefore are financing the election campaign. In the four years of the party's existence, Zhirinovsky has several times run out of funds and been on the verge of bankruptcy. Usually Zhirinovsky himself, in bursts of unrestrained candor, has signaled the moment when the party coffers are running dry or are already empty. In May 1992 the LDP was again in desperate straits. In June, Zhirinovsky complained in a conversation with Alexander Yanov that the only barrier in his path to power was the lack of funds: "Give me a billion dollars and I'll become the president of Russia." Former shadow-cabinet minister Eduard Limonov, now a political rival, confirmed that Zhirinovsky was being financed by Russian business capital: "The resourceful Vladimir Volfovich received his first money from sympathetic businessmen—banker boys in motley-colored suits, from those whom the Yeltsinites had cut out when they divided up the rich pie of Russia."

The trip to Paris to meet Le Pen was paid for by one of these nouveau-riche businessmen, and arranged by Limonov, who has French citizenship and contacts in Paris. Limonov reported a curious detail about this trip. One morning Zhirinovsky called him and expressed a wish to meet with Rothschild. "Which one? There are dozens of Rothschilds," said Limonov. "Well, the main one, the one who's the banker," explained Zhirinovsky.

Rothschild is to this day a symbol of fantastic wealth in Russia, and according to the common folk's understanding, a Jew will help a Jew regardless of any ideological or political disagreements. Therefore, a conversation between the Jewish banker Rothschild and the Russian nationalist Zhirinovsky was easy to imagine. Alas, to his great chagrin, it must not have taken place, since by fall the party's coffers were empty again. When a correspondent from *New View* pestered Zhirinovsky about who his finance minister was, Zhirinovsky replied, quite in earnest:

> No, we have no general manager in our cabinet, it's too early. We are still assigning the portfolios to the

ministers. We have Kruchina's[4] party post, but we don't have the millions of rubles. When we have our millions, we will have our Kruchinas as well, we'll install them. For now we only have kopecks enough to fit in my right jacket pocket. But we will have money, have no doubt about it.

After Zhirinovsky's trip to Baghdad, anti-American propaganda multiplied and his complaints about lack of funds decreased—although his expenses increased drastically. In 1993, Zhirinovsky planned to visit thirty-two cities in Russia, but he included even more in his schedule when Yeltsin unexpectedly set parliamentary elections for December 12. About a million dollars went for television appearances alone, which were destined to play a decisive role in the outcome of these elections. Zhirinovsky clearly was not sparing anything; indeed, he spent more than any other party or bloc. Money appeared, after his meeting with Saddam Hussein, and he had more than enough for a year, when once again he ended up on the verge of bankruptcy and even appealed in 1994 for financial aid from the government.

Journalists renewed their search for his financial sponsors in late 1993 and early 1994, and the name of the Iraqi president continued to crop up more frequently than others. It's quite possible that the rumors of the LDP's cash flow problems were deliberately circulated to disguise the traces of Zhirinovsky's actual income. One thing is certain: Zhirinovsky himself personally raises funds for his party, not disdaining anything in the process. As the saying goes, money doesn't stink, whether it comes from Rothschild, Saddam Hussein, the KGB, nouveau-riche businessmen, or German or Austrian neo-Nazis. It is all the same to Zhirinovsky.

Zhirinovsky's casual assertion that Russia's economy can be fixed with the help of eight to ten Iraqi billions is perhaps explained psychologically by his personal experience of financial transactions with Saddam Hussein. In the fall of 1992, Zhirinovsky retreated for a time to the shadows, squeezed offstage

---

4. Nikolai Kruchina was the Communist Party chief treasurer and general manager. He committed suicide by leaping from a window after the August coup.

by the struggle between the president and the parliament. The political acoustics were not so deafening, however, that Zhirinovsky's shrill voice could not be heard over the din. A Moscow journalist who had developed the habit of visiting LDP headquarters for an interview with its chairman justified what democratic colleagues called an "unhealthy interest" in a "future dictator" by saying: "Is it really necessary to explain that, unlike many other political figures today, who have frozen in static positions, Zhirinovsky is mobile and that in itself is interesting?" In the many years of virtual anarchy in the country, the Zhirinovsky phenomenon developed into the Zhirinovsky factor, as he has grown politically stronger and has matured into the most popular national politician after Yeltsin. We now see the quintessential Zhirinovsky, perpetual pretender to power, a hardened veteran of a protracted election campaign, who has honed his strategy and tactic to attract voters to a fine art. Zhirinovsky's entire internal mechanism—slogans, ideas, programs, and advertising gimmicks—has operated without a hitch and has finally led to his enormous popularity among the common people.

4

ULTIMA RATIO

(SEPTEMBER 21–OCTOBER 4, 1993)

Zhirinovsky is not afraid to seem ridiculous, unlike the usual would-be tyrant. No wonder *Time* magazine started a regular column in early 1994 titled "ZhirinovskyBeat," and had plenty of material to fill it for some months. The real question is: Is Zhirinovsky being deliberately ironic? Or is he actually serious? This makes him the most colorful, fascinating, and unpredictable of Russian politicians.

Without detracting in the slightest from Zhirinovsky's uniqueness, it should be noted that political buffoonery began in Russia in the early 1990s. Since then, drama and farce not only have existed side by side but have intertwined and sometimes become indistinguishable. Hegel said that history repeats itself, first as tragedy, then as farce. Marx took the maxim even further: history bids farewell to its past by parodying itself.

Obviously farcical in nature, the August coup of 1991 seemed to prove Marx's metaphor. Russia parted easily and happily with its communist past; communism's last defenders turned out to be harmless clowns, who tried to play dramatic roles but were laughed and booed off the historical stage. Their foolishness somewhat demythologized Yeltsin: it was one thing to kill a dragon, like Saint George did, but quite another to imprison several middle-aged Brezhnev-era bureaucrats with high blood pressure and trembling hands (and to jail them only temporarily, as it turned out). Even the military's blockade of the rebel White House, and Yeltsin's appeal to the crowd from atop a tank that had crossed over to the side of the democrats, seem, in light of the peaceful denouement of this show, a little like an operetta. At the time it seemed to us that Russia had been lucky in all respects with this three-day coup: the farce prevented a tragedy from happening. It was a kind of vaccination—a mild incapacity instead of a dangerous illness.

We were mistaken, as it turned out, in our optimism, as Marx was mistaken in his. Farce did not follow tragedy: tragedy followed farce. Two years after the coup, in the fall of 1993, the standoff between the Kremlin and the White House was repeated, with Yeltsin in the Kremlin and his former comrades in arms defying him from the White House. Although Yeltsin's battle against the parliament had by then degenerated from ideological conflict into political slapstick, his siege on the White House turned the comedians occupying it into potential heroes, who might follow Yeltsin's model into power. The same false analogy provoked fear and panic in Yeltsin's Kremlin. How history will regard the participants in this battle of Moscow in the fall of 1993 depends on who will write the history. History is written by the victors, but this battle had no clear moral or political victor; even the military victory turned out to be Pyrrhic. A mere two months later, the people replaced what Yeltsin called the "red-brown" legislature with one no less red (communist) and even more brown (fascist). The real victor to emerge from this skirmish was Zhirinovsky, who hadn't taken any part in it at all.

Throughout the protracted conflict between the president and the parliament, Zhirinovsky rebuffed all questions as to which side he was on. In fact, he wasn't on any side except his own. Like Mercutio, his attitude was "A plague on both your houses!" Zhirinovsky had every reason to wish for the defeat of both sides, in order to rid himself of political rivals. He would be a third force who would take power in his hands to restore law, order, and peace in the land. That, at any rate, was how he explained it to the hordes of journalists seeking interviews.

"They're all like each other," he said about Yeltsin, Rutskoi, speaker of parliament Ruslan Khasbulatov, and Valery Zorkin, chairman of the Constitutional Court:

> I dislike all four of them, because they are former Communists and, wittingly or unwittingly, profess the old ideology. Look at how Yeltsin appealed to the IX Congress[1] "Well, you remember, we used to be comrades, we can get together to solve these problems." Perhaps I haven't cited it properly, but that's how the Communist Party Congresses are remembered. Zorkin is not the chief of the Constitutional Court, he's always on a leash. You feel [his] connection with the former Communist Party and its ideology. It's the same with Khasbulatov and Rutskoi—and what they all have in common is a tendency toward betrayal. First they betrayed their party. They left it and founded new ones. People don't do that. If you don't like it, leave and remain partyless. You have to have ethical norms. Rutskoi says to Yeltsin: "Boris Nikolayevich, I'm with you to the end, you have my word as an officer." Where's his word now? Perhaps the parliament can give him shelter? In a word, all four Communists betrayed their party. The whole bunch came in together, and they should all leave together.

Despite a certain ideological kinship with Khasbulatov and Rutskoi—patriotism, restoration of the USSR, national interests directing international obligations, and so on—Zhirinovsky is more inclined toward Yeltsin, even though Yeltsin is an ideological opponent. For Zhirinovsky, strong authority is more important than any idea, and Khasbulatov, Rutskoi, and Zorkin, with their backtracking and betrayal, are weakening the very foundations of power, leading to paralysis, anarchy, and collapse.

In that sense Zhirinovsky and Yeltsin differ only in rhetorical style. For example, Yeltsin commented in a televised speech on March 20, 1993: "It is impossible to govern a country and

---

1. The Congress of People's Deputies, the full parliament.

its economy, especially in a time of crisis, with voting, heckling at the microphone, parliamentary gabfests, and meeting-mania. That's anarchy, that's a direct route to chaos, and to the demise of Russia." Zhirinovsky's March interview in *Argumenty i fakty* went in part as follows:

AIF: Imagine you are sitting in the presidium[2] of the Congress in Boris Nikolayevich's place. He is hunched over and gloomy. How would you behave in that situation?

ZHIRINOVSKY: I would cut off the speaker, come out and say, "Deputies, either elect a new speaker right now, or we will live in a different country tomorrow." It is intolerable that a chairman of a parliament should act this way, behaving rudely, cutting people off, labeling them, ridiculing them, and smirking all the while.[3] This is a case where the deputies don't realize where they're headed. A speaker should only open and close the session.

AIF: What levers would you use?

ZHIRINOVSKY: I would not permit the convening of the Congress.

AIF: That's against the Constitution.

ZHIRINOVSKY: Is Manezh Square closed for reconstruction?

AIF: Yes.

ZHIRINOVSKY: I would close the Kremlin and the White House for reconstruction.

AIF: But they'd convene anyway in Voronovo outside Moscow.

ZHIRINOVSKY: I would send the deputies on vacations, they wouldn't convene anywhere. If you are president, you have three powers: money, the army, and authority among the population.

AIF: If Yeltsin were to bang his fist on the table now and say "I'm kicking you all out," would the people support him?

---

2. The presidium is the speakers' platform, where the chairman, or speaker of parliament, and other officials are seated.

3. The reference is to Ruslan Khasbulatov's behavior.

> ZHIRINOVSKY: You cannot simultaneously conduct both reform of the state and reform of the economy. You first have to make a strong state, reinforce its power, remove everything that is unnecessary from Moscow, from the parliament, and then start economic reform. But he started with economic reform, and now everyone's poor. As a leader of a political party I understand: I would rather have the Russian Yeltsin than the Caucasian Khasbulatov, after all.
>
> AIF: What comes next for the current congress? Is it capable of doing anything or will it quietly die out like the Soviet Congress?
>
> ZHIRINOVSKY: The current Congress is in its death throes. When a sick man dies, the rattle begins.
>
> AIF: Can you help Yeltsin?
>
> ZHIRINOVSKY: I am ready to help and I have told his advisers: "Let him conduct presidential elections and help bring to power a president who will not put him up against the wall." Then his name will remain as the first president of Russia.

Zhirinovsky's promise not to execute Yeltsin (or in another version, to send him back to his home village in the Urals to pick potatoes) is not an entirely empty offer. Khasbulatov's parliament had become a powerhouse of hatred of Yeltsin, reforms, and democracy. Yeltsin had been called everything there—from a traitor to the Motherland to an enemy of the people to a CIA agent to a tool of international Zionism. At the end of March 1993, a majority of deputies had voted for Yeltsin's dismissal from office. The total was only a few dozen votes shy of impeachment, although the Kremlin was overjoyed with this slight edge as if it were a victory. More and more calls were being heard to try Yeltsin as a traitor or even to assassinate him without investigation or trial. In such an atmosphere, Zhirinovsky's promise sounded merciful albeit condescending.

This interview signaled Zhirinovsky's position to the Kremlin. From all indications, the signal was accepted. After obtaining support at an April referendum on economic reform and governance, Yeltsin called a Constitutional Convention in the Kremlin that summer, with Zhirinovsky among the participants. He behaved in a businesslike fashion, making constructive proposals and echoing Yeltsin in every way on the need to draft a Constitution that would provide for firm presidential power and a parliament with curtailed rights, more consultative than executive. Zhirinovsky's support was important to Yeltsin because not only Khasbulatov and his deputies opposed the strengthening of presidential power, many democrats did as well, fearing that a new Constitution drafted under Yeltsin would sooner or later be inherited by someone else—Zhirinovsky himself, for example. But the Yeltsin camp did not take Zhirinovsky's political ambitions seriously, although on May 18, at a luncheon with journalists, Zhirinovsky had announced his intention to run for president in the 1996 elections.

He also convened the next congress of the LDP, whose membership indicated the nature of Zhirinovsky's party. The number of members hovered at about one hundred thousand, making the LDP the largest of all the parties and groups in Russia except the Communist Party, which after a brief pause was once again legalized. More than 40 percent of the members were white-collar workers, including many engineers and technicians. Every tenth member was a scholar or a scientist. There were workers, students, entrepreneurs, and industrialists—each group added approximately another 10 percent. The remaining 20 percent was a mixture of other social groups.

The average level of education among Zhirinovsky's party members was (and remained) surprisingly high. More than two-thirds of the delegates to the Congress had at least begun higher education. More than 90 percent of the members were men. Half of the members were in the politically active age range of thirty to fifty, 15 to 20 percent were over fifty, and the remaining third were under thirty. They were hardly lumpens and outcasts, as the liberal press portrayed the LDP, but rather a quite respectable part of society.

Yeltsin, however, could do nothing but ignore the future threat possed by Zhirinovsky—he had a more proximate enemy at the time and could not wage a battle on two fronts. He was battling the red-brown parliament not for life but to the death, and the immediate, concrete help from Zhirinovsky was more important than the hypothetical damage in the remote future. This is characteristic of Yeltsin. He never looks far into

Vladimir Volfovich Zhirinovsky
Photograph that he likes to give out with his autograph.

(ABOVE) Favorite activity: with pointer at a map, Zhirinovsky tells about his geopolitical plans and the most recent restructuring of the world order (December 1992, photograph by Vladimir Kozlovsky).

(LEFT) The coat of arms of the Liberal Democratic Party hangs in Zhirinovsky's office—an eagle surrounded by rays of the sun above a map of Russia with its borders as they were during the last century, containing Finland, Poland, and Alaska within them (photograph by Vladimir Kozlovsky).

Triumph in the parliamentary elections (December 13, 1993, cartoon by Kusko of the Moscow *Izvestia*). Zhirinovsky jumps over those favored to win—the two vice premiers Yegor Gaidar and Sergei Shakhrai, reformer and member of the opposition Grigori Yavlinsky and mayor of St. Petersburg Anatoly Sobchak.

Zhirinovsky at the Duma. On February 23, 1994, Fatherland Defenders Day, he appears at the session in a lieutenant's uniform and manages in the end to get the political amnesty accepted.

As a result of this law, the leader of the anti-Yeltsin rebellion, former vice president General Alexander Rutskoi, emerges into freedom and immediately announces his intention to run for president.

(RIGHT) Astride a horse in downtown Moscow: there was no white horse to be had for the victor, so he donned a white suit instead.

(BELOW) Zhirinovsky with David Frost before an interview (March 1994, photograph by Vladimir Kozlovsky).

Demonstration of Russo-Serb unity. Zhirinovsky with a machine gun in hand in Bosnia.

In Helsinki. From an international conference directly to King's Kakadu Club.

With an Orthodox priest. Zhirinovsky kisses a cross.

the future but instead reacts to events at the last minute, immediately, impulsively. Zhirinovsky is his complete opposite here—calculating the majority of his moves in advance and planning, where possible, his political future.

At the Constitutional Convention, Yeltsin encountered serious opposition to his draft Constitution, primarily from the parliamentary group led by Khasbulatov. Zhirinovsky and he were allies willy-nilly, although their alliance was temporary and forced on both sides. Zhirinovsky would help Yeltsin, but Yeltsin would not remain indebted to him.

After two weeks of working in groups, a plenary meeting was convened. To speak at the meeting was not only an honor but also an opportunity for extremely useful publicity. When the names of the speakers were announced, Zhirinovsky was not on the list, but at the plenum, to everyone's amazement, the floor was given to Zhirinovsky instead of to the chosen speaker. His energetic persuasive speech in defense of a presidential republic was greeted with applause.

Meanwhile, Yeltsin's battle with his conservative opponents took a new turn. General Rutskoi made use of compromising material he had obtained on Yeltsin's closest aides during a period of close relations with Yeltsin, when at the president's urging he had launched a war against corruption. Rutskoi threatened to expose the contents of eleven suitcases full of documents. In reply, the Yeltsinites made countercharges of corruption against Rutskoi. In the end Yeltsin unilaterally, in violation of the Constitution then in effect, removed Rutskoi from the office of vice president. Yeltsin's loyal security detail, headed by General Alexander Korzhakov, barred Rutskoi from the Kremlin, even from his own office. "Alexander Rutskoi has no assignments at the current time," announced Yeltsin's press office. "In the absence of such assignments, the authority of vice president has no legal status." Subsequently, the corruption charges against Rutskoi would turn out to be unfounded and the materials compromising him false. Minister of Security Viktor Barannikov, whom Yeltsin suspected of dual loyalties, was also removed and he joined Rutskoi in the opposition.

In late August and early September, Yeltsin finally decided to disperse the parliament, but for the time being kept his plan secret, carefully sounding out the opinion of some of his immediate subordinates. He increased the wages of military people several times over, visited the Taman, Kantemir, and Dzerzhinsky divisions and the 119th Paratroopers' Regiment to check the mood and combat readiness of the troops. The newspapers carried photos of Yeltsin in camouflage fatigues, carrying an automatic rifle and surrounded by military people. He apparently believed, naively, that he could flex his muscles in this fashion to demonstrate his determination and battle-worthiness. Another demonstration was the return to the government of reformer Yegor Gaidar, who was absolutely loyal to Yeltsin even though Yeltsin had removed Gaidar as prime minister under pressure from the parliament eight months before.

The straw that broke Yeltsin's patience was Khasbulatov's "obscene" act, as Yeltsin put it, of hinting at the president's love of drink:

> We have to do something about this national curse—drunkenness, alcoholism. It is intolerable when officials go out of their way to demonstrate that there's nothing wrong here supposedly. If someone drinks, that means he's our kind of guy! But if he's "our kind of guy," then let him remain as such and let him do peasant's work and not the state's.

With that, the speaker snapped his fingers at his throat and nodded toward the Kremlin, a gesture that every Russian understood to mean that Yeltsin liked to knock back a few now and then.

Three days after Khasbulatov's rude remarks, Yeltsin dissolved the parliament. His doubts, however, grew as the last hopes of a peaceful outcome to the political conflict began to disappear. In his self-justifying memoirs, Yeltsin reflected:

> On that morning as I rode to the Kremlin, for the first time in my life I was tortured by the thought, Had I done the right thing? Was there another option? Could it have been done another way? Had I exhausted all the alternatives? Russia was drowning

in lawlessness. And here I was, the first popularly elected president breaking the law—albeit bad law, cumbersome law that was pushing the country to the brink of collapse, but the law, all the same. I rolled back the mental tape of all the events in the last month, hour by hour, day by day, trying to see if I had been mistaken.

The situation was legitimately ambiguous: disbanding the parliament on September 21, Yeltsin had violated the Constitution first. His act automatically allowed parliament to dismiss him from office and to transfer total authority to the vice president, which is exactly what parliament did while occupying the White House: former Vice President General Alexander Rutskoi, took the oath of office as president and appointed his own ministers of defense, security, and internal affairs.

By the end of September, the situation was not only ambiguous but also tragicomic: two presidents, two defense ministers, two security ministers, and so on. Without military intervention, the two-year standoff between the Kremlin and the White House would have been practically impossible to settle.

Yeltsin placed himself and the whole country at an impasse when he issued his ill-fated Decree No. 1400, which (like many other presidential decrees) no one intended to fulfill. Oddly enough, in dispersing the parliament, Yeltsin was certain he could resolve the crisis peacefully and, a week before the publication of the decree, told his closest aides that "we will not allow any casualties." Whether he was sincere or prevaricating is not clear. Did Yeltsin truly not realize what he was doing when he issued his unlawful, unconstitutional decree? Did he really think that the deputies would obey him and peacefully disperse to their homes, giving up their citadel without a fight? After all, he, defender of the White House in August 1991, knew that there were enough weapons stockpiled in the White House to arm hundreds of its defenders.

Rutskoi and Khasbulatov could no longer contain themselves. Exploiting the indecisiveness and inaction of the Kremlin after the decree on the dissolution of parliament, they sent bands of fascistic thugs to seize government buildings. Military and police divisions gave up without a fight or even crossed

over en masse to the side of the White House. There the oc-
cupiers not only were certain of their victory but believed they
had already won. "If Yeltsin opens fire, he will be hung from
the walls of the Kremlin!" Ilya Konstantinov, leader of the nationalist faction of parliament, announced through a megaphone from the balcony of the White House. Intoxicated with
impunity, combat detachments and an angry crowd under the
direction of General Albert Makashov (who had run against
Yeltsin and Zhirinovsky in the 1991 presidential elections)
stormed the Ostankino television station, to proclaim victory.

On Sunday, October 3, 1993, power in Moscow was transferred into the hands of the red-browns.

President and Commander in Chief Yeltsin, following the
latest events from his dacha in Barvikha, outside Moscow, flew
back to the Kremlin that evening in a helicopter. His relatives
saw him off as if we were going to war, which he believed was
in fact the case—a civil war. Security measures were taken: the
helicopter made a dogleg before landing in order to throw any
Stingers off course.

Yeltsin gave the order to storm the White House. Defense
Minister Pavel Grachev reported that troops were already moving on Moscow, but the head of the Russian traffic police informed Yeltsin that no troops were in Moscow yet; the columns
had halted in indecision on the Moscow Ring Road surrounding the city. Radio reports that evening said that military units
loyal to the president were moving toward the center of the
capital, although in reality they entered Moscow only at dawn
on the following day.

The commander was rushing into battle without being certain that the army was supporting him. Yeltsin could no longer
rely on his security ministries, just as the ministers could not
count on their generals, nor the generals on their officers, nor
the officers on their soldiers. Since August 1991, the democrats had been calling on the army to stay out of politics and
maintain neutrality, which it now demonstrated to its commander in chief, refusing to obey his orders. Attempts to draw
the army over to the side of the rebels also failed. "You've
made your bed, now lie in it," replied General Alexander
Lebed to Rutskoi, who had called on the telephone to ask his
friend and fellow believer for military support (Lebed had

defended the White House in August 1991 along with Rutskoi, Yeltsin, and Khasbulatov, and was now commander of the 14th Army, deployed in the Transdniestr Republic, the Russian-speaking region of Moldova that had declared its independence.) Still, the army's refusal to intervene played into the hands of the White House generals, who bit by bit won some of the troops over to their side. By the beginning of October, the Dniestr and Delta special-assignment battalions from the Transdniestr Republic were among the defenders of the White House, along with the Baltic OMON, the parliament building's security, defectors from the police and state security, and finally Barkashov's Nazi storm troopers, who were former military men. Of course, there are the commanders of the White House themselves: "Among the organizers of the disorder there are many military people: Rutskoi, Achalov, Makashov, Urazhtsev," explained former KGB General Oleg Kalugin. "These people know how to behave during combat maneuvers and how to organize them. But our government is still only a civilian government."

Finally, through persuasion, threats, cajoling, and cunning, Yeltsin got what he wanted, and the tanks and special divisions were sent to storm the White House. "He was striking not at ideology with the tanks, but at the black spot of hatred," wrote Leonid Radzikhovsky of Yeltsin's shelling of the parliament. As Jose Ortega y Gasset commented appropriately:

> It is really too bad that human nature is forced in such situations to resort to force, but on the other hand, it cannot be denied that this is the highest tribute to truth and justice. Because such a form of force is nothing more than a gesture of desperation. Force is supplied literally as an *ultima ratio.*

The journalist Veronika Kutsylo was an impartial observer of the events. She stayed in the White House until the bitter end, and on the morning of October 4 was on the sixth floor, where she made her report:

> At five minutes to seven on Monday someone wakened me. . . . I looked out: armored assault vehicles

were standing outside the window and were shooting at the barricades, cars, and canvas tents, where defenders of the parliament had spent the previous night. People could be seen lying on the square, either wounded or dead. People dragged one person by his arm to the White House; a bloody trail was left behind on the square. No one could manage to get to the rest; they lay there, and tracer bullets arced over their heads. It looked to us as if the shots were only coming from the outside. I went along the corridors: I couldn't see a single person shooting out the window. . . .

The automatic-weapons fire continued until evening with rare silences. About 10 o'clock in the evening, there was a powerful and deafening crash, the glass flew out of the windows in the White House, and there was a terrible draft. Looking through the windows onto the embankment, tanks could be seen on the bridge, their cannon barrels smoking. It is terrible when tanks are shooting at you. The mortars exploded somewhere above, I think, in the tower, but the whole building echoed from the explosions. Then there was a thunderous crash, and several explosions followed one after another n the hallway of the sixth floor, near the press center. It seemed to be rounds from a small-calibre rapid-fire BMP-2 [armored assault vehicle] artillery. The main pipeline was burst from the explosions, and water poured into the hallway.

The tanks continued to strike the White House methodically. The first was targeted: new explosions kept resounding in the tower.

There would have been far more casualties if a slow, wait-and-see tactic had not been adopted by Pavel Grachev and his generals; if the OMON had not only begrudgingly taken part in the operation with their obvious ideological sympathies for the defenders of the White House; and finally, if it had not been for the pacifist order of General Rutskoi, who led the White House defense:

> Is it possible even to imagine that you would shoot your own son? I have two sons: the younger is nineteen and the older is twenty-two. The soldiers who stormed the building were the same age, and I saw my sons in them. How could I raise my hand against them? For what reason? No, it's unthinkable to fight with your own children. Therefore I gave the command not to shoot at people, but only to have defensive fire in front of the attackers so as not to let them at the building. But can you really keep back such numbers of troops, if more than twenty-thousand people were deployed from the president's side with armored vehicles and special troops as backup?

By overstraining himself as well as overdeploying state resources, Yeltsin finally managed to wrest the capital back from the forces of Russian reaction. He decided he would use the advantage achieved from the military victory that had required such effort and cost so many casualties (the officially acknowledged number was 145), and called parliamentary elections for December 12.

Yeltsin won the battle, but that scarcely affected the overall political war under way in Russia. His enemy was so discredited in society's eyes that Yeltsin felt his authority strengthened and ignored the real enemy, Zhirinovsky.

Gennady Ponomaryov, Moscow procurator and a Yeltsin supporter, said of the post-October situation:

> We have apparently wrapped up the first act of the civil war. And there could be no victors in it. From all accounts we have overstepped the boundary beyond which we have got a new situation. And it is worse than before . . . the number of angry people has increased, the sum of anger has increased. And it will break out somewhere again.

Four days after the White House capitulated and its leaders were arrested, Vladimir Kozlovsky went to LDP headquarters on Rybnikov Lane to see his former schoolmate and find out why Zhirinovsky, who was always in the middle of the action, had been neither seen nor heard. In fact, during the October events, Zhirinovsky had holed up in his headquarters, kept himself out of sight, and waited. He explained to Kozlovsky:

> Our party is not a party for which weapons or an armored personnel carrier is a means of achieving ends. We will never come out on the barricades, and will never call the people to the barricades. Once again, it was done at night, once again on the night of the 3rd to the 4th, that's how the Bolsheviks came to power in October 1917, and that is how they are leaving seventy-five years later. The first attempt to leave was in 1991, and then in 1993, in October, October again, once again October. See, October 1917 and October 1993. Seventy-five years [*sic*]. The regime came at night with bloodshed and by night with bloodshed it left.

"When we were kids, we used to say, who are you for, the moon or the sun? Who are you for, Yeltsin or Rutskoi?" asked Kozlovsky. Zhirinovsky replied:

> Not for either one. We supported the idea of the elections, and from that some journalists drew the conclusion that I was for Yeltsin. In this case the names do not play a role, but the practice of our political life. We supported the [decree of] September 21; we did not support [the actions] of October 3 of either side. The decree was correct because it was time to come out of the impasse. In that sense we supported the president's decree of September 21 until these bloody events.

Further on in the interview, Zhirinovsky noted:

> The position of our party on the events of October 3–4: we support neither side since in the White House, and at the last Congress and the last parliament, the Constitution was violated and in the final analysis they moved to an armed methods of struggle.

The Kremlin also violates the Constitution and also uses armed methods of struggle with the opposition. Therefore we took a neutral position, we proposed to function as mediators, and we were always for a settlement of the issues peacefully, in the form of a discussion. And the best way out of any such dead end is through elections! Therefore we supported the idea of elections, and we will take part in the elections of the new Russian parliament, the State Duma.

5

THE SECRET OF VICTORY

(DECEMBER 12, 1993)

Elections for the new parliament were held simultaneously with a referendum on the new Constitution, drafted under Yeltsin's guidance and granting the president expanded, if not extraordinary, powers.

Naturally Zhirinovsky, advocate of a regime of personal power, supported Yeltsin's Constitution, which provided for strong presidential powers and a toothless parliament. The new parliament was to consist of two houses, the lower of which was called, in the Russian tradition, the State Duma. Journalists who were on the ball immediately dubbed it the Fifth Duma, counting the first four before the revolution, under Emperor Nicholas II. (The first two Dumas demonstrated insubordination to monarchical authority and were dissolved by the tsar.) Under the new Constitution, Yeltsin would also be granted the right to disband the Duma if his disagreement with it led to a political impasse, as had happened with him and the previous parliament. Election to the Duma was possible in two ways. Half of the deputies were elected as individuals, that is, each one personally ran for his seat in parliament. The other half gained seats in parliament from their party list, which was supposedly to the advantage of the Kremlin's ministers and bureaucrats who wanted to get into the Duma without having to lower themselves to running a campaign. As it happened, however, this system played into Zhirinovsky's hands, since he carried faceless and unknown fellow believers into parliament on his coattails.

Democratic critics of Yeltsin's Constitution saw it not only as an attempt by Yeltsin to expand his powers but also as a danger to fledgling Russian democracy in the future—no one knew who would come after Yeltsin and how his heir would wield these extraordinary powers. In contemporary political practice there are democracies with nominal presidents or without presidents at all, but no democracy is without a parliament or a nominal parliament. After the constant clashes with parliament over a period of two years, a routine interrupted only by his use of force, Yeltsin wanted some insurance. He had no doubt that the elections would give him a tame and obedient new parliament that would consolidate his unconstitutional October victory. The referendum on the Constitution was a kind of vote of confidence (or not) for the president. Perhaps in part because of Zhirinovsky's support of the Constitution, Yeltsin decided to let him take part in the elections—although Zhirinovsky's ideas differed from those of banned parties only in their more reckless form of expression. Throughout the campaign, Zhirinovsky supported the president on the constitutional issue, and the president's bureaucracy didn't get in Zhirinovsky's way—which was well within its capabilities—as if there were a silent pact between Yeltsin and Zhirinovsky. Thus, paradoxically, two parties at opposite extremes of the election struggle—Russia's Choice, headed by Yegor Gaidar, the fiercest reformer in the government, and the ultra-conservative LDP of Vladimir Zhirinovsky—supported Yeltsin's Constitution.

These elections, which Yeltsin's enemies instantly dubbed "elections on the blood,"[1] were conducted on a political stage cleansed of extraneous players. Much of the opposition was crushed and its leaders were awaiting trial in Lefortovo prison, their parties and newspapers banned. All media were in the hands of the Kremlin and functioned in good working order—

---

1. After the famous Russian church "Savior-on-the-Blood."

to the point of indecency—as official government propaganda organs. With such favorable conditions, the democrats and reformers were sure that they would gain a crushing victory.

The democrats, however, had been unable to design a new Russian state polity or stabilize the economy. Moreover, the population was increasingly feeling the pain of its exclusion from fundamental political processes, from its outsider status in democratic Russia. Worse, the infighting that broke out up above from the very first days of the new government was incomprehensible and alien to the masses at large, occupied as they were with their own survival. Yeltsin, until only recently the indisputable popular leader, had become insensitive to popular needs. He ceased communicating with the people altogether, and, like his onetime political rival Gorbachev, locked himself up in the Kremlin, the leader of the new nomenklatura. Once again, society was broken down into those at the top and those at the bottom without any interaction between the two.

The populace sunk into confusion and discord. With a strange distancing of himself from events, Yeltsin writes of this sharp contrast between the democratic expectations and the real outcome: "People expected paradise on earth [after the August revolution] but instead got inflation, unemployment, economic shock, and political crisis." Stripped of their illusions, hopes, and prospects, the masses were increasingly overcome with feelings of abandonment and rejection.

The split among the democrats worsened, and even Yeltsin's ministers did not form a united front, running under different party groups. They emphasized their loyalty to Yeltsin but disassociated themselves from his unpopular actions, such as dispersing the opposition parliament. They distanced themselves from each other even further: comrades in arms and colleagues became political rivals. There were the democrats who had remained outside the chosen circle of the Kremlin elite and were angered by its claims to exclusive representation of Russia's liberties and reforms—St. Petersburg mayor Anatoly Sobchak; former Moscow mayor Gavriil Popov; businessman Konstantin Borovoi, leader of the Party for Economic Freedom and the richest man in Russia; and finally, Grigori Yavlinsky, the author of the ill-fated "500 Days" economic plan. Yavlinsky did not hide his intention to replace Yeltsin as president sooner or later, or at least to become his prime minister. "Democratic government cannot exist without a normal constructive opposition," said Yavlinsky. "The opposition is a safety valve for the government. It notices the government's mistakes and tells it about them."

The Communists and their rural allies, the "agrarians," were allowed to take part in the elections, although their reputation made them harmless. There was also Zhirinovsky and his "make-believe" Liberal Democratic Party.

Zhirinovsky was seemingly the only person who doubted that the democrats would win in the upcoming elections. He confidently predicted victory for himself and his party, but few took him seriously. Few recalled his unexpected third-place showing in the presidential race two and a half years before; however, he had predicted it at the time. Since that time, Zhirinovsky had seemed to fade.

Thanks to Yeltsin's trouncing of the opposition, however, Zhirinovsky was left without competitors, alone in a political vacuum. The October defeat of the "Communofascists" had cleared the decks for Zhirinovsky to play the only patriot, the only defender of the poor and unhappy, the last, great hope of the desperate.

Unlike the leaders of the other twelve parties and blocs, Zhirinovsky personally plunged into the election race. He worked from dawn until dusk, traveling all around the country, organizing rallies, speaking in front of any audience, agitating, persuading, assuring, exhorting, calming, flattering, and, most important, promising, promising, and promising.

His promises are as close as they can come to a political program, haphazard and cynical as they are.

The Pied Piper

Zhirinovsky's main secret of success was still his slogans and promises, his differentiated approach to voters, his subtle stratification of the population by income, sex, age, profession, religion, and other factors. Appealing separately to each individual group, Zhirinovsky accentuated the most burning issue for that group and proposed a means of resolving it rapidly. Teachers and doctors, traditionally paid poorly in Russia, were promised salaries commensurate with skilled workers; officers were offered social security and the opportunity of receiving several acres of land on retirement; the poor were offered shelters and free soup kitchens so they would not be picked up by police or left on the street. "Zhirinovsky's campaign is a battering-ram," pronounced Gary Kasparov, world-class chess champion.

Zhirinovsky promised to restore the empire, to return the savings Russians had lost due to inflation, and to guarantee everyone a comfortable and well-fed life. The two hundred thousand homeless officers returning from postings abroad would instantly be given nice apartments; collective farmers would have deliveries of fertilizer and firewood for the winter. Single women would be given husbands, men would be given cheap vodka. All women would get free bras. Old people would get affordable coffins, now in short supply, when they died. Students would receive enormous stipends, soldiers would get huge salaries, and so on. Zhirinovsky offered gifts for every social and age group of the population, from Pioneer to pensioner. But if voters preferred another candidate to him, there would be "civil war and dictatorship, the like of which no scholar has ever described," World War III, the demise of Russia and the extinction of the Russian people.

His boldest economic promise was to double the actual wages of the population. The question of how to do it didn't stump him in the least. First, he would end the free aid to countries of the near and far abroad, but would trade with them at world market prices and accept only hard currency from them. "Why must we create headaches for ourselves? Let's make headaches for other people."

Second, he would stop the conversion of military factories and resume the sale of arms to other countries, which would give Russia thirty to thirty-two billion dollars a year: "We left the market ourselves. We had twenty-four thousand tanks sitting idle in the Volga-Ural District. India had need of them. But we didn't sell them to India—we chopped them up and sent them to be melted down."

Third, Zhirinovsky would demand countries that owed Russia debts to repay them, but would not repay Russia's debts: "Let the Russian navy patrol up and down the shores of countries that owe us. A ship with our flag should stay there. It should approach and prepare for landing. In Nigeria. After all, two hundred million dollars is money. Isn't it?"

On closer examination, of course, all three putative sources of riches are fictitious and utopian. The economies of the former Soviet republics are extremely intertwined. The newly independent states—Zhirinovsky has them mainly in mind—have no hard currency to pay for vitally needed oil and gas from Russia. All purchases are made on a barter or credit basis. If Moscow were to stop its deliveries, industry would simply grind to a halt in these countries.

As for profit from exporting Russian armaments, the old Soviet clients used to receive weapons on credit. The sum of such deals reached 130 billion dollars, and no one intends to return the debts. Cuba alone received weapons from Moscow totaling eighteen billion dollars, and now is laughing up its sleeve at its creditor, the USSR, which no longer exists. Moreover, Moscow did not entirely leave the market on its own; it was squeezed out by more successful competitors. The profits for Russian arms sales in 1992, for example, were barely two billion dollars.

Just as unrealistic are his other economic formulas, from extracting debts from other countries to supporting state-run factories, which will inevitably lead to inflation, regulated prices, and a wage freeze. He promised the simplest and most dazzling solutions of the most complex and hopeless Russian problems. To overcome the economic collapse, Zhirinovsky proposed plundering Russia's rich neighbors by threatening them with nuclear weapons. He cited Iraq, India, and Mongolia among the countries fervently wishing to feed, clothe, and shod Russia in exchange for Russian armaments. He even cites "long-suffering" Serbia, which, in his words, has been "plundered, robbed, and blockaded": "We could have excellent relations, because there is an enormous number of factories in Serbia producing garments, footwear, and food. They are prepared to clothe, shod, and feed us. Serbia alone. There is such a large number of factories making consumer goods."

Zhirinovsky proposed a foreign solution not only for Russia's failed agriculture and light industry for also for heavy industry still in crisis: "At the end of the century we will come out of the state of sickness, and early in the century the whole Near East region will work for Russia. For our industry."

Even for such a specific and exclusively domestic issue like unemployment, Zhirinovsky proposed exotic, foreign options if he comes to power:

> There will be no unemployment! Tens of thousands of specialists are needed now in Iraq. And we are artificially holding them back. Our military-industrial complex workers could work there. There are testing grounds already built there, and our equipment. There will be wages, warm weather, and the south. The sale of weapons [is the solution].

Zhirinovsky's foreign policy was based on his frenzied anti-Americanism and an endlessly reworked strategy of nuclear blackmail and intimidation of the United States. In his manifesto in *Liberal*, the party's organ, he said:

> I will terrorize them. . . . Because we are hungry, angry, humiliated, and offended. . . . The American won't fight—he can't. He couldn't fight in the Gulf, where there was a desert, but we have mountains, forests, and guerrillas. We already have battle stations in space. They don't know where they are. And there are weapons on them aimed at the U.S. If Yeltsin has told them that he supposedly gave the order to retarget part of the missiles away from America, I will do the opposite; I'll tell Clinton that we'll target all the missiles on America. All the space stations will be aimed at America. Submarines will be all over America's shores. If their two submarines come near Crimea and Murmansk, we'll sic our whole fleet on them. If they destroy them in the Hudson Bay near New York, New York will fry. So the danger of World War III is ruled out.

Zhirinovsky proposed to partition the world anew with the help of nuclear intimidation, keeping his finger on the firing button. He asserts that the West will surrender and make any geopolitical concessions under the threat of mutual destruction. On this score, it seems to us better to believe Zhirinovsky's plans to threaten the West than *not* to believe them—just to be on the safe side.

The LDP leader's plans to restore Russia's national pride and power boiled down to his old formula: restoring the Russian empire's borders, preferably those of 1913. Imperial restoration is Zhirinovsky's idée fixe, a panacea for the collapse of the state and the demise of the Russian nation. As always with Zhirinovsky, his imperial ambitions have a personal motivation as well as a historical one, and are all the more emotionally powerful for being so. This comes from his childhood trauma.

When democrats warned that if Zhirinovsky were to carry out his imperialist plans it would mean war, Zhirinovsky himself always replied unequivocally: "There will be no war. All of these territories—the Baltics, the Bessarabia, and the Caucasus—have historically belonged to Russia. I am taking the beginning of history and you're taking the end. Nobody has to be conquered." How should the separated republics be brought back? As always the recipe is extremely simple: they must be strangled with an economic blockade, Russia must stop selling fuel to them, and then "they'll come back to us themselves, or actually, they'll crawl back" and ask to be let back into Russia:

> Everything's very simple. We stop delivering timber to Ukraine, and all the coal mines in the Donbas will collapse. We stop delivering to Ukraine everything that we're delivering now, and within three months they will be on their knees and the Kravchuk government will collapse. We will stop the aid, including the military aid, to Tadzhikistan, and Rakhmonov [president of the country] will flee to Moscow, he'll get there on any form of transportation he can find, and he'll beg: "Take us back into Russia, as the Dushanbe [capital of Tadzhikistan] *guberniya* take us, I beg you.

The old Russian empire, as it was at the turn of the century, is attractive to Zhirinovsky as an ideal model for modern Russia not only because of its far-reaching and firm borders and enormous centralized possessions, but above all for the division of the country by administrative rather than national or ethnic principles. The administrative partitioning of Russia into *gubernii* was introduced by Peter the Great in 1708 and lasted until 1924. By the time of the October revolution, there were 101 *gubernii* and regions.

In Zhirinovsky's notion, the division of the country by the ethnic principle, established under the first Soviet Constitution of 1924, destabilized the entire Russian region because of constant nationalist tension and fratricidal wars. "We should remove the ethnic issue from the agenda," maintained Zhirinovsky. *Gubernii* would indicate not an ethnic or national affiliation but merely a territorial one. Thus, instead of Estonia, Latvia, and Lithuania, there would be the Baltic *guberniya;* instead of the republic of Ukraine, there would be two dozen *gubernii* subordinated directly to the center; instead of the national autonomous regions in the North Caucasus, there would be a North Caucasus *guberniya* with its center in the Russian town of Rostov and a Russian governor-general; and so on. In Zhirinovsky's notion, this system would guarantee political stability, territorial integrity, and durable borders, since an individual territory would not be able to declare sovereignty and leave the whole state, as the national republics withdrew from the USSR.

Restoration of the Russian empire was Zhirinovsky's minimum program. But he also had a long-term geopolitical scheme that he will fulfill at the beginning of the next century. He himself gave it the flashy title "the last push to the south" in his partially autobiographical but largely sloganeering book of that name. Why did he need the epithet "last"? From Zhirinovsky's point of view:

> This will be the last partitioning of the world, and it has to be done in a state of shock therapy, suddenly, quickly, and effectively. It will immediately solve all problems because we will acquire peace. We will acquire a four-sided platform. When we will abut the

Arctic Ocean on the north, the Pacific Ocean on the east, the Atlantic via the Black Sea, the Mediterranean Sea and the Baltic Sea, and finally, in the south, we will wash up against the shore of the Indian Ocean like a huge pillar; then we will acquire peaceful neighbors as well.

The "last push to the south" serves as a panacea for all troubles and misfortunes besetting Russia in recent years: "The last push to the south . . . is really a task for the national salvation of the Russian nation." Other times it serves as military doctrine:

New armed forces can be reborn only as a result of a combat operation. . . . I see Russian commanders in the headquarters of Russian divisions and armies, tracing the routes of movement for troop formation and the final destinations of the routes. I see airplanes in airfields in the southern districts of Russia. I see submarines surfacing at the shores of the Indian Ocean and landing ships approaching the shores, along which soldiers of the Russian army are already marching, with assault vehicles and huge numbers of tanks rolling forward. Finally Russia is completing its last military march.

Still other times it is an economic task:

All of this will provide a stimulus for development of the economy, transportation, communications; for procurement of raw materials for production, consumer industry, and cheap manpower; and for opportunities to build new highways.

Finally, it is used as a geopolitical concept, a Russian version of the Monroe Doctrine:

Until now the Americans have managed to hold sway over all corners of the planet. But the idea of world domination is flawed. Regional cooperation is

better. Division into spheres of influence is better,
and by the principle of north–south. If we cross
paths again, we will once again get in each other's
way. We must come to an agreement, and let there
be such a world agreement, that we divide the whole
planet, with spheres of economic influence, and operate on a north–south axis. There's the Japanese
and the Chinese, and below are Southeast Asia, the
Philippines, Malaysia, Indonesia, Australia. There's
Russia, and Afghanistan, Iran, and Turkey to the
south. There's Western Europe, and the African
continent to the south. And finally, there's Canada
and the U.S., with all Latin America to the south.
And everyone is equal. No one has any advantages
here. The direction is the same—toward the south.
The territories are contiguous. . . . Therefore a system based on such a geopolitical formula would be
very favorable for all of humankind.

Zhirinovsky's geopolitical ideas arise from Russian history,
and they are part and parcel of Russian political thinking at
least since the times of Peter the Great. From his reign until
the beginning of World War I, Russia increased its territory *per
day* on an average of fifty-five square miles, more than twenty
thousand square miles annually.

In the fourteenth century, Ivan Kalita, Prince of Moscow,
began to acquire lands around Moscow, ultimately creating the
Russian state. Subsequent acquisitions either by a peaceful
treaty imposed on a neighbor (Ukraine, Georgia), or a half-
geographical, half-military expedition (as under Ivan the Terrible, the Siberia was annexed, that is, conquered by Cossack
Ataman Yermak), or through outright military action (Crimea,
Chechnya, Central Asia). Territory has always been the chief
form, if not the only form, of political capital for Russia.
Chaadayev was right: if Russia had not sprawled out from the
Bering Strait to the Oder River, no one would have noticed it.
Nor would it have become a full-fledged member of the club
of great powers.

Moreover, thanks to its vast stretches of territory, Russia
cannot be conquered all at once. The capitulation of Paris

automatically means the fall of France, but the seizure of Moscow would not mean the defeat of the whole country. (This happened repeatedly in the past: the Tatars burned down Moscow; the Poles ran rampant over it; Napoleon took a stand there; and even Hitler by sheer accident did not traverse the thirty kilometers remaining until the Russian capital.) Although the Russian winter has been called the greatest military campaigner, with its severe frosts alone, Commander Russian Winter could not win a single war if it did not have the great Russian outdoors to help it. Russia at one point saved Europe by swallowing and rendering harmless the Tatar hordes with its territory, barricading Europe from them with its own land. Even Hitler first bogged down in the great Russian expanses.

Russia will be threatened again, Zhirinovsky says, if his fellow citizens do not elect him as their *vozhd'*, so that he can restore the Russian empire to its former borders—either to its Soviet borders, as they were before the fall of the USSR, or even better, to its prerevolutionary borders with Finland and Poland, or better yet, to the borders of the last century, including Alaska.

No wonder it is the last push, since it is the end of history, the vision beyond the grave, the waking dream, the forbidden, necrophilic dream of paradise on earth and a golden age, a Russian Nirvana, which is why Zhirinovsky's speech sounds at times like an incantation:

> How I dream that Russian soldiers would wash their boots in the warm waters of the Indian Ocean and change to their summer uniforms forever. . . . That would be a cleansing for all of us. And the ringing of bells in the Russian Orthodox Church on the shores of the Indian Ocean and the Mediterranean Sea would proclaim peace to the peoples of this region. . . . This is not my whim. This is the destiny of Russia. It is fate. It is Russia's achievement. We must do it, because we have no choice. We cannot do it any other way. It's geopolitics. Our development requires it. Like a child who has outgrown his clothes and must put on some new ones.

The last poet of the Russian empire, Zhirinovsky sees the only opportunity for the survival of the Russian nation in renewing and expanding its realm.

Under democratic conditions, so utterly new for Russia, Zhirinovsky was the first and is so far the only politician to exploit the situation in society so openly for his personal career goals. An oddity in his own country, Zhirinovsky was perceived quite differently by those more accustomed to electoral politics. Richard Nixon told Zhirinovsky that he saw a "purely American approach" in his campaigns. Some American journalists have compared Zhirinovsky to the maverick outsider Ross Perot. Despite all his flamboyance, Zhirinovsky fits into a familiar type, as Michael Dobbs of the *Washington Post* commented: "His political strategy is simple: to attract as much attention as possible by screaming as loud as he can. He is a cynical and unscrupulous politician who will say and do almost anything to win votes."

There is one substantive difference, however. In older democracies, the voters are more experienced and do not so easily fall for demagogy and cheap tricks. Russia's embryonic democracy, directed from above and without deep roots, allows a talented and charismatic demagogue to be taken for a serious leader.

Even in the first presidential elections of June 1991, Zhirinovsky foisted on voters the image of a resolute *vozhd'*, an iron fist, a "third force": "I never deceived you because I was never in power . . . I have no previous mistakes." In a polarized society tired of political games, it was a fail-safe position even then. This pose of an independent politician unmarked by the sins of either the communists or the democrats was an inexhaustible source of popularity for Zhirinovsky. It has become his refrain at rallies:

"I am from below, from you people. But I have enough education to understand what has to be done."

"There's only one of me, only one! I am the only one who is clean, fresh, independent, untied—I was never in the Communist Party!"

Indeed, there was a striking and paradoxical similarity between the political situation in the late 1980s and in the early 1990s, between the struggle of Yeltsin with Gorbachev and

Zhirinovsky with Yeltsin: both would-be presidents attracted the masses to their side. Yet, despite the external similarity, there is a substantive difference. Yeltsin promised a democratic paradise; Zhirinovsky, a return to dictatorship and the empire. In an extraordinarily brief period by historical standards, the political situation in the country turned upside down. Zhirinovsky copied and parodied Yeltsin to such an extent that the parody began to cast a shadow on the original. Doubts began to arise not about Zhirinovsky's motivations but about those of Yeltsin himself. Was Yeltsin camouflaging his own selfish aims to remove Gorbachev? Or was Yeltsin's success the result of historical necessity, as he understood it at the time? If so, why did restorationist sentiments immediately appear at all levels of national consciousness after the collapse of the USSR, so that Zhirinovsky could ride them, amplifying them and eventually taking charge of them?

Despite Zhirinovsky's protests (and even litigation) against comparisons of him to Hitler, both leaders manipulate mass psychology in similar ways. Their rhetoric is of militant nationalism, with the obligatory scapegoat of an ethnic origin different from the native population; and appeal to aggressive and revanchist sentiments; and hence a militarist doctrine with a promise of a final partitioning of the world (Hitler's *Drang nach Osten* and Zhirinovsky's *Drang nach Suden*); the promise of miraculous means to restore the economy; impossible pledges based on an exact knowledge of the most painful issues for society; and finally, the idea of the führer, the *vozhd'*, who leads his people to the radiant future.

Zhirinovsky often used to speechify at Moscow street rallies in a frenzied style reminiscent of Hitler. He played the role of the hard *vozhd'*, promising, to the crowd's exultation, to settle scores with the former Soviet republics that were mistreating Russians in their countries:

> I will end the humiliation of Russia. . . . Not a single hair will fall from a single Russian head! . . . If Moldavian bandits have put a Russian through a sawmill, I will destroy all the industrial plants of Moldavia! If a Russian was bound up with reins in Kyrgystan and the horses were sent off in different

directions, ripping him to pieces, I will destroy that region!

On hearing these words, a man in the crowd instinctively raised his hand in the Nazi salute, solemnly intoning: "I am a representative of the regular officers' corps. My friends and acquaintances support you." Zhirinovsky himself was slightly embarrassed, but possibly flattered, by the comparison. Several Zhirinovsky watchers have independently remarked on the un-witting similarity of Zhirinovsky and Charlie Chaplin's Hitler in *The Great Dictator.*

Zhirinovsky quite publicly created links between himself and Hitler. Following his trip to Germany, he defended the führer's ideology. At rallies he will say, "I am all-powerful! I am a tyrant! I will follow in Hitler's footsteps!" He declared himself a national-socialist, and in *Zhirinovsky's Falcon,* the theoretical foundations of Russian national-socialism are studied in two issues. *Liberal* developed—also theoretically—a joint Russian-German *Drang nach Osten.* During 1992 both Zhirinovsky and his party press ranted about the threat to the "white nation" and to "white civilization" from the "nonwhite majority." Zhirinovsky dressed his falcons in military uniforms with fake holsters on the belts, reminiscent of the Nazi uniform. Journalists instantly began to call them storm troopers. One Zhirinovsky falcon, V. Akhimov, leader of the LDP's youth section, was only too happy to describe the similarity of the Russian liberal democrats to the Nazi Party:

> Our party emerged in a time of troubles, seemingly from nowhere, and is winning over its adherents with confident measures. It is exactly the same way Hitler's party arose in its day. And it similarly won over its adherents until it came to power. Second, we have another point in common. Hitler came to power through constitutional means, through elections. We did, too; we have a party of law, we intend to come to power only through constitutional means. Third, Hitler conducted a tough national policy. He did well for the German race within Germany. We are carrying out the same policy in the

new Russia. We want things to be good for Russians in Russia.

The party slogans Zhirinovsky declaims in the mass rallies are developed not inside the party but by Zhirinovsky himself on the run, or more often are devised by his party comrades, the way effective reprises are written for a showman by a hired copywriter. Some were written by two former ministers in Zhirinovsky's shadow cabinet—Andrei Arkhipov, minister of information, and Sergei Zharikov, minister of culture—who were at the extreme right within the LDP. Now parted from the *vozhd'*, they described how they "dressed Zhirinovsky, the emperor with no clothes, in their slogans." Arkhipov recounts:

> Almost all the slogans that Zhirinovsky put out were conceived by me and Zharikov. . . . Ten minutes before his speech at a rally we would write them out in large letters on sheets of paper; for example: "America, give Alaska back to Russia." As I held up the sheet of paper, Zhirinovsky would eloquently expound the slogan right on the spot. His chief trait is the ability to pick up an idea on the fly and immediately give it to the public in the right form.

Zharikov also tells a story:

> In Murom, where the LDP held a rally two years ago, the crowd was in ecstasy from Zhirinovsky. We stage-managed it: when he got to rambling, we would immediately cross our arms as if to say "stop," and Zhirinovsky would shut up. On the whole, he has a wonderful sense of the crowd's mood, and he works himself up from it.

These former comrades may be exaggerating their role in the creation of Zhirinovsky, but obviously he was not the only one to concoct his inflammatory slogans. In the two years since Zhirinovsky collaborated with his ultra-right-wing stage prompters, the arsenal of slogans has obviously been enhanced by Zhirinovsky's very own sound bites, such as "We will wash our boots in the Indian Ocean"; "We will cut off the oxygen supply of the near abroad"; "We will put a bomb fuse in the far abroad"; "War is a good thing"; and "The whole nation, I promise you, will have an orgasm next year." And throughout all of Zhirinovsky's slogans and political rhetoric can be heard the persistent, hypnotic refrain: Vote for me.

Because his virtuoso demagoguery serves the most diverse population groups, and because of his inexhaustible wish to please all social strata at once with his promises, it is impossible to judge Zhirinovsky's real opinions or program (if he indeed has one). Zhirinovsky is both war and peace; he is a tyrant and a dictator but a democrat to the marrow of his bones; he is a national socialist but a liberal democrat; he is for pluralism but also for a tough regime; he is a strict pragmatic but also a visionary idealist; he advocates law and order but seizes other people's territories and threatens global blackmail; he opposes destroying the state sector and supports 100 percent the private sector; he is against dismantling the collective farms but is for private farmers.

No politician with the slightest bit of self-respect could seriously promote all these contradictory positions. It is not a problem for Zhirinovsky, however. You cannot trip him up with logic. You cannot get at him with the facts. You cannot learn the truth from him. It's as if he knows Henry Adams's formula for political pragmatism by heart: "Practical politics consists in ignoring facts." Zhirinovsky is beyond morality, rules of behavior, political conventions. "I cannot give you such assurances that tomorrow, on the twelfth, I will come to power, and on the thirteenth, you'll have a better life," dourly commented Arkady Volsky, one of the leaders of the military-industrial complex, on Zhirinovsky's success in the elections to the Duma, "because I am guided by common sense and I have an internal brake. Zhirinovsky has neither." Volsky concluded, "The phenomenon of the LDP leader is explained only by unbridled populism." Having begun his first election campaign in May 1991 with vulgar populist ploys like promising cheap vodka, a well-fed life, and enormous salaries for soldiers, Zhirinovsky quickly cottoned to the fact that in a situation of total collapse, it was easier to arouse the masses with an idea rather than with self-interest. British economist Walter Bagehot wrote of this feature of mass psychology: "The masses of men are very difficult to excite on bare grounds of self-interest; most easy if a bold orator tells them confidently they are wronged."

We must give the bold orator his due; he has intuitively perceived the Russian mass psychology and its need for national dignity. Zhirinovsky recounted confidently to an American journalist how he exploited the national idea in his campaign: "I was the first politician who said that he would defend Russians. I got six million votes just for saying that. The next election, I will win." A heartrending paradox arises: the masses all over the country see Zhirinovsky as he portrays himself—a defender of the Russians, a miracle-working politician, a wise guardian of a troubled people. Zhirinovsky, however, sees in them only potential voters. He plays on national sentiments, or in fact imposes them on the country, because in a worsening socioeconomic crisis, when the people are fighting for their survival, they have no time for patriotic contortions.

Zhirinovsky's secret of success is not only in his slogans but in the genre he has selected, more stage performance than politics. He is the only Russian politician to have taken the mood of the common people into account. They treat the elections as a spectacle more than anything, a show, expecting entertainment and humor from politicians as they would from actors. After Zhirinovsky's 1993 election victory, even his sworn political enemies were forced to admit that he had accurately guessed the tastes of the people, known from the times of Emperor Augustus, when the ancient Roman mob demanded—and got—*panem et circenses*, bread and circuses. The former prime minister Yegor Gaidar, in comparing Zhirinovsky with Hitler, emphasized a distinction: "Hitler was serious in the German manner. Zhirinovsky is the opposite, he tries to make people laugh, knowing that it is easier to get at the Russian popular consciousness that way, with laughter."

The film director Nikita Mikhalkov made the point in explaining Zhirinovsky's success: "Zhirinovsky is a folkloric man, he put everything very simply, as if spelling it out in capital letters. . . . Here is one person who went and relied on the popular traditions of the people who want to vote for him."

Yevgenia Albats calls Zhirinovsky a "genius of kitsch," and

Eduard Limonov writes about the "language of the street" in which his former party boss speaks:

> It was Zhirinovsky who introduced the language of the street into politics. After the wooden speech of the party, he spoke with the common man in his own language, and the fellow in the street liked that. Zhirinovsky never takes credit for his street argot, but that's his strength. . . . His caricaturized talk sounds normal to the common man and easily penetrates his consciousness.

The Zhirinovsky people did not conceal the folkloric mixture and genesis of their leader. Alexander Vengerovsky, Zhirinovsky's closest aide and deputy chairman of the Duma from the LDP, accounted for the party's triumph in the parliamentary elections in this way:

> In ancient Russia, there has always existed a legitimate opposition. Under the tsar, it was the jester. And the people always treated members of the opposition as holy. Our people understand why our agitation and propaganda was conducted in just this way, and not another. We speak the same language as they do, in a single linguistic system.

In March 1994, when Richard Nixon met with Zhirinovsky, Vengerovsky explained to the former American president that Zhirinovsky deliberately chose for himself the extravagant image of a *yurodivy*, who alone is allowed to speak the truth with impunity. Nixon translated this as "holy fool," the jester in *King Lear*.

Giles Fletcher, Queen Elizabeth's envoy to the Moscow court, wrote in his travel diary that the holy fools in old Russia were allowed to say everything they wanted, without any restriction. "At the present time, among others, there is one in Moscow who walks the streets naked and incites everyone against the government. The people very much love such blessed simple people, since like a pasquinade, they point to the shortcomings of the higher-ups."

All of his ensuing sensational capers, from his nuclear threats to his fistfights with other politicians, from his solo dance with a broom in Slovenia to his spitting at Jewish demonstrators in France, are of this slapstick genre. Commentator Boris Paramonov, who has called him "the carnival king," is correct. Even the cult of Zhirinovsky's personality is an obvious parody, humorous tomfoolery. There are the party publications with his name in the titles (*Zhirinovsky's Truth, Zhirinovsky's Word, Zhirinovsky's Falcon,* and *At Home with Zhirinovsky*); the rock-music store named "Chez Zhirinovsky" in his honor; "Radio Zhirinovsky" with the list of his favorite songs or songs about him, such as "Hey, Vladimir Volfovich, Life's No Bowl of Cherries"; and even a vodka named "Zhirinovsky" with his portrait on the label.

Zhirinovsky has not reached the point where he is walking the streets buck-naked like Fletcher's holy fool. But he has appeared on the cover of the *New York Times Magazine* in his birthday suit, taking a shower, for an article titled "Why Russia Loves This Man." His exhibitionism, both physical and mental, comes from this same jester's nature. There is never a dull moment with him—he's a prankster, a clown, a buffoon, and a juggler. It is this image of low comedy—contrasting with the stolid Yeltsin in his Kremlin splendor—that has won him the love and recognition of the crowd. In Yeltsin, however, this image is a mask—he's also acting, but in another genre: the dramatic and the pompous.

Zhirinovsky is an entertainer and a comedian. His gigantic audience, increasingly inclined to slapstick humor and farce, seems not only gullible, but disenchanted with politics as such, and not only with Yeltsin personally. The voters preferred a parody of a *vozhd'* to the real thing because they stopped believing in real *vozhdi'*, regardless of who they are. Zhirinovsky is a mirror, a distorted one, of Russia's current hard times. As folkloric fool or the real thing, he has won himself the right to behave as he likes and say everything he thinks. And here is the paradox: the odder Zhirinovsky is with his deliberately silly manners, scandalous capers, and loose tongue, the more warmly and more seriously the audience of the people treated him, laughing all the while.

Is Fascism Always Wrong?

To some extent it was easier for Zhirinovsky to campaign than his rivals. Ever since he put himself on the ballot in the presidential elections in the spring of 1991, Zhirinovsky had never stopped running. He was tireless. Who else among the candidates to the Russian parliament hit thirty-two cities in eleven different time zones before the elections? Zhirinovsky even managed to be in several of them more than once.

He visited the ancient city of Vologda, with its population of four million, four times in the course of his three-year campaign marathon. (None of the other twelve leaders of his rival parties and groups bothered to stop there.) On this last trip through town, Zhirinovsky held a two-hour rally on the city's central square. By comparison, the local branch of Russia's Choice held its founding conference behind closed doors and kicked all journalists out of the hall.

Among Zhirinovsky's best supporters was the Vologda Popular Movement, the most powerful organization of the province, founded by young entrepreneurs whose slogan was "Capitalism with a Russian face." In putting their theory into practice, they had chased all their rivals—peddlers "of the Caucasian nationality"—out of the market and thus gained popularity with the local people. During the election campaign, the Vologda Popular Movement distributed leaflets warning that they would take "all measures to retaliate against a person or representatives of the mass media who attempt to discredit the person and activity of V. V. Zhirinovsky." The threat had some teeth to it given that the movement had its own detachment of gunmen.

Moreover, Zhirinovsky's emissaries traveled throughout Vologda Province agitating for LDP candidates. One of them was the party gauleiter, Vladimir Chashchin of Cherepovets, a city within Vologda Province that exceeds Vologda in population and in the number of factories and their industrial importance:

> CHASHCHIN: The party of which I am a member has been called fascist . . . I have to agree, although it

Prior to the elections, Gavriil Popov confidently stated that Russia's Choice would take first place with a large gap between them and other parties, and would garner about 20 to 40 percent of the vote.

If the polls can be believed, Zhirinovsky began with little better than zero support, but by the end of October, 2 percent of those surveyed backed him. No one ascribed any significance to this increase. Nevertheless, Zhirinovsky kept attracting new supporters, breaking them away from other groups (reformists, communists, even agrarians) or drawing into his ideological orbit those who had no set opinion.

By November, Zhirinovsky had 9 percent, and after that he shot up the charts.

Two weeks before the elections, trying to demonstrate his neutrality, Yeltsin received the leaders of all thirteen parties and blocs in the elections. Perhaps accidentally, or more likely because of his own agility, Zhirinovsky ended up sitting next to the president. Most people noticed this only later after the startling results of the elections led them to interpret the seating arrangement as greatly symbolic.

"We will fight for the Constitution. I ask you not to touch the Constitution," said Yeltsin at that meeting, warning that if candidates criticized the draft Constitution on television, "the broadcast will be shut off." Zhirinovsky's demand that opponents of the proposed Constitution withdraw their candidacy from the elections resounded in unison with the president.

When the campaign speeches were on television at the same time as good movies on other channels, people watched the movies. But when the candidates were on all three channels, the majority of viewers chose Zhirinovsky. His speeches were more visual, theatrical, and original than the others; he was unpredictable, never disappointing his audience.

His ratings jumped several times during these last two weeks, when he aired constant television advertising. Zhirinovsky was the first candidate in Russia to realize fully that these were not just democratic elections, but first and foremost *televised* elections.

Stylistically, Zhirinovsky was the most modern politician of all those in the elections, and was better prepared than the others for the medium of television. On some days Zhirinovsky contrived to be seen on all channels, and, in *Izvestia*'s exaggerated comment, "his mug was almost permanently stuck to the television screen for a month." Yegor Gaidar, with his bald pate, round face, and academic manner, wasn't ready for prime time or any kind of close-ups. With the help of psychoanalysis on his team, Zhirinovsky was well briefed on how to communicate intimately with voters through the television screen. Furthermore, according to a report in *Argumenty i fakty*, British campaign experts coached him in Moscow. They held special seminars for Russians open to any parties, but most candidates sent third-rank representatives. Zhirinovsky came in person and studied hard, asking questions, taking notes, participating in the tests, and amazing his teachers with his industriousness and receptivity.

Zhirinovsky acquired half of his votes during the end of the campaign. One-fifth made their selection at the last minute. This striking growth in popularity was due not only to his own television appearances but also, paradoxically, to the attacks on him.

Pavel Chukhrai's propaganda film *The Hawk* was supposed to destroy Zhirinovsky politically. The democrats had not taken Zhirinovsky seriously for much of the campaign, becoming concerned only in the last days before the election as his ratings in the polls soared. They did not stoop so low as to debate him, but they did air the film. It ended up having the opposite effect.

Chukhrai's *Hawk* was a subtle attempt to parody its subject by showing him in action. One scene showed the chairman's birthday, celebrated with Cossack songs, drinking and carousing, and greetings from the Iraqi ambassador and Gerhard Frey. Another scene followed Zhirinovsky, surrounded by a tight ring of bodyguards and supporters, as he went out on the streets to meet people. Another showed Zhirinovsky unleashing his usual tirade of populist demagoguery at a rally. The last scene found Zhirinovsky leaning on a barrier, gazing pensively at the Kremlin.

Since the figure the LDP chairman cuts already contains an element of caricature, to ridicule him would seem to require no extra effort. Simply showing his as he is—how he walks, how he talks and gesticulates, how he eats and drinks—would allow viewers to realize that he is hollow, a liar and poseur, a demagogue and a fascist. But the large mass of viewers were unsophisticated, naive, politically ignorant, and aesthetically undeveloped. Judging from the reactions the next day during the elections, the hero of this film made a strong and immediate impression on people. Even his pensive gaze at the Kremlin was effective, as if it were his future residence, where sooner or later he would celebrate his birthday before the entire population, as a supporter confidently predicted in the film.

Some material on him in the film could have been compromising. The worst blows to his image were his Jewish roots, on the one hand, and on the other, his fascist ideology. The first catered to traditional Russian anti-Semitism, and the second to the nation's historical memory of the relatively recent war with Hitler that had cost, even by the most conservative estimates, twenty-five million lives. There was every reason to believe that the Russian people had received a historical inoculation against fascism. The democrats were wrong on both accounts, exaggerating both popular anti-Semitism and the historical memory.

As we have noted, all sorts of people had been called Jews in recent times, from President Yeltsin to Dmitri Vasilyev, the head of the anti-Semitic Pamyat. The word had become so overused and devalued that it no longer worked against Zhirinovsky. Moreover, Zhirinovsky's own anti-Semitism outweighed his Jewishness. What difference did it make what roots he had if he was determinedly against the domination of Jews in the Kremlin, in culture, and on television, where he promised to replace them with blond, blue-eyed newscasters?

The historical memory of fascism turned out to be shorter in Russians than was supposed. After the elections, a clear formula was discovered for what had happened. "Fascism in Russia is terrifying today not because it is strong. It is terrifying because it's right," said the liberal economist Mikhail Delyagin. The journalist Alexander Burtin picked up on this observation and extended it: "A fascist engaged in demagoguery— that's normal. A fascist who speaks the truth—now that's real trouble." Another common aphorism, "The worst is if fascism comes, and we don't recognize it," turned out to be untrue on close inspection. In fact, people recognized the face of fascism even before its arrival.

Homo sovieticus did not have complete immunity to fascism. Many traits nurtured in him during the Stalin era had a striking similarity to the early signs of fascism: the demand to be taken care of by the government; a history of strong, one-person rule; paternalism; primitive political and social thought; ethnocentrism; and chauvinism. Essentially, Stalin's barracks socialism was the Russian national model of fascism. The Russian political soil of the 1990s was increasingly reminiscent of Italy or Germany in the 1920s and 1930s, when the *fleurs du mal* first grew: the impoverishment of the masses; the fall in industrial production and the threat of unemployment; corruption and the paralysis of power; rampant crime; a feeling of national humiliation; Russians who have found themselves outside of Russia; a thirst for revenge; hatred of foreigners; and universal inflation—of money, ideas, words, moral values, and life itself.

Moreover, like the word *Jew*, the very meaning of the word *fascist* had become eroded in the Russian political battles. It lost its original sense and turned into a political label, a gutter curse. Democrats called the Old Believers occupying the White House the "Communofascists." Not to be outdone, the conservatives called the democrats "demofascists," especially after the bloody massacre at the center of the capital. In his essay "Politics and the English Language," George Orwell claimed that many words used in political discussions become meaningless because they are not used to refer to something particular and identifiable but only for effect. As the most vivid example, he cited the word *fascism*, which "has now no meaning except insofar as it signifies 'something not desirable.'" In the minds of the masses who were dissatisfied with the government, Zhirinovsky was labeled a fascist simply because he criticized the Kremlin.

The words *fascist* and *Jew* were no longer bogeymen for the voter. Nor could Zhirinovsky's friendship with the Iraqi dictator bother them. Zhirinovsky was a Teflon candidate; criticism never seemed to stick and only had the reverse effect.

Ignorant of these changes in the public mind, the democrats still felt they had the victory in their pockets. Certain of their success, they were already in a relaxed state. Not superstitious by nature, they saw no reason why they shouldn't celebrate the victory publicly even before the tallies were in. A banquet reception was organized at the Kremlin, televised live nationwide on the night of December 12 (after all, the Kremlin had control of the airwaves) as the results began to come in from the electoral districts. The title of the television show was "Meeting the Political New Year," which turned out to be more than apt.

As the first returns were put on the screen of Ostankino's computer, the democrats who had gathered in the Kremlin's banquet hall grew more and more gloomy. Many took advantage of the noise and confusion of the party to sneak out the door. Meanwhile Vladimir Volfovich felt as if he were the birthday boy. His Liberal Democratic Party was coming in first in the elections, with a total of fourteen million votes—one in every four voters chose Zhirinovsky. Taken together, the Zhirinovsky followers, the communists, the agrarians, and other conservatives gained a majority of seats in the State Duma, the lower house of the new parliament.

It was at this banquet that the prominent democrat Yuri Karyakin couldn't restrain himself and shouted over live television:"Russia, come to your senses! Have you gone mad?" Then Telman Gdlyan tried to spoil Zhirinovsky's celebrations by reminding him of his Jewishness, and got socked in the ear for his trouble.

The democrats' blitzkrieg had obviously failed, the October victors turned out to be the December losers; the people had spoken decisively and unambiguously, rejecting the government's reform program. It was an utter political defeat for the democrats, and only Yeltsin formally escaped the rout because of his neutral position as the "father of the nation"—as if he were above the fray in which, in fact, he was the chief participant.

Yeltsin's Constitution was approved, although by a narrow majority, which his political opponents immediately began to carp at him about. A little more than half of those who voted were in favor of the Constitution, but since only a little more than half of those eligible to vote turned out for the elections, 31.5 percent of the whole electorate voted for the

Constitution, or less than one-third of the adult population. Yeltsin's Constitution would never have done even this well, however, if Zhirinovsky hadn't called for his followers to support it. Stanislav Govorukhin predicted that in time it would be called "Zhirinovsky's Constitution." The weekly magazine *Stolitsa* [Capital] wrote that Zhirinovsky had snatched up almost all the trump cards, and his strongest card was Yeltsin's Constitution.

It was not the defeat of the democrats but Zhirinovsky's victory that made the greatest impression in Russia as well as abroad. President Clinton tried to downplay the significance of Zhirinovsky's victory—which was a fiasco for White House Russian policy—and hastened to declare the Russian elections result a protest vote. That superficial explanation of what had happened in Russia, however, did not account for the main issue: why disgruntled voters preferred Zhirinovsky instead of democrats who were in opposition to Yeltsin—for example, Yavlinsky, who was called a "Zhirinovsky for the intelligentsia," or at least the communists and agrarians, their ideological mates in the countryside who received fewer votes than Zhirinovsky's falcons.

Russian democrats, shaken by the LDP's election success, reacted violently to the "triumphant march through the country of Zhirinovsky's fascist party hand in hand with the communists." An oft-quoted saying from the era of the transition from Gorbachev's Soviet Union to Yeltsin's Russia, "We woke up in a strange country," once again became current, perhaps even more appropriate than before.

The ultra-liberal Valeriya Novodvorskaya demanded that the authorities immediately arrest Zhirinovsky and annul the mandates of his party's deputies—more than sixty people whom the chairman of the LDP had carried into the State Duma along with him. Foreign Minister Kozyrev swore never to shake Zhirinovsky's hand (there is a notion in Russia of an untouchable), and Deputy Prime Minister Gaidar instantly cobbled together an antifascist bloc to liquidate "Vladimir Adolfovich," as he began to call Zhirinovsky.

The comparison to Hitler became a cliché of anti-Zhirinovsky propaganda, and if he were Hitler, then Yeltsin was by political and physical analogy the weak Hindenburg, ready to turn over the reins of government to Zhirinovsky at any moment. Russia seemed more and more like Weimar Germany. The only thing that wasn't clear was which year in Germany—1929, 1932, or 1933, on the eve of the führer's coming to power.

The reasons for the political emergency were sought in the most unlikely places, from the billion Zhirinovsky allegedly received from his friend Saddam Hussein for the campaign, to bad weather and the broadcasting of the soccer supercup on election day, which prevented commonsense voters from turning out. Even parapsychological reasons were cited: some credited Zhirinovsky's sexual influence on the female half of the audience or even on both sexes. His entire campaign had supposedly been an appeal to subconscious fears and base instincts, a kind of mass hypnosis session, "elections under hypnosis," as one of the losers, Konstantin Borovoi, declared them.

Because, since time immemorial, someone has to be blamed for everything in Russia, Vyacheslav Bragin, head of television, was removed from his position by presidential decree for giving Zhirinovsky 220 minutes of airtime. Other blocs had just as much access to television, and Gaidar's party, Russia's Choice, had even more airtime—it was just a question of how it was used.

The democratic candidates also took a beating from the democratic press for the split in their ranks and for ceding to Zhirinovsky the ideals of social justice, patriotism, statehood. Yeltsin himself was attacked for withdrawing from the party fray instead of identifying himself unabashedly with Russia's Choice (this criticism came from Gennady Burbulis, formerly his closest adviser).

Based on polls of its most distinguished readers, the journal *Golos* [Voice] declared Zhirinovsky "man of the year," even with a minus sign, that is, an antihero and even the Antichrist. The humorist Arkadi Arkanov was perhaps most pointed of all: "Zhirinovsky is at the same time a hero and an antihero. He is a fascist, and so full of shit! But we have to admit: he won this year. Perhaps because the people who played against him are even more full of shit!"

To this day the question as to who funded Zhirinovsky's campaign has not been answered. Was it Saddam Hussein?

Gerhard Frey? The International Bulgarian adventurers Dmitry Klinkov and Svetoslav Stoilov? The Dutch firm GMM? The Berlin firm Werner Girke? The KGB—directly and by proxy, through cutouts? Russian businessmen with a keen interest in establishing order in the country, who were therefore betting on Zhirinovsky? Or perhaps the LDP itself was successfully pulling off financial deals through dummy corporations? In the past, the LDP's commercial operations were run by Andrei Zavidiya; now they are managed by Valentin Minakov, officially the party's general manager working under Zhirinovsky. Is he unofficially its "grey cardinal"? There are numerous theories but no solid proof, and our own research along these lines has been inconclusive. In any case, Zhirinovsky himself could not have afforded to pay for the trips around the country, the campaign literature, and the television advertising, which alone cost him nearly a million dollars. "Most parties gave letters of credit to a special account at the Central Bank, but some dummy corporations paid for Zhirinovsky," said Kirill Ignatyev, deputy chairman of the Ostankino television company. Although he seemed to be on the paper trail, his discovery has only clouded the issue further. But whatever the identity of Zhirinovsky's fairy godmothers, neither television nor money alone created him; he created himself. Commenting on the results of the elections, Moscow film director Alexander Mitta wrote:

> Zhirinovsky is not crazy; his diagnosis is the same as all the social psychoses of the little man of Russia today.
> The insanity of Russian life has only one figure who could express it as it is—and that's obviously not Yeltsin. It's Zhirinovsky. Because Russia in fact (all of its except the major cities) is pregnant not with democracy but with fascism. It dreams of dictatorship, of order, and of its lost greatness. Zhirinovsky is an expression of these dreams. He is the right man at the right time. I think in the near future we will see how he grabs the presidential seat he needs. Yeltsin has prepared a fabulous present for him— unlimited power enshrined in the new Constitution.

> . . . A powerful beast has broken into Russia's po-
> litical forest. A real wolf with sharp teeth. He will
> strangle all the sick and weak, and fight all his
> equals. Only now we remember that a healthy forest
> needs a strong predator. Without him the forest
> grows decrepit, wilts, and dies.

Perhaps the most surprising and revealing insight into Zhirinovsky's success comes from a look at the people who voted
for him. In the two and a half years after the 1991 presidential
elections, Zhirinovsky not only more than doubled the number of his voters but qualitatively changed his electorate. They
were no longer pensioners and drunks, as the first time, but
younger people, mostly employed, primarily men. The haven
for pensioners nostalgic for the recent past became the Communist Party, whereas the LDP, with only 10 percent of its vote
coming from the aged, was the "party of the future." More
than two-thirds of Zhirinovsky's followers worked, half in the
state sector and 43 percent in industry. A third of his electorate were semiskilled workers with average wages. In the three
months before the elections, one in five Zhirinovsky fans was
laid off from his factory, one and a half times higher than the
national average.

Fifteen percent of Zhirinovsky's people made additional
earnings on the side, and about a third, when asked, intended
to make some extra cash in the next month. In other words,
Zhirinovsky's supporters were relatively young, enterprising,
energetic, and even aggressive people. Although the most dis-
contented people were found in Zhirinovsky's camp—people
dissatisfied with the government, the bosses at their factories,
the state of labor discipline, the size of their pay packets, and
so on—almost none was a pessimist, depressive, or a whiner. In
short, Zhirinovsky gave ordinary people a political outlet for
the social and political anger.

Besides the general problems troubling all Russians regardless of their political preferences (the rise in prices, the growth
of crime, and the state of the economy), the primary problem
for Zhirinovsky's people is the loss of Russia's status as a great
power and the weakness of its government. Their number-two
concern is bribery, corruption, and the squandering of

national resources, all of which began to flourish under the democrats. Sociologists also noted that Zhirinovsky voters identified themselves with the "Soviet people," a notion that had supposedly lost its point after the collapse of the Soviet Union.

According to surveys, Zhirinovsky's electorate was formed under the influence of his active campaign. Men between the ages of twenty-five and forty were the first to be attracted to him; then they brought in older age groups, and women joined at the last moment.

Finally, there is one more important indicator: the geopolitical factor inside Russia. From the very start, 70 percent of Zhirinovsky's supporters were residents of small provincial towns with populations under one hundred thousand. By voting day, the geographical spread had evened out somewhat, but the majority of Zhirinovsky's voters—56 percent—were still from industrial towns that were small by Russian standards. Zhirinovsky did poorly in the largest cities—Moscow, St. Petersburg, Arkhangelsk, Nizhni Novgorod, Ekaterinburg, and Khabarovsk.

The political and economic reforms that enriched the large metropolitan centers simultaneously led to a greater impoverishment of the Russian hinterland—which is exactly why the changes were so unpopular. Now not just people but whole cities and regions were lumpenized: at the time of the parliamentary elections, thirty-five million Russians lived below the poverty line, all of them potential votes for the opposition. And just as the 1991 Zhirinovsky electorate consisted largely of lumpen, the same occurred again, only this time not lumpen people, but lumpen cities and lumpen villages, that is, cities and towns doomed to bankruptcy.

To them were added the "new Russians," get-rich-quick and nouveau-riche provincials. These were those "young wolves," in Zhirinovsky's expression, to whom he had promised that when he came to power he would "destroy the bureaucratic mechanism of access to resources," and would lower taxes and curb racketeers. A confidential analysis prepared in Moscow for the political and commercial elite said that Zhirinovsky's party was lobbying on behalf of some influential and wealthy groups: "And what is particularly important, their combined financial clout will enable the party to implement a wide-scale, ambitious political strategy." Thus, paradoxically, Zhirinovsky's electorate is an alliance of the poor and the rich, equally interested in a powerful state and a strong government."

In its heyday the Soviet state was a political dictator, owner of the economy, sponsor, employer, nourisher, protector from criminals—in short, a lord exercising total control over his subjects from birth to death. Former Soviet citizens now feel orphaned. "We are like people who have been in prison for a long time," wrote Moscow psychologist Sergei Agrachev. "Released outside the gates, overwhelmed by the noise of the street and the possibility of moving in different directions, we are in a neurotic state." As in Byron's image, this is the syndrome of the prisoner of Chillon who became agitated and confused when freed, and dreamt of returning to prison, under the protection of law and order.

In a fit of temper, Valeriya Novodvorskaya denounced those who had voted for Zhirinovsky as not a people but a mob. In fact, she was talking about that other Russia, the geographically remote and politically marginal Russia that had made itself known in these elections and spoken up for its rights to representation in the highest echelons of power.

The elections finalized the polarization of society (in the absence of a stable political center). Russia split into two countries, into "clean" and "unclean," "white" and "black." Both these Russias treated each other with suspicion and growing enmity. With the elections the Russian provinces threw down the political gauntlet to metropolitan Russia by ensuring Zhirinovsky his victory.

Mikhail Poltoranin traveled through the towns outside of Moscow immediately after the elections. He cites an incident that he believes is typical. In a relatively wealthy village— wealthy as a result of the economic reforms—voting was heavily in favor of the LDP. Poltoranin asked the farmers why. Their answer: "It's gotten hard to breathe—the criminal groups are torturing us with their extortion rackets. If you don't pay up what they demand, they threaten to retaliate against your family. The authorities look the other way. But Zhirinovsky is promising strict law and order."

Fryazino, where Zhirinovsky had held rallies before the elections, is home to the flower of the technical intelligentsia. There are four scientific research institutes and four military factories, but the town is now an economic anachronism. A third of the residents of Fryazino voted for Zhirinovsky—exactly the number of people who are unemployed, underemployed (working three days a week), or temporarily suspended due to lack of work. The average wage in Fryazino is now far lower than in the rest of Russia, although several years ago it was higher. When asked why the people of Fryazino voted for Zhirinovsky, they said: "He promised to help us." "He promised to defend us." "He's one of us and understands us."

Quite a few Fryazinos languish around the country, where people who worked in the military-industrial complex have found themselves idled. They form an additional stream of people into the Zhirinovsky camp.

When General Rutskoi was released before trial from Lefortovo in March 1994, his assistant, Andrei Fyodorov, spent days on the phone calling the "red directors" (the heads of the military-industrial complex factories) to enlist them for his boss. Here is now he described their mood:

> They're not so interested in the stuff Zhirinovsky is spouting. Scientists and engineers proceed from a very correct principle: whatever he's spouting isn't so important. What's more important is that when he comes to power, he'll give them money and give them purchase orders. And what will happen after that doesn't concern them. I was speaking just now with one of the directors who voted for Zhirinovsky. He is the director of a major defense plant. He said outright that he was voting for Zhirinovsky now, because in another six months his factory will have disappeared. And then nobody will bring it back—not Zhirinovsky, nor any Tom, Dick, or Harry. So I'm voting for Zhirinovsky now because Zhirinovsky at least won't let that factory die.

The people of Fryazino or Perm are against war, but Zhirinovsky promised them work and won additional votes for that. Seven and a half million people work at the some fifteen hundred military factories in the country. Counting their families, that's twenty-five million people. Not all of them are of voting age, but nevertheless, it is a powerful reserve of votes for Zhirinovsky.

The most surprising group of followers (and the most ominous or depressing for the democrats) was Zhirinovsky's military electorate: his percentage of the army votes was more than 70. An equal number voted for the Constitution that would ensure extraordinary powers for the president. The military voted for a strong president, and acknowledging that man to be out of the available politicians, picked Zhirinovsky. His absolute triumph in the Russian army was perhaps no less a sensation than his victory—relative, to be sure—in the country as a whole. In short, if the military had the right to choose their commander in chief, it would be Vladimir Volfovich Zhirinovsky, a lieutenant in the reserves. "He hasn't become [commander] yet, but formally he already is," wrote a military expert for *Novaya yezhednevnaya gazeta* [New daily news].

Valeriya Novodvorskaya, shaken by the results of the military vote, announced that we had the Russian fascist army after the elections, instead of the Russian army. She proposed that a national guard be formed immediately from Yeltsin supporters and that it be outfitted with planes and tanks.

The Kremlin was so frightened by the news about the army's vote leaking to the press that it tried to squelch it, deny it, and distort it. In some army divisions, the numbers were forged to portray the army as more loyal that it was in reality. A few days later, Defense Minister Pavel Grachev ordered, all documents concerning the elections on army bases were strictly classified, and a report with deliberately lowered figures was placed on Yeltsin's desk. At a press conference immediately after the elections, although Yeltsin admitted the alarming fact of the preference shown by the army for Zhirinovsky, he still cited a percentage lower by half.

But the reality was far from reassuring for the democrats. In the strategic missile forces, 27 percent voted for Zhirinovsky; 16.5 for the communists; and only 5.8 for Russia's Choice. Two tank divisions, Kantemir and Taman, that had been considered pro-Yeltsin and had helped to suppress the October rebellion turned heavily pro-Zhirinovsky: 74.3 in the Kantemir

Division and 87.4 in the Taman Division. In Kronshtadt, the chief base for the Baltic Fleet, 73 percent of the residents voted for Zhirinovsky. He gained 40 percent of the air force's vote (Russia's Choice took 10 percent; the communists, 8 percent). Even in the Moscow Military District, with its traditional leanings toward the central political and military elite, Zhirinovsky did far better than Russia's Choice (13.7 percent) or the communists (8.5), walking off with 46 percent of the vote. There were landslide votes as well, for example, at the Russian Military Academy, where 93 percent of the students and teachers voted for Zhirinovsky.

The right-wing newspaper *Sovetskaya Rossiya* gleefully pronounced the army's vote for Zhirinovsky a "ballot salvo." Military analyst Lieutenant General Alexei Smirnov stated that Yeltsin could no longer count on the support of military people. Major General Vladimir Dudnik, leader of an organization called Army and Society, put it more bluntly: "These results clearly show that the army has said 'farewell' to Yeltsin."

In fact, the situation was more complicated and contradictory. In voting for Zhirinovsky, the Russian army had not *yet* left the Kremlin's command and had not *yet* turned into a fascist army, but, as the army newspaper *Krasnaya zvezda* [Red star] soberly explained, had voted for its own interests:

> The army voted for itself, for its own corporate interests, which are not narrow or trivial, but the government's interests. It voted for a strong, united, and patriotically oriented Russia; for politicians not to drag the army into their games in the future; to be respected and socially secure; for a decent service for new recruits and a dignified life for its veterans.

Although *Krasnaya zvezda* represents the army's corporate interests, there is a grain of truth in its commentary. The army simply turned out to be more conservative and patriotic than civilian society, a trait it has in common with all the armies of the world.

In addition, the complicated Kremlin intrigues that dragged the army unwillingly into Yeltsin's battle with the "red-brown" had an effect on the results. Although caught between two

along with World Zionism and Russian Jewry, plus those countries that had only recently been part of the Soviet empire, as
well as their intelligence services (the CIA, the Mossad, the
British Intelligence Service, and even the state security of
Zhirinovsky's homeland, Kazakhstan, which was personally
staging an operation against him). Zhirinovsky's personal enemies become mixed with and finally merge entirely with the
"enemies of the people."

The Jews occupy pride of place in Zhirinovsky's list of enemies, either as such, or under their equivalent terms: "Israel,"
"the Israeli trap," the "Zionist plot." These propagandistic
stereotypes would seem to belong in the historical archives of
Hitler's and Stalin's time, but no sooner were they taken down
and dusted off than they immediately resumed their function
of unifying the masses. There is evidently a vestige of Stalinism
in him (more likely than Hitler). This ultra-modern figure
with "planetary thinking," as he himself puts it, turns out to
be old-fashioned, even archaic. His almost maniacal obsession
with "Russia's enemies" echoes perfectly with Stalin's persecution mania. No wonder Zhirinovsky recalls Stalin well for creating a strong state and forcing everyone to fear Russia, and
"when they fear, they respect," as Zhirinovsky is convinced.

> Stalin the Red Monarch was not inherently a blood-
> sucker. At the end of the 1920s he was the bewil-
> dered leader of an enormous peasant state with a
> primitive industry, and accordingly, a poorly armed
> military and a machinery of government grown cor-
> rupt under the influence of NEP.[2] Stalin understood
> that Russia did not have the right to be weak, other-
> wise it would be eaten up. . . . We now have a situa-
> tion like Stalin had at the end of the 1920s. The
> collapse of the economy, the empty state treasury,
> the loss of our outlying territories. But we don't
> need terrible persecution, we are not in a hurry the
> way Stalin was, because we do not fear external

---

2. NEP, New Economic Policy, was a brief period in the 1920s when the
Kremlin was forced temporarily to tolerate private enterprise and free trade,
but then banned them once again until the 1990s.

enemies the way Stalin did. We have nuclear missiles and other forms of weapons of mass destruction.

Zhirinovsky knows how to rule the weak-willed Russian masses but also knows that these masses are passive, inert, and apathetic. Their instinct for self-preservation is worn to a frazzle, although that is what the orator is persistently and passionately appealing to, proclaiming his mission to save the fatherland: "I would really like it for millions of Soviet citizens to understand how serious, how tragic the situation is, for them to awaken from their indifference." Elsewhere Zhirinovsky noted that the Russian masses may be rallied to a cause only by extreme means: "and in Russia, in order to arouse the Russian nation, you have to arouse it with bloodshed." Zhirinovsky's speeches began by whipping up horrors, followed by instilling hopes.

More than anything, Zhirinovsky peddles hope to people who have lost everything, who have nothing to lose, humiliated and disenfranchised, furiously nostalgic for the imperial past. The professional politician Zhirinovsky offers buckets, tubs, tanks of hope—as much as his future voters can handle. If they bring him to power, he also promises to return them Russia's lost greatness, to restore the powerful empire, and to instill terror in Russia's enemies. The democrats promised nothing good, but instead told people the harsh truth that things would not be better, that they would be worse and no one knew when they would get better, if at all.

Unconsciously, Zhirinovsky had taken into account a corrective to Francis Bacon's formula for "wise government": "It is a certain sign of a wise government and proceeding that it can hold men's hearts by hopes when it cannot by satisfaction."

Yeltsin's October conquest of the red-brown parliament, achieved at such bloodshed, turned out to be in vain. In December he got a new parliament with the same dominant color scheme. Apparently, the old parliament had more or less accurately reflected the moods in society. "Was it worth shelling Khasbulatov with tanks in order for Zhirinovsky to pop up!" exclaimed Leonid Radzikhovsky. *Nezavisimaya gazeta* wrote about the "boomerang effect—the strike delivered returns with greater power." It seemed as if the armed battle in the center of the capital and the billions of rubles spent on the new elections were all done for the sake of only one man: Zhirinovsky. Free of his rivals from the right-wing camp (they were in prison), he arranged a one-man show on Russia's empty political stage, charming one-fourth of the audience with his acting and prevailing in the country's first democratic elections to parliament.

Two days after the elections, Zhirinovsky held a press conference packed with journalists at the international press center in the hotel Radisson-Slavyanskaya. The victor was dressed in a tuxedo, bow tie, and cummerbund known to be the present from Saddam Hussein, although at the press conference Zhirinovsky flatly denied any campaign contributions from the Iraqi leader. His mood was uplifted and he spoke of an impending audience with Yeltsin and his assurance that the meeting would be successful. But even if the president did not propose, as the aging Hindenburg once offered Hitler, to form a government (made up 99 percent ethnic Russians, promised Zhirinovsky), he was not disappointed: "We're a party of compromises—we're prepared to form any blocs."

Zhirinovsky bragged about the president's good attitude toward his party and toward him personally, which he attributed to his centrist views. He confirmed that he intended to run in the Russian presidential elections in 1996, when Yeltsin's term in office would expire.

"If the elections take place in 1996, that will be a nice present for my fiftieth birthday," added Zhirinovsky, without a trace of humor. Deprived of his birthday in childhood, Zhirinovsky was preparing to celebrate it in the Kremlin.

6

THE ZHIRINOVSKY FACTOR

(1994–EARLY 1995)

How Can Democracy Be Saved from the Demos?

On December 12 the voters rejected not just one democratic group in particular, nor all the democrats, but democracy itself at least as it had developed in the two years of Yeltsin's leadership. In fact, they voted twice: first for the Constitution that provided for a strong president with virtual dictatorial powers, and second, personally for Zhirinovsky, whom the people sensed was the most appropriate candidate for the role of dictator. All in all, they spoke out unequivocally against "nomenklatura democracy."

We are borrowing the term "nomenklatura democracy" from an article by Yury Burtin and Grigory Vodolazov, published during the summer of 1994 in *Izvestia*, that constituted the Kremlin's official position. This is important to emphasize because it is one thing when a fierce enemy of Yeltsin, Stanislav Govorukhin, calls the upheavals in the country "the great criminal revolution," and another when the pro-Yeltsin press comes to a similar conclusion:

> There has been a decentralization of state property and a distribution of it to personal ownership by those who previously only managed it as government employees. As a result, an extraordinarily original phenomenon has occurred on the basis of the plant directors and local administration: a class of individual owners of state property has been formed. . . .
>
> The basis of social relations under "real socialism" has essentially remained unchanged—the system of the exploitation of the majority of the population by the ruling bureaucratic groups. Only now, the former system of collective or corporate exploitation has added new forms, and the license for their use is almost unlimited.

Such is the nature of nomenklatura capitalism in the economy and its corresponding political cover—nomenklatura democracy, which is what people voted against in December 1993. "Although they are free, they simply cannot find a place for themselves in the democratic structures of the government," noted Adam Michnik in an article on the crisis of the "elite democracy," and the alienation and loneliness of the "mass person" under the new circumstances. By a most democratic method Russia rejected democracy and capitalism, without ever having learned what it was all about, confusing freedom with anarchy and corruption. The discontent, dispersed throughout the enormous country, did not reach the ruling elite in the capital until the elections.

The question that now preoccupies Russian political and intellectual leaders, "What is to be done?" can be formulated in a paradoxical way: How can democracy be saved from the demos?

Berthold Brecht once suggested, tongue in cheek, that in the event the people's will is not to the liking of the powers-that-be: "Relieve the people of their duties and elect a new one."

That was what many democrats first suggested. "I would

propose to Boris Nikolayevich that he forget the word *democracy*. Russia has shown its incapacity for democracy," Valeriya Novodvorskaya stated adamantly, calling everyone who had voted for Zhirinovsky a "mob." Leonid Radzikhovsky was more cautious in his statements but even more definitive in his judgments. He recalled that in the free elections to the Constituent Assembly of 1917, the Bolsheviks won in the cities, but the Socialist Revolutionaries prevailed in the villages, where the majority of the population lived at the time. The Socialist Revolutionaries, Radzikhovsky reminds us, were the party of terrorists. He comes to the depressing conclusion that the people have not changed since that time:

> Universal suffrage is a general mechanism conceived for the peaceful resolution of civil and political conflicts. Alas, in our country, it doesn't work. Universal elections threaten to turn into a general catastrophe for those who do the electing. . . . Russia needs a period of authoritarian rule, without any elections or parliament.

Commentator Valery Lebedev cited the historical experience of British democracy for comparison:

> Universal suffrage in Western Europe was the fruit of a long (hundreds of years) political development. When Margaret Thatcher visited Moscow during the height of perestroika, she explained the stages of the maturation of democracy in England using the following scheme: First, the peers and barons attained the right to vote (that was the famous Magna Carta, which King John was forced to sign in 1215), then urban residents attained this right (who had certain property and education qualifications), then the rural people (also with certain qualifications). Then all men were granted suffrage, without qualifications. And finally, the entire adult population, starting with all persons who reached the age of majority. All of this took more than six hundred years!

In other words, Lebedev would deny the majority of Russians the right to vote—probably the same people who voted against the democrats in the parliamentary elections.

Fazil Iskander, one of the most talented Russian prose writers of our time, even coined a special term—"freedom-phobia"—and believes that the Russian people are seriously ill with this condition:

> If the nationalists seize the upper hand in the presidential elections in two years, Russia will plunge into an utterly insane situation. . . . I believe that in this crazy chaos, when society has been overwhelmed with freedom, the criminal elements have sensed their historical chance. . . . In our sick state universal elections can be a tragedy.

It is almost verbatim what Zhirinovsky himself says: "Without dictatorship you could not rule my country."

These comments were typical of democrats in 1994. It was even hard to say who was suffering more from freedom-phobia, the demos or the democrats. The democrats declared the demos to be the chief enemy of democracy, and the demos believed that these democrats wanted to take democracy away from them.

In fact, the situation grew even more complicated as the democrats suddenly found themselves in the company of traditionalist conservatives. From Herzen to Solzhenitsyn, Russians had declared Western democracy to be anathema, and feared that it would infect Russia. Truth should not be debased by being put to a vote, believed Herzen, and his contemporary, political philosopher Konstantin Leontyev, claimed that the Russian nation was especially not created for freedom. The first thing Solzhenitsyn did on returning to Russia after more than twenty years in exile was to urge that in the next elections, "no current parties should be believed, and the party lists should be torn up and thrown in the garbage."

A Pole, not a Russian—Adam Michnik—captured the essence of the problem in the above-mentioned article in *Der Spiegel:*

> The louder the voices of the populists resounded in the parliament and on the streets, with nostalgic

Bolsheviks and Great Russian fascist Black Hundreds denouncing reform, the more frequently the democratic intelligentsia muttered something about the need to settle scores with the opponents of reform, about Russia's insufficient maturity for democracy, and that for reform of the state an enlightened dictator is needed.

Russia today is faced with a dilemma, the intelligent solution of which no one knows. What is better: to violate the rules of democracy and ban parties professing totalitarianism while they are still fairly weak, or respect democratic order and open the way to power for these parties?

The Moscow intelligentsia's hope that Yeltsin would save fledgling Russian democracy (along with the democrats) by taking back the freedoms granted the people, and establishing something like an enlightened absolutism in the country, proved infeasible. The means for establishing a regime of personal power were simply not at the disposal of the president— Yeltsin could not rely on either the army, or the police, or even, as a last resort, public opinion. Russian democracy was helpless and defenseless in the face of encroachments upon it. It has survived only because of public inertia, exhaustion, and lack of responsibility. Only a little more than 50 percent of those eligible voted in the December 1993 elections, and the local elections in the spring of 1994 lacked the necessary quorum. This political apathy seemed to extend to potential dictators as well. "Dictatorship in Russia has outlived itself. . . . It's just that after all the recent events no one can be found who would dare to take upon himself that huge responsibility," admitted Deputy Defense Minister General Boris Gromov.

Only the general apathy can explain the political calm that befell Russian in the spring of 1994, interrupted only by Zhirinovsky's flamboyant escapades and statements. The real question was which of the politicians would benefit most from this time-out, and who would make better use of this enforced breather to regroup and prepare his forces for the new battle for power.

Perhaps even more paradoxical is Zhirinovsky's attitude

toward democracy. The democrats fear a democracy that leads to dictatorship, whereas Zhirinovsky is vitally in favor of democracy—in order to become a democratically elected dictator.

Some of the moderate democrats hoped that once Zhirinovsky got into the *Duma* as head of its most influential faction, he would come to his senses, settle down, and turn into a respectable politician. Such hopes were quickly dashed.

Starting with the incident with Telman Gdlyan at the Kremlin banquet in honor of the "New Political Year," Zhirinovsky stepped up his shocking behavior, outrageous proclamations, and fistfights. Indeed, taking advantage of the international media attention, Zhirinovsky now broadened his show on the road.

Without waiting for the parliament to open formally in January in 1994, Zhirinovsky began his blitz-raids on European countries, where his appearances were so successful that they often ended in a diplomatic fiasco. He irritated Germany with references to Chernobyl and Hiroshima and promised to use a supersecret and superpowerful weapon of mass destruction called Elipton if Germany interfered in Russian affairs. Perhaps as a gesture of reconciliation, he then proposed that Germany and Russia divide Poland between them once again. He denied the Romanians the right to exist as a nation, stating that they were all Italian gypsies by origin. He advised the Bulgarians to annex Macedonia and proposed that their lawfully elected president Zhelya Zhelev be exiled to Siberia and replaced by Zhirinovsky's friend and financial adviser Svetoslav Stoilov.

The Bulgarians were the first to lose their tempers and told Zhirinovsky to leave the country within twenty-four hours. He was forced to obey, but at the airport he threatened to return when he becomes the Russian president. Austria and Germany refused Zhirinovsky permission for a return visit to their countries.

Zhirinovsky's close associates suspected his restrictions and denials of visas were due to the meddling of Russian foreign minister Andrei Kozyrev, who had personal as well as ideological reasons to dislike Zhirinovsky, who has also demanded Kozyrev's resignation: "My job is to take him out of the Russian government." For his part, Kozyrev noted that Zhirinovsky's speeches were interesting not so much from a political but from a psychiatric perspective. Despite Kozyrev's supposed pressure on his colleagues in the Eastern European countries, Zhirinovsky was allowed into Poland, the Czech Republic, Slovenia, Serbia, and Bosnia, where he was not shy about speaking his mind.

Zhirinovsky had often threatened the existence of the Czech Republic: "Slovakia will perhaps remain, but Czechia's industry is already in the hands of the Germans, and Moravia—the greater part of Czechia—will go to Germany. And by the beginning of the next century you'll forget the word 'Czech' forever." Upon arriving in Prague, he announced that soon the Germans would multiply throughout their country, that the Czechs would be forced to learn German and forget their own language, and that Slavic people will be forced to go to the German *kirche* and polish the boots of German soldiers. When Zhirinovsky learned that President Vaclav Havel had said something unflattering about him, he responded that he had never approved of "that no-talent playwright" and predicted that in ten years, Czechs would curse the name Havel.

In the former Yugoslavia he was photographed surrounded by Russian soldiers in the UN contingent, holding an automatic rifle, and met with Radavan Karadjic, leader of the Bosnian Serbs, to emphasize the Slavic and Orthodox ties:

> I came here as a victor, as the chairman of a party that has received three times as many votes as the people who are now ruling Russia. I want to warn the governments of the Western countries, that the bombing of any cities of Bosnia will mean a declaration of war with Russia. . . . Let them not forget that Russian troops are still in Europe and they can remain there for a long time.

Zhirinovsky chose Slovenia for a brief vacation, where he danced a waltz with a broom, kicked up his feet in a solo *kazachok*, and advocated the withdrawal of Russia from the UN. Zhirinovsky disdainfully remarked, referring to Slovenia's size, that "any shtetl can call itself a state." His comrades smashed wineglasses in the Russian tradition, and one fellow even downed his drink and then ate his glass. The Slovenians then refused their hospitality to Zhirinovsky and his comrades, explaining that they had destroyed hotel property, large quantities of which were heaved in the lake (although to be sure, some of it was fished out of the water by Zhirinovsky's bodyguard, who turned out to be a pretty good diver).

Zhirinovsky then stopped off in Budapest, where he explained to the Hungarians that they had no hope of exporting their local apples and *Icarus* buses and the only way out of the situation was to restore the Warsaw Pact and create a zone of Eastern European cooperation like the Comecon that had previously existed under Soviet communism. (Only a few months after Zhirinovsky's visit to Hungary, the local communists returned to power after winning democratic elections. Hungary became the third East European country, after Poland and Lithuania, to reject capitalism, and it was not the last).

Back in Moscow, Zhirinovsky's first appearance in the Duma almost ended in tragedy: crowds of domestic and foreign reporters and photographers hurled themselves at him, almost injuring themselves and the new superstar. Ever since, they have dogged him constantly, even following him into the toilet.

"My trip to Europe for only two days threw the whole planet on its ear, all the diplomats, all the ministers," Zhirinovsky bragged to the deputies. In reply there was the laughter from the democrats' section, but Zhirinovsky was not bothered by hostile ridicule. He was thrilled, as always, by negative publicity. Parliament, however, was not an easy audience. Gaidar's bloc, Russia's Choice, interfered with Zhirinovsky's speeches in the Duma in every way they could, interrupting, laughing, catcalling. It was easy to rile Zhirinovsky, the self-described "ordinary and calm person."

On his nomination to the post of speaker of parliament, Zhirinovsky said:

> All over the world, the position is the same—the leader of the party that gained the largest number of votes in the elections is automatically appointed head of the state, he is assigned to form the government, or he automatically becomes head of the

government. . . . Of course I would be happy to fulfill this function of leader of the Russian parliament, and that would be an example not only for our country, not only for Europe, but for the whole world.

Zhirinovsky grew more and more wound up as the noise and laughter and remarks from the democrats became more aggressive. When he proclaimed, "For you, war means the defeat of Russians. When Russians are mocked and killed, that's democracy for you!" there was noise in the hall. "Don't bother me! Shut up!" Zhirinovsky yelled, pounding his fist on the podium with all his might. "I'm speaking, and you will sit down!" As a sign of protest, several democrats begin to leave the hall. "Get out of the room, get out of the room!" Zhirinovsky shouted after them.

> Everyone out of the room! You're all candidates for a psychiatric hospital! . . . The communists didn't keep you in jail long enough. Just look how many of you there are, that's the faction that is disrupting the State Duma session. Some deputies and ministers will be apologizing before the Russian people after the Russian Supreme Court verdict that will definitely be issued in the fall of this year. You will definitely be apologizing.
>
> I have one minute left. On the sixtieth second I will definitely tell you my decision.

"Our time has begun and your time is finished," said Zhirinovsky to the democrats. "On December 12, the voters of Russia let you know. . . . And your voice will die out all over Russia's political horizon."

Deputy Prime Minister Anatoly Chubais, Gaidar, Kozyrev, and Boris Fyodorov, then finance minister, pointed to their watches, signaling to the session chair that Zhirinovsky's time was up, according to the rules of order.

"Mr. Chubais, you'll be pointing to your watch in Lefortovo prison. You'll be pointing in your cell, so they'll give you lunch!"

Defrocked priest Gleb Yakunin of Russia's Choice got up to leave the room. Despite having fallen from favor with the church hierarchy for refusing to leave his seat in parliament, he was still wearing his clergyman's robes.

"So, the priest Yakunin is walking around!" exclaimed Zhirinovsky. "He has been stripped of the right to wear the robes and cross, and yet he goes around in them, offending the Russian Church. And Mr. Chubais is waving his arm because these are his last days at liberty."

> As long as there are people like Kozyrev, Chubais, Gaidar, and Fyodorov, and the small number, literally 30 percent, of the same kind of deputies, and I see their faces everyday, it will have a bad effect on my health. And the whole Russian people need my health, people who do not lisp [a reference to Jews] and who do not have dual citizenship. I temporarily withdraw my candidacy and wait for the presidential elections in Russia. Then we'll talk!

Zhirinovsky had no alternative but to withdraw his candidacy for the post of speaker of parliament—he could not count on the votes of the majority of the Duma's deputies.

Deputy Prime Minister Sergei Shakhrai, who spoke after him, recommended that the Duma's treasury be replenished by selling tickets to Zhirinovsky's shows.

"The last train car is headed to the north, the stop is Taimyr, the station is the tundra," Zhirinovsky threatened those who disagreed with him at a press conference, implying they would be exiled to Siberia. "It's kind of light banter, black humor, which unfortunately the journalists don't get," said Grigori Serebrennikov, Zhirinovsky's press secretary, explaining his boss' escapades, including his threats of war and atomic bombs.

On the fourth day of the parliamentary session, Zhirinovsky got into a fight in the Duma cafeteria with a deputy from St. Petersburg, the entrepreneur Mark Goryachev. According to Goryachev, the cafeteria workers were not serving anyone, and instead had lined up behind the counter quietly waiting for Zhirinovsky. Then they immediately waited on the "boss" when he finally made an appearance. "How can this be tolerated? Zhirinovsky's wrong," Goryachev said in indignation. "If you mention my name once more, you'll go to jail," Zhirinovsky shot back. After a brief exchange of insults, Zhirinovsky shoved the St. Petersburg entrepreneur. Goryachev boxed Zhirinovsky on the ears in reply and grabbed a chair, but Zhirinovsky's bodyguards intervened and dragged Goryachev away.

In the beginning, Zhirinovsky had some trouble restraining his motley crew of party members. Viktor Kobelev, head of the party office and labor minister in Zhirinovsky's shadow cabinet, came into the Duma only on the strength of the party list—that is, exclusively because of Zhirinovsky. Later he disagreed with him and left the faction. Zhirinovsky, indignant at the ungrateful renegades and fearing further splitting of the party, repeatedly proposed that the parliament adopt a decree that would allow party blocs to recall renegades: "Under our faction's bylaws, a deputy who voluntarily quits the faction automatically relieves himself of his powers as deputy," Zhirinovsky explained in connection with the departure of yet another deputy, the nationally popular hypnotist and television therapist Anatoly Kashpirovsky, who later went back to Zhirinovsky and apologized.

By a small majority (173 to 150), the deputies voted down Zhirinovsky's proposal, considering it to impose a kind of serfdom within the Duma. In desperation, Zhirinovsky then physically beat the recalcitrant former party member as an object lesson to the other members of his party.

On April 2, the Fifth Congress of the LDP took place with a full house—343 deputies, 250 journalists, plus guests from fourteen countries. Zhirinovsky was elected chairman of the party for ten years and given extraordinary powers. "The *vozhd'* and the party are a single whole," proclaimed Zhirinovsky. "This regime is in its death throes. And when the patient is on the operating table, he needs one and only one surgeon, not a whole consultation."

The *vozhd's* ninety-minute speech was in the usual extravagant style. He said he intended to disband the UN. He admitted a "weakness for border posts," which, he said, "ought to be put back in the holes where they used to stand"—his old notion of restoring the empire, but in a new image.

uproot tulips from a flower bed and threw them at the demonstrators, shouting "We won't let ourselves be Zionized, Americanized, or Islamicized!" To journalists he said that he had been attacked by extremists, and that the French police had not provided proper protection. He declared the demonstration to be "a war against me, paid for by NATO or the French secret police."

On returning to Moscow, Zhirinovsky grandly celebrated his forty-eighth birthday at the Budapest restaurant. The table was set for five hundred people. Bottles of a new brand of vodka called "Zhirinovsky" sported his picture on the label and a map of the Russian empire with the last century's borders, including Poland, Finland, and Alaska. During the presidential campaign, Zhirinovsky had promised the people cheap vodka when he came to power. Now the demand for the vodka named in honor of the most popular Russian politician was guaranteed. It is difficult to imagine a more effective means of political advertising in a country where alcoholism is the national disease and vodka the national drink. People say in Moscow that if the new vodka is put into mass production, Zhirinovsky will be a shoo-in in the next presidential elections.

In short, the democrats' hopes that Zhirinovsky would be kept busy by the routine work of the Duma proved unfounded. They then pursued any means to neutralize Zhirinovsky politically, from blacking out his television broadcasts to instigating criminal charges against him. He was accused of war propaganda in *The Last Push to the South*, of unlawful receipt of campaign contributions from foreign companies, of assault. Because Zhirinovsky was immune as a member of parliament, however, the matter did not reach the courts.

As the presidential election set for 1996 draws near, the anti-Zhirinovsky campaign is being joined by the Kremlin, which now more and more resembles a "mixture of court and machinery of state," as Vitaly Tretyakov, editor in chief of *Nezavisimaya gazeta*, remarked. In the summer of 1994, when Yeltsin and Zhirinovsky, each on their own cruise ship, went on campaign tours up the Volga River stopping at major cities and meeting voters, the authorities played all sorts of tricks on Zhirinovsky (the ship broke down or was delayed at the check gates). In the fall, when Zhirinovsky and an LDP delegation flew to

North Korea for a meeting with the new leadership of that country, his plane was denied a stopover in Kemerovo. Even the pro-Yeltsin press attacked the government for such a risky incident, and the liberal paper *Moscow Times* ran an editorial headlined ZHIRINOVSKY IS RIGHT. Meanwhile, the democrats demand more and more from the Kremlin—even the abolition of democracy—naturally for the sake of saving it, since in the opinion of the democrats it is dangerous to entrust Russians with Russia's future. There is a proposal to postpone the presidential elections and extend Yeltsin's term in office another two years. Some would like to abolish elections altogether and decide the question of the next president privately through backstage intrigue and deals. If there were no Zhirinovsky, he would have to be invented: he serves the Kremlin nomenklatura as a pretext and an excuse for antidemocratic measures. They are clinging to power, not wishing to yield to anyone—regardless of whether it is Yavlinsky, Rutskoi, or Zhirinovsky.

Initially, Yeltsin continued to play the role imposed on him of "father of the nation," pretending that he had won the elections when he got approval for his Constitution. Yeltsin's first response to Zhirinovsky's victory was to remove several reform-minded ministers and advisers, notably Gaidar. Zhirinovsky was not allowed to form a government as leader of the winning party.

Yeltsin acted as if the results of the December elections were a kind of public opinion poll that he was forced to take into account but not obey. Although the voice of the people was more important to him than acquired principles, he was still not the desperate populist that Zhirinovsky was.

We have constantly given Yeltsin his due (including in this book) for an ability rare at his age to undergo ideological metamorphosis. But his gift is a two-edged sword: if he turned from a communist true believer and boss into a democrat, there is no guarantee that he won't undergo further changes. He could be swayed in any direction, although it is quite unlikely to be far from the center. The range of motions of this old pendulum is not what it used to be. And that's one reason (although not the most important) that Yeltsin is not likely to be the man for the job of saving democracy from the demos through the help of a personal dictatorship.

Judging from the polls in 1994, Yeltsin had no prospects for the presidential elections; his unpopularity had reached record highs. The more or less reliable All-Russian Center for the Study of Public Opinion conducted surveys by telephone and in person from March 3 to April 4, 1994, with a total of 3,776 respondents throughout the country: 19 percent were in favor of Yeltsin; 79 percent were opposed. By comparison, in an October 1993 survey immediately after Yeltsin cracked down on the parliament, he had 39 percent in favor. In the fall of 1991, after his victory against the August coup plotters, 70 percent of those surveyed were on his side.

A confidential analysis performed during the same period in 1994 by an anonymous group of experts, on special orders from the business and political elite, determined that Yeltsin's rating was even lower:

> The chances of being elected for the politically isolated and physically weakened Yeltsin are extremely low. No more than 16 percent of the voters would vote for him now, and obviously, every passing day works against Yeltsin . . . [1] Everyone realizes that the president has landed in a difficult situation and that the politicians should prepare for any unexpected developments.
>
> After the October "coup," the political life of the president of Russia entered a dramatic stage. This sixty-three-year-old figure who had until only recently been a model of robust health and enormous popularity began rapidly to deteriorate, politically and physically. . . . Power began to slip from his hands, and his influence on political processes weakened. The president increasingly finds himself on the sidelines of Russian political life. . . .
>
> The major political failures resulting from the collapse of the radical program and the events of October—Russia's Choice loss of the December elections

---

1. This prognosis was confirmed several months later in the heat of the military adventure in Chechnya, when Yeltsin's popularity plummeted even further, to eight percent.

and the January reorganization of the cabinet of ministers—changed drastically the system of relations between the president and the political environment. He no longer possessed reliable channels for governing effectively, and his most accustomed style of political behavior now seems outmoded and anachronistic, not in keeping with the spirit of the times. . . . There are more and more signs that in certain circles of the Russian government Yeltsin is perceived more as a hindrance than as a condition for resolving urgent matters of state.

Even the democratic and pro-Yeltsin press wrote sadly of the "autumn of the patriarch." Rumors of Yeltsin's illnesses and plots to overthrow him multiplied. Yeltsin himself provides fertile ground for such conjectures by appearing less and less frequently in public, removing himself from politics and handing over almost all governmental affairs to Prime Minister Viktor Chernomyrdin, leaving himself in charge only of the security ministries.

The amnesty to the president's enemies was the first blow Zhirinovsky dealt Yeltsin after winning the elections in December. It had been a campaign promise and Zhirinovsky had insisted on it in the Duma, although the amnesty was voted down several times before passing on February 23 (formerly Red Army Day, and now Defenders of the Fatherland Day), an absolute majority (253–67). Yeltsin tried to sabotage the parliament's decision and gave the order to Procurator General Alexei Kazannik, whom he had just appointed, not to obey the Duma's resolution.

Kazannik reported to his colleagues his decision to carry out the amnesty declared by the Duma. "But since the president has appointed me, and the president in principle has the right to give me orders, I will resign." On the morning after he had turned over the lease to the Moscow apartment that had been provided him, Kazannik flew back to his native Omsk. He bitterly concluded that:

The current government is lacking a moral foundation; only narrow, self interests reign there. If I had violated the law and overturned the amnesty, I would have most likely been useful to the president. . . . The only job of those around Yeltsin is to make a daily demonstration to him of their feelings as loyal subjects. Although it is regrettable, Boris Nikolayevich never got beyond the methods of a regional party secretary.[2] He does not understand the many facets and complexity of life and believes that pounding his fist on the table is enough to turn the country around.

Zhirinovsky met the amnestied Rutskoi at the gates of Lefortovo prison with a bouquet of flowers. He called on the crowd to vote for his party, which "keeps its word, and just as it promised, so it delivered—not a single political prisoner will remain in Russia's prisons." Not at all concerned about the logical non sequitur, he immediately went on to say that the empty cells at Lefortovo would come in handy for Yeltsin and his advisers. "Well done, guys! This is our day today. When Russians choose their next president, the choice is between me and Rutskoi," Zhirinovsky predicted.

Later he even announced that if Rutskoi received more votes than he in the first round of elections, he, Zhirinovsky, would withdraw his candidacy in the second round.

Zhirinovsky's releasing of his future rival seems odd. As soon as he was released, General Rutskoi launched his campaign for the president, which will not only split Zhirinovsky's voting bloc but steal from him some covert as well as overt sponsors in the military-industrial complex, the KGB, the army, and the so-called patriotic business, new entrepreneurs with nationalist views.

Moreover, Zhirinovsky personally dislikes Rutskoi. When Rutskoi was still vice president, Zhirinovsky declared:

Rutskoi, who, under the Constitution must replace the head of the country if necessary, is a poorly-

---

2. Before his move to Moscow at Gorbachev's request in the spring of 1985, Yeltsin was secretary of the Sverdlovsk Regional Party Committee in his native Ural Mountains.

suited figure. He has the same minuses dragging him down as Yeltsin—he's a former communist, a former Democratic Russia member. He has not done anything real in a year. He just sits and twirls his mustache.

Zhirinovsky's sudden change of heart has probably only one explanation—fear. Democrats have openly discussed his murder, and there is evidence that these conversations have provoked alarm in Zhirinovsky's circles. Press secretary Grigori Serebrennikov did not conceal his indignation at Alexander Gordon's film *How to Kill Zhirinovsky*—particularly the reaction of a former Gaidar aide to the staging of Zhirinovsky's assassination: "Why didn't you kill him?"

In other words, the threat that the democrats see in Zhirinovsky results in a direct physical threat to Zhirinovsky himself. The only way to deflect the blow from himself is to redirect it at another. Recalling his boyhood pranks and those of his friends, Zhirinovsky tells how after they had done something wild, they ran off in different directions as soon as they saw a policeman. Thus Zhirinovsky has used the general just released from prison as a kind of shield—instead of one mortal enemy, the democrats now have two, and it's a toss-up as to whom they consider more dangerous to themselves. Zhirinovsky's comment at the gates of Lefortovo, that the empty prison cells would still come in handy, served as a warning, that a revenge seeker was being released, which Rutskoi himself confirmed several months later: "The persons who have brought the country's economy to a crisis and its people to poverty and who have plundered national assets should be brought before the law to answer for their deeds. That is possible only if I become head of state. And they're afraid of me."

One indication of Zhirinovsky's success with this stratagem was Yeltsin's strong reaction to former president Richard Nixon's meeting with Rutskoi. Yeltsin did not react at all to Nixon's meeting with Zhirinovsky. The suspicious Yeltsin perceived Nixon's meeting with Rutskoi as a step aimed personally against himself and childishly got his revenge against the former American president. He canceled his own scheduled meeting with Nixon and forbade his prime minister, chief ministers, and advisers to meet with him. He canceled the VIP car and body-guards he had previously offered Nixon. On the square inside the Kremlin, Yeltsin gave an impromptu press conference, muttering and having difficulty putting his words together. Journalists and television viewers were reminded of Brezhnev in the last years of his rule, when he lost control of his legs and tongue. Yeltsin appeared sickly, his speech was slurred, and only one thing was clear: that he was terribly offended and leaned on the word *former* when speaking of Nixon. The offense Nixon dealt him was interpreted by Yeltsin as an insult to Russia as a whole: "Let him know that Russia is still a great country," he mumbled, his tongue thickened like a drunk's.

Nixon continued this last trip before his death to build bridges to the post-Yeltsin Russia, meeting with leaders of various Duma factions: Grigori Yavlinsky, Sergei Shakhrai, Gennady Zyuganov, and Vladimir Zhirinovsky. At first Zhirinovsky had joined Yeltsin and refused to meet Nixon, saying to reporters that the United States nearly "impeached Nixon and now Russia is impeaching him, too." But later his anger was replaced by graciousness. Zhirinovsky gave Nixon a copy of *The Last Push to the South.* Through Nixon he also passed on a copy for President Clinton, although only two months previously he had advised Clinton not to travel to Russia, but to stay home and play his saxophone (in retaliation for Clinton's refusal to meet with him).[3] Each copy was signed with an inscription. For Nixon: "Don't support the losers in the last election—there's no future in it," and for Clinton, "I don't want to be misunderstood by you," although Zhirinovsky should probably have switched the inscriptions.

Nixon spoke respectfully about Yeltsin, but noted that Yeltsin was no longer a superman and had "lost much of the mystique from his historic role in the destruction of Soviet Communism."

---

3. Despite the unpleasantness of the saxophone remark, Clinton was relatively lucky. Zhirinovsky said of Mitterrand, regarding his support of Western actions against Bosnian Serbs: "That old man has gone crazy. He doesn't understand that Napoleon already tried to build a French empire, and look what became of him. And now Mitterrand, who is old and is leaving his post in six months, is going back to the same stupid ideas."

As a wounded beast crawls to its lair, Yeltsin flew to Sochi to put himself together at his Black Sea resort. This unscheduled Sochi vacation, categorically opposed by his wife, Naina, but which General Alexander Korzhakov, chief of presidential security, insisted on, only incited further talk of the inevitable end of the Yeltsin era. Rumors of an impending coup were covered in papers all over the world. Prime Minister Chernomyrdin was supposed to head the conspirators, and then after a while an opposite rumor was circulated about Chernomyrdin's resignation.

Yeltsin returned to Moscow from his unexpected Sochi vacation with the idea of making peace with his political opponents. He proposed signing a temporary cease-fire, to take a breather in the endless, exhausting struggle for power, a battle he was already too tired to fight after suffering defeat after defeat, and seeing no light at the end of the tunnel. It was obvious how insecure he felt in his Kremlin fortress, despite its medieval walls and his faithful Praetorians headed by Alexander Korzhakov and Mikhail Barsukov, head of the Kremlin's security.

From master of Russia, Yeltsin has turned into master of the Kremlin, treating this medieval residence, in the tradition of his predecessors, as his own inherited estate. Paradoxically, under the democrat Yeltsin the Kremlin is more reminiscent of Stalin's Kremlin than under the party dignitary Brezhnev or Gorbachev. Partly this is a result of democratic changes, with Russian anarchy and the direct physical threats against the president, including General Rutskoi's call to storm the Kremlin—neither Brezhnev's nor Gorbachev's Kremlin required such reinforced security as has flourished in the two and a half years under Yeltsin.

However, another reason for the irreversible changes in Yeltsin is the Kremlin itself—the citadel of the Russian autocracy has a historical atmosphere that has far from the best effect on its occupants. "Oh, how heavy you are, Cap of Monomakh!" exclaimed in despair Tsar Boris Godunov in the play of the same name by Pushkin. The Cap of Monomakh with which the Russian rulers were crowned was heavy for each one of them. Each one of them, from the first Tsar Ivan to Ivan the Terrible, from Boris Godunov to Boris Yeltsin, regardless of their personal qualities, was tormented and driven out of his mind from the power he attained, as if the very air of the Kremlin were poisoned by a virus of fear. This virus apparently still runs rampant behind the Kremlin walls, and no resident is immune to infection. Yeltsin, who has withdrawn into the Kremlin like a snail into its shell, is the latest example. In 1994, he quite rapidly turned into a hostage of the Kremlin, a prisoner of his own power. Unlike Stalin or Ivan the Terrible, however, Yeltsin does not execute his political opponents, but concludes truces with them, which neither side has any intention of keeping.

On April 28, 1994, in the Kremlin's St. George Hall, the leaders of the Duma factions and political parties, the leaders of the constituent regions and republics of Russia, clergy, civic, and trade union leaders gathered to sign the Agreement on Civic Accord in Russia, as it was called. The communists, agrarians, Yavlinsky bloc, and two regional bosses refused to sign the agreement. Zhirinovsky dragged out his decision until the last minute, first insisting on a personal meeting with Yeltsin, and then arriving with two bottles of the vodka named in his honor. Admiring his own picture on the label of his vodka, he said that he would sign the agreement only if Yeltsin would smile at him. "I was convinced he would come here and sign it, and then he would [expletive deleted] on his own signature," recalled Vladimir Lukin, former Russian ambassador to the United States and now an associate of Yavlinsky in his parliamentary faction.

Yeltsin might have preferred that Zhirinovsky not sign the agreement because his mere presence with the two bottles of Zhirinovsky vodka put everyone in a frivolous mood and gave the Kremlin event a farcical aspect, despite all the pomp and circumstance. Politically, morally, and psychologically a broken man, Yeltsin vitally needed the breathing space the accord could provide to restore his strengths. That was why he had made compromises with his rivals, if only they would agree to be patient another two years and not demand premature presidential elections.

Zhirinovsky went to the signing ceremony as if with a light heart. Several days before, he had published his article in *Izvestia* entitled "On the Acquisitive Role of Russia and the Young

Wolves." At a time when most newspapers were carrying premature political obituaries for Yeltsin, Zhirinovsky was composing panegyrics to him:

> He has won two coups, and he has outfoxed and beaten Gorbachev. What a party he destroyed![4] He is simply a hero from a Russian fairytale. . . . Yeltsin goes about politics not by Friedman's blueprints, but by intuition. There you cannot catch him with logic. Like me. Both of us are mystics. By the laws of logic I also couldn't have won the parliamentary elections and come in third in 1991. Therefore among the candidates for the new presidency Yeltsin is my most threatening rival. The rest of them are rural schoolteachers and kids from the capital's elite schools.

Although fully approving Yeltsin's current political line, Zhirinovsky wrote that there were two "pushes" that Yeltsin was not capable of making—restoring Russia to the borders of the USSR and dividing it into *gubernii*, in order to become the "Father-Tsar." The final push to the south "will be my chance, my mission," concluded Zhirinovsky. As for the latter, events would soon show that Zhirinovsky erred—Yeltsin put into practice even this famous slogan, throwing the Russian army into the Caucasus in order to restore the Kremlin's power over secessionist Chechnya.

Power Without Portfolio

Aside from tactical considerations, the primary reason for Zhirinovsky's turnabout was Yeltsin's own political rebirth. Yeltsin had begun to change the course of the ship of state in the direction spearheaded by Zhirinovsky. Yeltsin himself admitted that in these elections, Zhirinovsky "had revealed to us ills we had never suspected." Zhirinovsky's influence on the course of affairs of state was indisputable: the Kremlin met his campaign demands, removing people he disliked from the

---

4. The reference is to the Communist Party.

government, borrowing his ideas and slogans, and changing the direction of domestic and foreign policy.

Immediately after the December elections, Yeltsin's press secretary Vyacheslav Kostikov noted several points in Zhirinovsky's program—including his "great-power" proclamations—on which Yeltsin and Zhirinovsky could find some common ground: "In Yeltsin's policies there are many points overlapping with Zhirinovsky's platform." Even Yeltsin himself made a cautious statement: "So far we have only heard Zhirinovsky's words. Let us see what kind of deeds he and his party will do. What if suddenly they are for the good of Russia? Especially because our people have yearned for a strong hand and order."

Yeltsin's supporters—present and former—were not far behind, as if Zhirinovsky had untied their tongues with his win. Mikhail Poltoranin, who had just stepped down as press minister, spoke rather incoherently but anti-Semitically about "labor-camp Hebrew," a language Russian journalists supposedly used, implying that Jews dominated the media. Democrats now fell all over each other to see who could be more patriotic and nationalist. Foreign Minister Kozyrev, heartily loathed by all Russian chauvinists as pro-Western and pro-American, definitely came out in front in this competition. Because of his reputation he had to try harder than all the rest to prove his ethnic patriotism.

Only a year ago, Kozyrev had shaken the world with a half-hour speech at an international conference in Stockholm full of great-power rhetoric and imperial threats. He demanded that the United States withdraw sanctions against Serbia, that NATO cease its interference in Yugoslavia and the Baltics, and that new independent states on the territory of the former USSR immediately join a new federation under Moscow's aegis. If these demands were not met, added Kozyrev, Russia was prepared unilaterally to take the necessary measures, including military and economic, to protect its interests.

Shocked diplomats and journalists raced to telephones to inform their governments and newspapers of this return by the Kremlin to the cold war. Then Kozyrev once again took the floor and explained that it had all been an instructive hoax, so to speak, to illustrate what would happen on a global scale if

Yeltsin's enemies came to power: the speech, he warned, was "a fairly accurate compilation of the demands made by the far-from-extremist opposition in Russia."

But after the December elections, Kozyrev began in earnest to defend things that until recently he had denied or ridiculed: Russia's superpower status and its special role in the "near abroad" (with a temporary freeze on the withdrawal of Russian troops there); the priority of national interests over international obligations; the protection of Russians in the former Soviet republics and the Serbs in Bosnia. On the latter issue he approached Zhirinovsky: when the U.S. Congress voted to remove the arms embargo to Bosnia Muslims, Kozyrev warned that the conflict would spill over Bosnia's borders and would escalate into World War III.

Many people began to get the impression that Kozyrev, who continued reflexively to curse Zhirinovsky, was now in fact working as his foreign minister. "In their essence, Kozyrev's politics overlap more and more with Zhirinovsky's," commented Yelena Bonner, widow of Andrei Sakharov. "This politics is oriented not at human values but geopolitical, geostrategic interest. It is dangerous, because it will inevitably lead to aggression." Moscow journalist Natalya Ivanova put it even more tersely: "These days, Zhirinovsky is just Kozyrev in caricature. I very much fear the beginning of a new state ideology."

Kozyrev himself denied that he was acting at Zhirinovsky's prompting: "Russia's foreign policy remains consistent, and it will not be changed under pressure from Zhirinovsky," he said on the Bosnian issue, hastening to disassociate himself from Zhirinovsky. In Kazakhstan, where Zhirinovsky is the national idol of the local Russians and persona non grata at the official level, Kozyrev conducted lengthy negotiations with President Nazarbayev about the fate of the Russian minority. At a press conference he spoke in detail about his differences from Zhirinovsky:

> People sometimes say that I am playing on Zhirinovsky's field. But if Zhirinovsky is using this problem to aggravate the political struggle for demagogic purposes, then his field is chaos and lawlessness. Our

field is the area of legal regulation, where it is necessary to find a civilized answer unlike the lawless field of nationalist dictatorship signifying war. I belong to the party of peace.

Despite these hasty disassociations, the Kremlin's international policy became increasingly independent of the West and increasingly similar to Zhirinovsky's program.

The Kremlin was forced to cancel the planned radical reduction of the three-million-strong army, which Russia could no longer afford and furthermore did not need as much as before. And Yeltsin went to Eastern Europe and triumphantly announced that Moscow has nothing against its former satellites joining NATO, but was forced to disavow his own statement. Complete membership in NATO for Eastern European countries was replaced with a vague Partnership for Peace, to which Russia had to be grudgingly invited. Then Russia dug in its heels and demanded a special superpower status, which the West would not countenance. Statements from Russian officials about "division of spheres of influence" began to sound completely in keeping with Zhirinovsky's geopolitical agenda.

Along with these shifts in foreign policy, the Kremlin began to shift on the domestic front as well—again in line with Zhirinovsky's statements, or with the will of the people, which in this case coincided. The chief reformers, headed by Yegor Gaidar, left the government, along with foreign advisers like Jeffrey Sachs. The very word *reform* virtually disappeared from the Kremlin's vocabulary, along with the word *democrats*, which by that time has been transformed from the original Russian *demokraty* into various and mocking puns such as *dermokraty* (the "dung-ocrats") and *demokrady* (the "demo-robbers"). Freed from reformers, technocrats, and new economic managers, Viktor Chernomyrdin's government began to turn back to a planned economy, seeing it as a panacea for all the country's myriad ills. Chernomyrdin stated that "bureaucratic experiments on people" would not be tolerated and accused the departing ministers of "market romanticism."

Mikhail Berger, economic commentator for *Izvestia*, seized on this phrase and defined the about-face in the economy as the replace of "market romanticism" with "industrial romanticism."

have stolen or bought from the army. Plans have become known of Mafia groups to steal or buy atomic weapons in order to terrorize the Kremlin and the world community. Russia has plunged into the abyss of anarchy, becoming a no-man's-land. Freedom has turned into the license to do anything that Dostoyevsky once warned about.

Armed skirmishes in broad daylight in the center of the capital have become common occurrences while the government looks the other way. Yeltsin did not dare to replace the interior minister, General Viktor Yerin, who has proven his loyalty to the president on many occasions.

The wave of crime has even reached the Duma. Deputy Andrei Aidzerdnis was shot near his home with a Maverick five-round airgun. The reason for this reprisal was likely the publication in a newspaper issued by Aidzerdnis called "Who's Who?", with a list of 266 major figures of the underworld, with their real names and nicknames.

At an emergency session of the Duma, Zhirinovsky demanded the immediate resignation of General Yerin. When Prime Minister Chernomyrdin rhetorically asked who would replace Yerin as interior minister, Zhirinovsky shouted "Me! Me!" from his seat. Yeltsin authorized Yerin and the minister of security—with the help, if needed, of the army—to take emergency measures to fight crime. The president's decree substantially broadened the powers and rights of the police to fight criminals, in particular allowing them to detain a suspect without a public prosecutor's warrant for thirty days, to conduct warrantless searches in homes and automobiles and check bank accounts and financial documents of those detained as well as their relatives—up to and including the imposition of states of emergency in the large cities. Russia's Choice, by that time renamed Russia's Democratic Choice, found this decree excessive. Zhirinovsky, on the contrary, found it insufficient: "Nothing can be changed as long as power is in the criminal organizations." And in place of the murdered Duma deputy, with Zhirinovsky's vigorous help, was elected the nation's best-known swindler, Sergei Mavrodi, thus reinforcing the LDP's faction in parliament. Several days after these reelections yet another deputy, Valentin Martemyanov, was murdered. And in the beginning of 1995 the third deputy, this time a member of the LDP, Sergei Skorochkin, was shot dead after being kidnapped.

Nevertheless, Zhirinovsky had every reason to be satisfied with the course of events. That explains Zhirinovsky's altruistic approval of the new line, although he did complain that Yeltsin was not taking into account the results of the elections and was not giving his faction ministerial portfolios appropriate to the election results. (Zhirinovsky and Prime Minister Viktor Chernomyrdin met about this in early May.)

After Yegor Gaidar, Boris Fyodorov, and Minister of Social Security Ella Pamfilova demonstratively left the government, Zhirinovsky confidently predicted that the remaining liberals there—Andrei Kozyrev and Anatoly Chubais, the privatization chief, would also soon leave: "Then I will gladly say—Long live the president of Russia! Long live the Russian government! Long live the Russian parliament!"

A correspondent of the St. Petersburg newspaper *Rush Hour* asked Zhirinovsky why he was now supporting Yeltsin.

> He has already tried two political forces. And they didn't work. He rejected the communists himself. And he virtually has left Democratic Russia. Now he is in such a state that he doesn't know what will happen next. It's worthwhile for him to pay attention to us. We are urging him: take a rest, give out awards, receive ambassadors, travel abroad, write memoirs—but don't get in the way. Let another party head the government. And life will be better—and why not better for you, too?

The democrats, bankrupted in the parliamentary elections, were understanding—at least at first—about Yeltsin's latest political metamorphosis. "The president is lonely, I sensed that he was hurting," said Ella Pamfilova, as she left office. Yeltsin had given her a farewell audience. Gaidar echoed her, and justified Yeltsin in the role of Zhirinovsky: "He was forced to deal with reality. In the final analysis, he is not god, nor tsar, nor even general secretary," that is, Yeltsin has less power and room to maneuver.

A democratic critic of Yeltsin, Leonid Batkin, chalked up the new developments as "the least of all evils":

> Zhirinovsky's success is an unexpected gift for the authoritarian and stagnant reformist regime. This real threat is a new justification for an inability and unwillingness to conduct deep social-political changes, to bring about an authentic democratic government, not an administrative-command "federalism." . . . Any consistent criticism of the regime will be cursed and paralyzed with calls to support "the lesser evil," only now it will be against Zhirinovsky's fascism.

That was how things stood in Russia before the Chechnya crisis when Yeltsin, unleashing on the eve of the new year a full-scale war in the Caucasus, began implementing Zhirinovsky's chauvinistic slogans. Indeed, why does one have to fear Zhirinovsky, if Yeltsin himself, using his (Zhirinovsky's) ideological arsenal and rejecting democracy and the democrats, tries to out-Zhirinovsky Zhirinovsky (according to the principle of "more Catholic than the Pope")? Which is now the lesser evil and which the greater?

On the other hand, who needs Zhirinovsky if Yeltsin is already playing his role for him?

Strictly speaking, this was the secret task of the Chechen campaign: to raise Yeltsin's faltering authority with the help of a military blitzkrieg. The blitzkrieg, however, became bogged down. With its attendant huge losses in life, it has become a humiliating war for the Kremlin: the violator turned out to be impotent, which in turn led to the cruel act of annihilating vengeance against the capital city of Grozny and the massacre of its civilian population. As the lawful heir to the defunct USSR, Russia has shown itself in the Caucasus to be the "evil empire."

One must take a sober look at the new arrangement of political forces in Russia, disregarding the Potemkin villages and sheep's clothing which the Kremlin traditionally uses when flirting with the West and coaxing credits from it. Beginning with Zhirinovsky's victory in the Parliamentary elections, the political situation in the country has changed radically: Yeltsin has quarreled stormily with the democrats, expelling them from the Kremlin and rejecting their ideas. In return he has brought the so-called "party of war," consisting of imperial bureaucrats and leaders of the "power ministries" (defense, counterintelligence and internal affairs) and led by a new Rasputin, the omnipotent General Aleksandr Korzhakov, a former Yeltsin bodyguard, closer to the throne. In other words,the democrats have gone over to the opposition, while Zhirinovsky—for the time being only ideologically—has come to power, and has consequently changed his tune from critic of the Kremlin to its adherent, blocking anti-Yeltsin resolutions in the Duma during the Chechnya crisis. Although still political foes in the Kremlin power struggle, Yeltsin and Zhirinovsky have become ideological allies. And that is precisely the union which Yegor Gaidar had warned against. In the summer of 1994 in an article entitled "Fascism and Bureaucracy," he wrote that "is it possible that the ruling bureaucracy will join forces with the Nazis," and "will hire bandits, truly repeating the Weimar catastrophe in Russia?" Only a few months ago such a situation would have been seen as hypothetical, but by the beginning of 1995 it began materializing. Maybe the Kremlin right now is only a velvet dictatorship, but where is the guarantee that it will not become an iron one? Maybe, to use Yeltsin's phrase, a "cold peace" between the West and Russia has set in, but to what level will their relations sink tomorrow? As far as Yeltsin personally is concerned, he is turning from Dr. Jekyll into Mr. Hyde, although it would be more correct to say, within the context of our book, from Yeltsin into Zhirinovsky.

What historical role does Zhirinovsky play on the domestic and international political scene? Is he a litmus test by which the changes, largely still invisible, can be judged in the life of Russia and those countries surrounding it? Is he a political yeast, accelerating the process of Russia's return to an imperial and chauvinist ideology, to its previous borders, to the status of a superpower, to the isolation and the cold war or worse? Or is he "the great midwife of history," the provocateur of Russian writer Ilya Ehrenburg's novel *Julio Jurenito*? "If you do not take me, the provocateur with the peaceful smile and hand ever in his pocket, another will come to perform a Caesarian, and things will be bad on earth."

Zhirinovsky is like a seismograph who first records underground shocks and then does everything to make the social earthquake really happen. The tendencies he represents exist in society on their own, but he gives them a name, a direction, a political shape, and takes charge of them.

Zhirinovsky is not the one to change the rules of the game, but is the most sensitive to the "din of the times," to use Osip Mandelstam's expression—and that means the most talented Russian politician. He was the first to accept the new terms of the political game and to adapt to them swiftly, as others were finally forced to do. Not even Yeltsin can rule against public opinion, or ignore political reality, social needs, and the popular will.

Similar political and social tendencies (minus the great-power nationalism) have emerged and grown stronger in the countries of the former Pax Sovietica. Through elections, communists were returned to power in Poland, Hungary, Bulgaria, Lithuania, Ukraine, Belarus, Azerbaidzhan, and other ex-satraps of the Kremlin. Economic collapse forced many of the former Soviet republics to restore economic ties with Moscow, and some even accepted its military aid. Georgia, until recently one of the most obstinate and freedom-loving of the republics, was drowning in the bloodshed of a civil war. Without Russia's help it would have ceased its independent existence. (If it were up to Zhirinovsky, he would prefer that Georgia go over to Turkey, although Turkey has few prospects under Zhirinovsky's redivision of the world.)

In fact, reunification has already occurred in recent Russian history. Right after the revolution of 1917, Russia collapsed like a house of cards. But first Lenin and Trotsky began putting it back together again, then Stalin restored its previous might and added territory by seizing substantial chunks from conquered and weakened countries or from falling empires— Germany, Poland, Austro-Hungary, and Japan. Now Zhirinovsky is confessing his "weakness for border posts" and dreams of returning them to the holes where they stood. Reunification could happen even without Zhirinovsky, since Russian troops remain in most former Soviet republics. Some have taken part in internal conflicts, as in Georgia and Moldova, or repelled external enemies, as in Tadzhikistan. They influence the "independent" countries by their mere presence. And finally the use of the army in crushing the Chechen separatism—regardless of how unprofessionally and artlessly the army displayed itself in this operation—has demonstrated the Kremlin's resolve to return prodigal republics to the imperial fold.

We are convinced that the restoration of the Russian empire—in its previous or near-previous borders—is only a matter of time, sooner rather than later, regardless of who will be head of state. As said in the Book of Ecclesiastes, there is a time for casting stones, and a time for gathering stones. The destructive period in Russia has reached a limit beyond which, as Rabelais said, can be glimpsed the Great Nothingness, that is, the death of the state. The instinct for self-preservation will operate in the state itself. Russia has never known any form of statehood except totalitarian or authoritarian empires in the last centuries, and its restorative tendencies will follow the historical direction.

Similar tendencies are occurring throughout Europe, along with the emergence of ever more ultra-right and extremist groups, the post fascists, as they call themselves in the recent right-wing government of Italy. There is a difference, however, between Italy, which has no nuclear weapons, and Russia, which is chock-full of atomic warheads. Although Zhirinovsky's threat to keep his finger on the nuclear button could be written off as black humor, as his press secretary does, some things are dangerous even to joke about. Russia is now the only country in the world where there is no antagonism, or even opposition, between the neocommunists and the neofascists. On the contrary, a compromise, or a political symbiosis, may lead to a red-brown dictatorship. The best candidate for dictator, as the results of the elections and polls have shown, is Zhirinovsky.

In any event, it seems that instead of the "new order" that was supposed to be established after the fall of the Soviet empire, a *new* new order is coming to the world, which suspiciously smacks of the old days of the "evil empire" and the cold war. Thanks to Zhirinovsky, it may be even more risky and explosive. There are no grounds for optimism.

Is there a way to prevent this man from coming to power, when he is now the most popular politician in Russia and invincible in the campaign television battles? The army, police, and state security are banking on him, and Zhirinovsky is counting on them no less than on the popular will as a whole. In an interview with the "patriotic" journalist Alexander Prokhanov in the newspaper *Tomorrow*, headlined I WILL RIDE INTO THE KREMLIN, Zhirinovsky transparently hints that he will come to power through a conspiracy. Reuters even quoted him as saying: "These two coups [of August 1991 and October 1993] took place without our participation, and that is why they failed. But if we participate, victory is certain. The third time it will be with our participation." In a March television program called "I Am the Leader," Zhirinovsky predicted that Yeltsin would assign him to form the government before the presidential elections, because he has brought Russia onto the firm road of order. So that Yeltsin will have no doubts, troops loyal to Zhirinovsky will surround the Kremlin during their talks. A woman can be raped, or she can be persuaded to give her favors willingly, explained Zhirinovsky, and promised Yeltsin a pension for life and a bust in his native village of Butka in the Ural Mountains. Former ministers Yegor Gaidar and Boris Fyodorov, and Anatoly Chubais, still Deputy Prime Minister, treated these predictions with utter seriousness. Chubais even called on the government to use security forces to prevent the conspiracy.

Political assassination, even if committed for the most noble intentions, would lead to even greater chaos, and Zhirinovsky's place would immediately be filled by others similar to him in views and no less dangerous than he. Nature abhors a vacuum. The only method of politically neutralizing Zhirinovsky is to give this bubbling and boiling energy some outlet. In our opinion, it would have been better to have accommodated him personally than to have adopted his slogans. It may not be possible to tame this lone political wolf, but why not try, when all other methods have proved ineffective? This method should have been tried earlier, and it may already be too late. Yeltsin's political mistakes, in our view, are that he did not give

Zhirinovsky's party several ministerial portfolios and did not appoint him personally as interior minister to fight crime, something Zhirinovsky had insisted on. Finally, only a few months after signing the truce with Yeltsin, Zhirinovsky announced that his party was withdrawing from the Agreement on Civic Accord, protesting the "state terrorism" of which, in his words, the LDP had become a victim. "Our party is pressured, stifled, and destroyed everywhere, and then they say 'let's cooperate.' We don't need that kind of cooperation."

It was also a mistake for Clinton not to have met with the victor of the December elections when he traveled to Moscow in early 1994. Such squeamishness does not befit a responsible politician. Nixon turned out to be wiser in meeting Zhirinovsky.

Zhirinovsky should be mobilized within the power structures, and his activity strictly limited by the framework of the law so that he doesn't commit follies. He has repeatedly shown that he knows how to obey the law and be constructive, as, for example, at the Constitutional Convention. If in politics and in life, the snake, the tiger, and the monkey can live in harmony, then in such a politician as Zhirinovsky other traits far more important may be missed behind the monkey grimaces.

Paradoxically, his path to the Kremlin Olympus may be barred only by bringing him closer to the peaks of power, by giving him a concrete and responsible assignment, which he does deserve for winning the elections. The most dangerous thing, in our view, would be to leave such a person politically unemployed, left to his own devices. It leaves him no other course but to seek revenge, to fight for the highest office in the land. He has every chance for victory—lawfully or not.

Zhirinovsky will continue to play his historical role, whether or not he becomes president of Russia. Even now he is the secret inspirer, the gray cardinal, the ideological architect of events occurring in Russia. It is already impossible to expel him from the political scene—it is too late. It would be senseless and immoral to remove him physically. The hope that he will burst like a soap bubble is only wishful thinking. Whether or not we like it, we must come to terms with Zhirinovsky. He is a major politician of the present who has a future that will, it seems, coincide with the future of his country.

Notes

As in our three preceding books, we list all references to sources in these notes, so as not to break the narrative flow. All references are presented here by chapter in the order in which quotations or details appear in the text. We purposely do not mention those infrequent cases where we quote a secondary source rather than an original one.

Preface: Pandora's Box

We quote Zhirinovsky (the AP bulletin from Vienna of April 5, 1994), Ivan Ilyin (his book *On the Coming Russia*, p. 67), Mikhail Zhvanetsky (*Novoye Russkoye slovo* [New Russian word], July 1, 1994), Yegoz Gaidar (Segodnya [Today], June 15, 1994), Nikolai Petrakov (*Nevskoye Vremya* [Neva Times], July 15, 1994), Alexei Mitrofanov (Eduard Limonov, *Limonov vs. Zhirinovsky*, p. 64).

1. The Man from Nowhere *(Summer 1991)*

Here and elsewhere we indicate Zhirinovsky's Liberal Democratic Party by the abbreviation LDP, although in party documents before the collapse of the USSR it was called LDPSU (the Liberal

Democratic Party of the Soviet Union), and, after the collapse, LDPR (the Liberal Democratic Party of Russia).

In this chapter, as in the following ones, we quote Zhirinovsky based on video and audio recordings that we have in our possession, shorthand transcripts of speeches at rallies (for example, a two-hour recording of a speech at Palace Square in St. Petersburg in April 1992), numerous interviews (by Russian as well as foreign journalists—Ted Koppel and Peter Jennings of ABC, Tom Brokaw of NBC, Dan Rather of CBS, David Frost of BBC, Charles Kraus of PBS, Yanna Witt of the Australian "60 Minutes," et al.), and the feature-length films *Mr. Zhirinovsky, Candidate for President, The Hawk*; and *How to Kill Zhirinovsky*. In this chapter we also used the following publications, which printed his speeches and statements: *Novoye vremya* [New times], no. 41, 1992; *Moscow magazine*, April/May 1992; *Novy vzglyad* [New view], no. 38, 1992; *Moya Moskva* [My Moscow, no. 10, 1991; *Izvestiya* [News], September 4, 1991; *Yevreisky mir* [Jewish world], February 24, 1994; *Sovetskaya Rossiya* [Soviet Russia], May 24, 1991; *Time,* July 11, 1994; *Krasnaya zvezda* [Red star], May 1, 1991; *Newsday*, November 28, 1992; *Argumenty i fakty* [Arguments and facts], nos. 2–3, January 1994; and the "party" brochure *The Zhirinovsky Phenomenon*, 1992, pp. 57, 11, 12.

From this same brochure the document issued to Zhirinovsky by the KGB was reproduced. Statements by Anatoly Sobchak and Mikhail Gorbachev on Zhirinovsky's links with the KGB are given as they were printed in *Literaturnaya gazeta* [Literary gazette] (January 12, 1994), *Novaya Yezhednevnaya gazeta* [New daily newspaper] (January 12, 1994), *Izvestiya* (January 13, 1994), and *Rabochaya tribuna* [Workers' tribune] (January 14, 1994).

We were able to trace the history of the registration of the LDP thanks to materials published in the magazine *Ogonyok* [Little flame], no. 2, January 11–18, 1992, and the question about the financing of LDP has been raised repeatedly by many Russian periodicals (*Izvestiya*, December 12, 1993, and April 21, 1994; *Segodnya* [Today], January 1, 1994; *Komsomolskaya pravda* [Komsomol truth], et al.

We quote Adam Michnik (*Novoye Russkoye slovo*, April 1, 1994), Andrei Zagorodnikov (*Izvestiya*, April 14, 1994), commentary from the newspaper *Soyuz* [Union] July 1991), Leonid Radzikhovsky (*Ogonyok*, August 7–14, 1991), Sergei Putin (*Izvestiya*, January 4, 1993), Andrei Arkhipov and Eduard Limonov (*Limonov vs. Zhirinovsky*, pp. 16, 113,

178, 171). We cite excerpts from Sigmund Freud's work *Psychology of the Masses and an Analysis of the Human Ego,* the Soviet edition (Sigmund Freud, *Psychoanalytic Studies.* Minsk: Belarus, 1991, p. 468).

2. THE SUPERMAN COMPLEX *(1946–1991)*

We gleaned information about Zhirinovsky's childhood in Almaty for the most part from his book *The Last Push to the South* (pp. 5, 6, 13, 12, 8, 21, 32, 35, 48–49, 12, and 13, 23, 8, 21, 141–142, 30, 24, 91, 42–43, 14, 25–26, 61, 25, 34–35, 38, 43, 41, 8, 41, 130, 14, 41, 47, 49—in order of their appearance in our book). All quotations are taken from the first edition of this book, although Zhirinovsky's literary aide Irina Sergeyevna Kulikova asserts that the book was pirated (*Izvestiya,* February 10, 1994). However, on comparison with subsequent editions, including those making up Zhirinovsky's trilogy *On Russia's Fates,* we discovered no substantial differences. Kulikova's repudiation of the first edition of *The Last Push to the South* is apparently connected with Zhirinovsky's prosecution for militaristic statements made in his book (*Izvestiya,* January 21; *Novaya yezhednevnaya gazeta,* February 4; *Rossiyskaya gazeta* [Russian newspaper], February 8; *Novoye vremya,* no. 5, February; *Srochno v nomer* [Stop the presses], no. 12, February; and other 1994 publications on this topic).

In addition to *The Last Push to the South* and video and audio recordings, we quote statements made by Zhirinovsky from the following publications: *Dyen* [Day] no. 1, 1992; *Moscow magazine,* April–May 1992; *Novoye Russkoye slovo,* December 30 and 31, 1993, and January 7 and April 7, 1994; *The Zhirinovsky Phenomenon,* pp. 60, 32, 84, 47, 51, 89; *Maariv,* January 11, 1994; *Novoye vremya,* no. 41, 1992; *Novy vzglyad,* no. 38, 1992; *Washington Post,* December 18, 1993; *Liberal,* no. 1, 1993; *Sokol Zhirinovskogo* [Zhirinovsky's falcon], no. 6, 1993; *Vanity Fair,* September 1994.

We reconstructed the awakening of Zhirinovsky's Jewish consciousness, which found expression in his unrealized attempt to emigrate and in two visits to Shalom, the Jewish organization, based on the following publications: *New York Times,* December 16 and 28, 1993; *Washington Post,* December 24, 1993; *Le Monde,* December 29, 1993; *Novoye Russkoye slovo,* December 30 and 31, 1993, and January 7, 1994; *Trud* [Labor, January 28, 1994; *Russkaya mysl* [Russian thought, February 3–9, 1994; *Stolitsa,* no. 9, 1994.

Many articles in the Russian press have been devoted to the problem of the Russian diaspora in the near abroad: *Pravda*, January 6, 1994; *Nezavisimaya gazeta* [Independent newspaper; January 12, 1994, *Vek* [Century], no. 4, 1994, et al.

We quote Anatoly Pankov and Evgeniy Kopyshta (*Kuranty* [Chimes], December 14, 1993), Lev Aleynik (*Russkaya mysl*, January 15, 1993), Victor Kobelev (*Novoye Russokoye slovo*, January 7, 1994), A. M. Rosenthal (*New York Times*, December 17, 1993), Mikhail Gorelik (*Novoye Russokoye slovo*, April 8, 1994), Eduard Limonov (*Panorama*, September 28–October 4, 1994; *Limonov vs. Zhirinovsky*, p. 171), Mikhail Pronin (*Panorama*, January 26–February 1, 1994), Nursultan Nazarbayev (ITAR-TASS, February 17, 1994; *Nezavisimaya gazeta*, January 6, 1994), V. Kuvaldin (*Izvestiya*, July 8, 1991), Vladislav Savitsky (*Panorama*, May 4–10, 1994), Galina Zhirinovskaya (*Novoye Russkoye slovo*, April 1, 2–3, 4, 1994), Nadezda Kozlovskaya (*Vanity Fair*, September 1994), Vladimir Isakov (*Sovetskaya Rossiya*, January 25, 1994), a "diagnosis" of Zhirinovsky (*Argumenty i fakty*, nos. 2–3, January 1994), Dmitri Makarov (ibid), Galina Starovoitova (*Vanity Fair*, September 1994), Mikhail Pronin (*Panorama*, January 26–February 1, 1994), Galina Volchek (*Novoye Russkoye slovo*, October 7, 1994), Yevgenia Albats (*Washington Post*, December 18, 1993), Victor Dashevsky (*Yevreisky mir*, January 21, 1994), Evgeny Kulishev and Vladimir Kartsev (*Washington Post*, March 6, 1994), Sergei Plekhanov (*The Zhirinovsky Phenomenon*, p. 86).

We also quote Erich Fromm, *Adolph Hitler* (Moscow: *Progress*, 1992), p. 199; Georg Christoph Lichtenberg, *Aphorisms* (Moscow: Nauka, 1965, p. 27; Vasily Shukshin, *Selected Works, Volume 1* (Moscow: Molodaya gvardiya [Young guard], 1975, p. 370.

3. THE UNEMPLOYED POLITICIAN (*August 1991–Early 1993*)

Sources of quotations of Zhirinovsky, as they appear in this chapter, are as follows: *Moya Moskva*, no. 10, 1991; *Komsomolskaya pravda*, August 10, 1991; *The Last Push to the South*, p. 58; the film *The Hawk*; *Dyen'*, no. 1, 1992; *The Zhirinovsky Phenomenon*, pp. 76, 87, 60; *The Guardian*, February 19, 1992; *Izvestiya*, December 5, 1991; *Moskovsky Komsomolets* [Moscow Komsomolets], December 30, 1991; St. Petersburg television broadcast, "Adam's Apple," December 29, 1991; *Sovetskaya Rossiya*, December 26, 1991; *Novy vzglyad*, no. 38, 1992; videotape of a rally at Palace Square in St. Petersburg, April 1992; *Novoye vremya*, no. 41, October 1992; *Liberal*, no. 1, 1993; *Novoye Russ-*

koye slovo, February 1, 1994; *Newsday*, November 28, 1992; *The European*, May 28–31, 1994; Reuters, December 26, 1992, 2nd December 14, 1993; *Novoye Russkoye slovo*, 23 August 1993; *Panorama*, January 26–February 1, 1994; *Newsday*, November 28, 1992; *Washington Post*, December 15, 1993; *Ogonyok*, no. 37, September 7–14, 1991; *Sokol Zhirinovskogo*, no. 2, 1992; *Novoye Russkoye slovo*, April 20 and March 4, 1994; *Pravda Zhirinovskogo*, no. 13, 1993.

We gleaned documents on preparations for Zhirinovsky's visit to Lithuania from the magazine *Ogonyok*, January 11–18, 1992, no. 2; on preventive measures taken by Mayor Anatoly Sobchak in connection with Zhirinovsky's trip to St. Petersburg from the broadcast "Radio Moscow-1," January 13, 1991, 12:00; about his trip to Iraq and meeting with Saddam Hussein (ITAR-TASS, December 29, 1992; *Izvestiya*, November 30, 1993; the film *The Hawk*; *Liberal*, no. 1, 1993; *The Last Push to the South*, p. 99; *Novy vzglyad*, no. 8, 1994).

We quote Moscow journalists' comments about Zhirinovsky (*Rabochaya tribuna*, November 20, 1991), an unnamed LDP functionary (*Izvestiya*, January 4, 1993), Andrei Arkhipov and Sergei Zharikov (*Sokol Zhirinovskogo*, no. 2, 1992), Alexei Mitrofanov (*Sokol Zhirinovskogo*, no. 3, 1992), Eduard Limonov (*Novy vzglyad*, no. 8, 1994), Elizabeth Rein (*The European*, May 28–31, 1992), a pun by two Moscow journalists (*Ogonyok*, no. 6, February 8–15, 1992), Leonid Kravchuk (*Wall Street Journal*, European edition, March 17, 1992), Anatoly Ivanov (*Sokol Zhirinovskogo*, no. 2, 1992); Richard Nixon (*New York Times*, March 25, 1994, and *Izvestiya*, March 31, 1994); Alexander Rutskoi (December 4, 1992); democrats' gloomy predictions for 1994 (*Segodnya*, December 16, 1993), Michel Tatu (*Le Monde*, September 29, 1992).

4. ULTIMA RATIO *(September 21–October 4, 1993)*

We cite statements by Zhirinovsky (*Novoye Russkoye slovo*, August 23, and December 24–26, 1993; *Argumenty i fakty*, no. 12, March 1993; *Vechernaya Moskva* [Evening Moscow], August 24, 1991; *Kommersant* [Merchant], no. 50, 1991), Yeltsin (his book *Notes of the President*, Russian edition pp. 347, 356, or American edition pp. 242, 250), General Rutskoi (*Pravda*, April 5, 1992; *Al-Kods*, no. 9, April 1994), Leonid Radzikhovsky (*Stolitsa*, no. 13, 1994), Ruslan Khasbulatov and Veronica Kutsylo (*Novoye Russkoye slovo*, October 6, and October 15, 1993), Oleg Kalugin (*Nevskoye vremya* [Neva Times], October 5,

229

1993), Gennady Ponomarev (*Obshchaya gazeta* [General newspaper], October 8–14, 1993).

We quote Marx from the Soviet edition of the works of Karl Marx and Friedrich Engels (vol. 1, p, 418), and Jose Ortega y Gasset from the Russian edition of his book *Uprising of the Masses* (New York: Chekhov Publishers, 1994), p. 78).

5. THE SECRET OF VICTORY (*December 12, 1993*)

In addition to transcripts and videotapes of Zhirinovsky's appearances (the rally in St. Petersburg and the film *The Hawk*), we also cite his statements from the following publications: *The Zhirinovsky Phenomenon*, pp. 14–15, 67, 44; *Washington Post*, December 15, 1993; *Nezavisimaya gazeta*, January 6, 1994; *Wall Street Journal*, European edition, March 17, 1992; *Kuranty*, December 16, 1993; *Newsday*, November 28, 1992; *Novy vzglyad*, no. 38, October 17, 1992; *Literaturnaya Rossiya* [Literary Russia , no. 7, February 18, 1994; *Liberal*, no. 1, 1993; *Izvestiya*, November 30, 1993; *Novoye vremya*, no. 41, October 1992; *Moskovskiye vedomosti* [Moscow register], no. 3, February 18, 1994; *Izvestiya*, April 23 and May 17, 1994; *Washington Post*, December 18, 1993; *Kuranty*, April 15, 1994.

Zhirinovsky's geopolitical statements in the last part of the chapter are quoted from his book *The Last Push to the South* (pp. 64, 63, 70, 142–143, 72, 71–72, 66, 75, 104); *Nezavisimaya gazeta*, December 8, 1993; *Kuranty*, January 5, 1994; *Izvestiya*, November 30, 1993, *Moskovsky Komsomolets*, December 18, 1993.

We quote Richard Nixon (*New York Times* March 25, 1994; *Izvestiya*, March 31, 1994), Michael Dobbs (*Washington Post*, December 15, 1993), Boris Yeltsin (*Notes of the President, Ogonyok*, 1994, p. 67; respectively, the American translation p. 42), Andrei Arkhipov and Sergei Zharikov (*Izvestiya*, January 4, 1994), General Alexander Rutskoi (*Rossiskiye vesti*, [Russian news], June 3, 1994), Yegor Gaidar (*Izvestiya*, May 17, 1994), Nikita Mikhalkov (*Novaya yezhednevnaya gazeta* [New daily newspaper], December 24, 1993), Yevgenia Albats (*Izvestiya*, August 5, 1994), Eduard Limonov (Limonov vs. Zhirinovsky, p. 36), Alexander Vengerovsky (*Argumenty i fakty*, no. 4, 1994), Boris Paramonov (*Panorama*, January 19–25, 1994). The photograph of Zhirinovsky in the shower was on the cover of the *New York Times Magazine* of June 19, 1994, accompanying the article "Why Russia Loves This Man," by Michael Specter.

Comparisons between Russia and Weimar Germany are frequently to be found in the Moscow press, but as far as we can tell, the first person to speak of this was Alexander Yanov; thus we refer the reader to two of his pieces on this topic–in the weekly *Stolitsa*, no. 52, 1993, and in *Izvestiya*, December 23, 1993. The expression "We woke up in a strange country" originally belongs to the writer Andrei Bitov (he wrote an article with this title, and subsequently also a book of his commentaries, published in 1991). We gleaned the information for our analysis of Zhirinovsky's constituency from Moscow newspapers; the most objective such report was published in *Izvestiya* (December 30, 1993). We learned the voting results in Fryazino from the newspaper *Kuranty*, January 5, 1994, and we obtained details of Zhirinovsky's press conference upon his triumph in the elections from the ITAR-TASS report of December 14, 1993, and articles in the Moscow press the following day (including coverage by his college classmate Alexander Shalnev in *Izvestiya*). Details and commentary on voting patterns among the military are taken from the *New York Times*, December 17, 1993; *Sovetskaya Rossiya*, December 21, 1993; *Segodnya*, December 15, 1993; *Novaya yezhednevnaya gazeta*, January 12, 1994, et al.

We culled reports about consultations with parapsychologists and psychoanalysts, and also with British electoral campaign consultants, from the Moscow weekly *Argumenty i fakty*, (nos. 4 and 5 for 1994). We cite Stanislav Govorukhin (*Pravda*, May 7, 1994), Grigory Yavlinsky, *Novaya yezhednevnaya gazeta*, January 21, 1994), Boris Yeltsin (*Nezavisimaya gazeta*, December 8 and 18, 1993; *Newsweek*, May 2, 1994), Mikhail Delyagin (twice: *Nezavisimaya Gazeta*, December 17, 1993), Alexander Burtin (*Novoye Russkoya slovo*, September 30, 1994), Gary Kasparov (*Novoye Russkoye slovo*, December 16, 1993), Arkady Arkanov (*Golos*) [Voice], 1994), Alexander Mitta (*Panorama*, January 5–11, 1994), Alexei Mitrofanov (*Time*, July 11, 1994), Vladimir Chaschin (Cherepovetsk newspaper *Ryech* [Speech], December 23, 1993), Andrei Fedorov (*Novoye Russkoye slovo*, April 12, 1994).

6. THE ZHIRINOVSKY FACTOR *(1994–early 1995)*

Most of Zhirinovsky's statements during his trips abroad in the winter and spring of 1994 are quoted from ITAR-TASS bulletins and AP and Reuters bulletins, and his speeches in the State Duma and his speech at the Fifth Congress of the LDP are from transcripts we have in our possession. Approximately half of these quotations have been checked against materials published in 1994 issues of the periodicals

BIBLIOGRAPHY

ENGLISH SOURCES

ALBATS, YEVGENIA. *The KGB: The State Within a State*, New York: Farrar Straus Giroux, 1994.

ALEXANDROV, VICTOR. *The Kremlin, Nerve Centre of Russian History*. New York: St. Martin's Press, 1963.

ATWAN, ROBERT, and VALERY VINOKUROV, ed. *Openings: Original Essays by Contemporary Soviet and American Writers*. University of Washington Press, 1990.

BESCHLOSS, MICHAEL, and STROBE TALBOTT. *At the Highest Levels*. Boston: Little, Brown, 1993.

BOBRICK, BENSON. *East of the Sun. The Epic Conquest and Tragic History of Siberia*. New York: Poseidon, 1992.

CARTER, PAUL A. *Revolt Against Destiny*. New York: Columbia University Press, 1989.

CHACE, JAMES. *The Consequences of the Peace. The New Internationalism and America*. New York: Oxford University Press, 1993.

CONQUEST, ROBERT. *Stalin, Breaker of Nations*. New York: Viking Press, 1991.

CORSON, WILLIAM R., and ROBERT T. CROWLEY. *The New KGB: Engine of Soviet Power*. New York: Morrow, 1985.

CRANKSHAW, EDWARD. *Khrushchev, a Career*. New York: Viking Press, 1961.

CUSTINE, ASTOLPH, MARQUISE DE. *Journey of Our Time.* New York: Pellegrini and Cudahy, 1951.

DORNBERG, JOHN. *Brezhnev: The Masks of Power.* New York: Basic Books, 1974.

DUNLOP, JOHN. *The Rise of Russia and the Fall of the Soviet Empire.* Princeton, N.J.: Princeton University Press, 1993.

FISCHER, LOUIS. *The Life of Lenin.* New York: Harper & Row, 1964.

FRANKLAND, MARK. *Khrushchev.* New York: Stein & Day, 1967.

HABBS, JOANNA. *Mother Russia: The Feminine Myth in Russian Culture.* Bloomington: Indiana University Press, 1989.

HITLER, ADOLF. *Mein Kampf.* New York: Reinal & Hitchcock, 1940.

HYLAND, WILLIAM, and RICHARD W. SHRYOCK. *The Fall of Khrushchev.* New York: Funk & Wagnalls, 1968.

IGNATIEFF, MICHAEL. *Blood and Belonging. Journeys into the New Nationalism.* New York: Farrar, Straus & Giroux, 1994.

KAISER, ROBERT. *Russia: The People and the Power.* New York: Atheneum, 1976.

————. *Why Gorbachev Happened: His Triumphs and His Failure.* New York: Simon & Schuster, 1991.

KENNAN, GEORGE F. *Sketches from Life.* New York: Pantheon Books, 1989.

KERBLEY, BASILE. *Gorbachev's Russia.* New York: Pantheon Books, 1989.

KLOSE, KEVIN. *Russia and the Russians: Inside the Closed Society.* New York/London: W. W. Norton, 1984.

LAQUEUR, WALTER. *Black Hundred. The Rise of the Extreme Right in Russia.* New York: HarperCollins, 1993.

————. *The Long Road to Freedom: Russia and Glasnost.* New York: Scribner, 1989.

LAQUEUR, WALTER, and others. *Soviet Union, 2000: Reform or Revolution.* New York: St. Martin's Press, 1990.

LINCOLN, W. BRUCE. *The Conquest of a Continent. Siberia and the Russians.* New York: Random House, 1993.

MALIA, MARTIN. *The Soviet Tragedy. A History of Socialism in Russia.* New York: Free Press, 1994.

NAGORSKI, ANDREW. *The Birth of Freedom.* New York: Simon & Schuster, 1993.

NIXON, RICHARD. *Beyond Peace.* New York: Random House, 1994.

————. *In the Arena.* New York: Simon & Schuster, 1990.

OWEN, RICHARD. *Comrade Chairman: Soviet Succession and the Rise of Gorbachev.* New York: Arbor House, 1986.

PECK, MERTON J., and THOMAS J. RICHARDON, ed. *What Is to Be Done? Proposals for the Soviets.* New Haven: Yale University Press, 1992.

PFAFF, WILLIAM. *The Wrath of Nations. Civilization and the Fury of Nationalism.* New York: Simon & Schuster, 1993.

PIPES, RICHARD. *Russia Under the Bolshevik Regime.* New York: Knopf, 1994.

———. *Russia Under the Old Regime.* New York: Scribner, 1974.

———. *The Russian Revolution.* New York: Knopf, 1990.

REMNICK, DAVID. *Lenin's Tomb. The Last Days of the Soviet Empire.* New York: Random House, 1993.

ROSITZKE, HARRY. *The KGB: The Eyes of Russia.* Garden City, N.Y.: Doubleday, 1981.

SINYAVSKY, ANDRE. *Soviet Civilization and Cultural History.* Boston: Little, Brown, 1990.

SMITH, HEDRIK. *The Russians.* New York: Quadrangle, 1976.

———. *The New Russians.* New York: Random House, 1990.

SOLOVYOV, VLADIMIR, and ELENA KLEPIKOVA. *Yuri Andropov: A Secret Passage into the Kremlin.* New York: Macmillan, 1983.

———. *Behind the High Kremlin Walls.* New York: Dodd, Mead, 1986.

———. *Boris Yeltsin. A Political Biography.* New York: Putnam, 1992.

STERNHELL, ZEEV. *The Birth of Fascist Ideology.* Princeton, N.J.: Princeton University Press, 1994.

TALBOTT, STROBE, ed. *Mikhail S. Gorbachev: An Intimate Biography.* New York: Time, 1988.

TATU, MICHEL. *Power in the Kremlin: From Khrushchev to Kosygin.* New York: Viking Press, 1970.

TAUBMAN, WILLIAM, and JANE TAUBMAN. *Moscow Spring.* New York: Summit Books, 1989.

TRAGER, OLIVER, ed. *Gorbachev's Glasnost: Red Star Rising.* An Editorials on File Book. New York: Oxford, 1989.

ULAM, ADAM B. *Stalin: The Man and His Era.* New York: Viking Press, 1973.

WALKER, MARTIN. *The Waking Giant: Gorbachev's Russia.* New York: Pantheon Books, 1986.

WREN, CHRISTOPHER. *The End of the Line: The Failure of Communism in the Soviet Union and China.* New York: Simon & Schuster, 1989.

YELTSIN, BORIS. *The Struggle for Russia.* New York: Times Books, 1994.

YERGIN, DANIEL, and THANE GUSTAFSON. *Russia 2010 and What It Means for the World.* New York: Random House, 1993.

BIBLIOGRAPHY

RUSSIAN SOURCES

ABALKIN, L. I. *Perestroika: Paths and Problems*. Moscow: Ekonomika, 1988.

AGAFONOV, V., V. ROKITYANSKY. *Russia in Search of the Future*. Moscow: Kultura, 1993.

AGURSKY, M. *Ideology of National Bolshevism*. Paris: YMCA Press, 1980.

The Anniversary Which Wasn't. Why the USSR Didn't Celebrate Its 70th Birthday. Moscow: Terra, 1992.

ARBATOV, G. A. *Prolonged Recovery*. Moscow: Mezhdunarodnye Otnosheniya, 1991.

BAKATIN, VADIM. *Getting Rid of the KGB*. Moscow: Novosti, 1992.

BATKIN, LEONID. *History Resumes*. Moscow: Moskovsky Rabochi, 1991.

BITOV, ANDREI. *We Woke up in a Strange Country*. Leningrad: Sovetski Pisatel, 1991.

BURLATSKY, FEDOR. *New Thinking*. Moscow: Izdatelstvo Politicheskoy Literatury, 1989.

BUYANOV, M. *Lenin, Stalin and Psychiatry*. Moscow, 1992.

CHAADAYEV, PYOTR, KONSTANTIN LEONTIEV, VLADIMIR SOLOVYOV. *Russia Through a Russian's Eyes*. St. Petersburg: Nauka, 1991.

Cherez Ternii: Perestroika, glasnost, demokratiya. [Per Aspera: Perestroika, glasnost, democracy.] Moscow: Progress, 1990.

Chernaya noch nad Belym Domom. [Black night Over the White House.] Moscow: Gazeta Rossiya, 1991.

239

CHERNYAEV, A. *Six Years with Gorbachev.* Moscow: Kultura, 1993.

CHURBANOV, YURI. *I'll Tell It Like It Was.* Kazan: Liana, 1993.

CUSTINE, ASTOLPH, MARQUIS DE. *Russian Under Tsar Nicholas.* Moscow: Terra, 1990.

DANILEVSKY, N. Y. *Russia and Europe.* Moscow: Sovremennik, 1991.

Eurasian Paths. An Anthology. Moscow: Russkaya Kniga, 1992.

FEDOTOV, G. P. *The New City, A Collection of Articles.* New York: Chekhov Publishing House, 1952.

FEDOTOV, GEORGI. *The Fate and Sins of Russia.* 2 vols. St. Petersburg: Sofia, 1992.

————. *Russia and Freedom.* New York: Chalidze Publications, 1982.

Forbidden Laughter: Soviet Underground Jokes. A Collection. Los Angeles, 1978.

FROMM, ERICH. *Adolph Hitler. A Clinical Case of Necrophilia.* Moscow: Progress, 1992.

GAUTIER, THEOPHILE. *Journey to Russia.* Moscow: Mysl, 1990.

Glasnost: Nasushchnye voprosy i neobhodimye otvety. [*Glasnost: Vital issues and necessary answers.*] A collection. Moscow: Politizdat, 1989.

GORBACHEV-YELTSIN. *1550 Days of a Political Standoff.* Moscow: Terra, 1992.

GORYUN, ANDREI. *Boris Yeltsin: Light and Shadows.* 2 booklets. Sverdlovsk. Clip, 1991.

GOVORUKHIN, STANISLAV. *The Great Criminal Revolution.* Moscow: Andreyevskiy Flag, 1993.

GROSSMAN, VASILY. *Forever Flowing . . .* Frankfurt: Possev-Verlag: 1974.

GUMILEV, LEV. *Ancient Russia and Great Steppe.* Moscow: Mysl, 1989.

————. *Entogenesis and the Earth's Biosphere.* Leningrad: Gidrometeoizdat, 1990.

————. *From Rus to Russia.* Moscow: Progress, 1993.

————. *Rhythms of Eurasia.* Moscow: Progress, 1993.

HAZANOV, BORIS. *The Myth of Russia.* New York: Liberty Publishing House, 1986.

HELLER, MIKHAIL. *Landmarks of 70 Years.* London: Overseas Publications Interchange, 1987.

HELLER, MIKHAIL, and ALEXANDER NEKRICH. *Utopia in Power: A History of the Soviet Union from 1917 to Our Day.* 2 vols. London: Overseas Publications Exchange, 1978.

ILYIN, I. A. *On the Coming Russia.* Jordanville, N.Y., 1991.

Inostrantsy o Drevney Moskve. [*Foreigners about Ancient Moscow.*] Moscow: Stolitsa, 1991.

KARAMZIN, N. M. *Legends of Old.* Moscow: Pravda, 1987.

KHASBULATOV, RUSLAN. *Choice of Fate.* Moscow: Respublica, 1993.

Khronika Putscha. Chas za Chasom. [*The Putsch Chronicle: Hour by Hour.*] Moscow: Russian Information Agency, 1991.

KHRUSHCHEV, NIKITA. *Memoirs.* 2 vols. New York: Chalidze Publications, 1979.

KLYUCHEVSKY, V. O. *Collected Works.* 9 vols. Moscow: Mysl, 1987–1990.

KOPELEV, LEV. *The Regime and the People.* Ann Arbor: Ardis, 1982.

LENIN, VLADIMIR I. *On Glasnost.* Moscow: Politizdat, 1989.

LIMONOV, EDUARD. *Limonov vs. Zhirinovsky.* Moscow: Konetz Veka, 1994.

NUIKIN, ANDREI. *We and They.* Moscow: Ayers, 1990.

Obratnogo hoda net: Perestroika v narodnom hozyaystve. [*No way back: Perestroika in a people's economy.*] A collection. Moscow: Politizdat, 1989.

OLEYNIK, BORIS. *The Prince of Darkness. Two Years in the Kremlin.* Samarsky Publishing House, 1993.,

Osmyslit kult Stalina. Lichnost i vlast. [*To comprehend the Stalin cult. Personality and power.*] A collection. Moscow: Progress, 1989.

PARAMONOV, BORIS. *Portrait of a Jew.* Paris–St. Petersburg: Grzhebin's Press, 1993.

Parties and Political Blocs in Russia. Moscow: Marco Media, 1993.

Perestroika i sovremeny mir. [*Perestroika and the modern world.*] A collection. Moscow: Mezhdunarodniye Otnosheniya, 1989.

PLATONOV, S. F. *A Time of Troubles.* Prague: 1924.

POKROVSKY, M. N. *Collected Works.* 4 vols. Moscow: Mysl, 1965–1968.

The Political History of Russia in Parties and People. Moscow: Terra, 1993.

Political Russia Today 2 vols. Moscow: Moskovsky Rabochy, 1993.

Political Science. An Encyclopedia. Moscow, 1993.

Program of the Liberal Democratic Party. (Brochure without publication information)

Russia. An Encyclopedia. Lenizdat, 1991.

The Russian Idea. Moscow: Respublika, 1992.

SAMOILOV, E. V. *Führers.* Kaluga: SELS Publisher, 1994.

SARNOV, BENEDICT. *Look Who's Here.* Moscow: Novosti, 1992.

SHAFAREVICH, IGOR. *Does Russia Have a Future?* Moscow: Sovetsky Pisatel, 1991.

SHTURMAN, DORA, and SERGEI TIKTIN. *Soviet Union Reflected in Political Anecdotes.* London: Overseas Publications Interchange, 1985.

SOBCHAK, ANATOLY. *Coming to Power.* St. Petersburg: Novosti, 1991.

SOLOVYOV, S. M. *Readings and Stories on Russian History.* Moscow: Pravda, 1989.

SOLOVYOV, VLADIMIR. *Operation Mausoleum.* New York: Liberty Publishing House, 1989.

SOLOVYOV, VLADIMIR, and ELENA KLEPIKOVA. *Mikhail Gorbachev: The Path to the Top.* Moscow: a pirated edition, 1989.

————. *The Kremlin Plotters: From Andropov to Gorbachev.* Moscow: Tsentr Isskustvo, 1991.

————. *Struggle in the Kremlin.* New York, Jerusalem, Paris: Vremya i my, 1986.

STEPANKOV, V., E. LISOV. *Kremlin Conspiracy.* Moscow: Ogonyok, 1992.

SUKHANOV, LEV. *Three Years with Yeltsin. Notes of an Aide.* Riga: Vaga, 1992.

Surovaya drama naroda. [The people's ordeal.] A collection. Moscow: Politizdat, 1989.

TELESIN, YULI. *1001 Anecdotes.* New Jersey: Hermitage, 1986.

V borbe za vlast. [In the struggle for power.] Pages from Russian political history. A collection. Moscow: Mysl, 1988.

Vekhi, [Landmarks.] Collection of articles about the Russian intelligentsia. Moscow, 1909.

VOSLENSKY, MIKHAIL. *The Nomenklatura: The Soviet Ruling Class.* London: Overseas Publications Interchange, 1984.

Who's Who? Political Moscow, 1993. Moscow: Katallaksi, 1993.

YANOV, ALEXANDER. *The Russian Idea and the Year 2000.* New York: Liberty Publishing House, 1988.

A Year After August. A Collection of Articles and Interviews. Moscow: Literatura i Politika, 1992.

YELTSIN, BORIS. *Confession on an Assigned Theme.* Moscow: PIK, 1990.

————. *Notes of the President.* Moscow: Ogonyok, 1994.

Yesli po sovesti. [Speaking openly.] A collection of articles on the problems of perestroika. Moscow. Khudozhestvennaya Literatura, 1988.

Zavisit ot nas. Perestroika v zerkale pressy. [It is up to us: Perestroika reflected in the media.] Moscow: Knizhnaya Palata, 1988.

ZHABA, S. P. *Russian Thinkers on Russia and Humankind.* Paris: YMCA Press, 1954.

The Zhirinovsky Phenomenon. Moscow: Kontrolling, 1992

ZHIRINOVSKY, VLADIMIR. *The Last Push to the South.* Moscow, 1993.

————. *On Russia's Fates, Part I. Lessons of History.* Moscow: Rite Agency, 1993.

————. *On Russia's Fates. Part II. The Last Push to the South.* Moscow: Rite Agency, 1993.

————. *On Russia's Fates. Part III. From My Point of View . . .* Moscow: Rite Agency, 1994.

ZHVANETSKY, MIKHAIL. *One Year for Two.* Moscow: Iskusstvo, 1989.

ZIMIN A. (pseud.). *Socialism and Neo-Stalinism.* New York: Chalidze Publications, 1981.

PERIODICALS

Christian Science Monitor
Economist
European
Guardian
International Herald Tribune
New York Times
Newsweek
Time
U.S. News and World Report
Wall Street Journal
Washington Post

In Russian

(Place of publication indicated only in cases where it is not Moscow)
Argumenty i fakty [Arguments and facts]
Armiya (Army)
Atmoda (later renamed Baltiyskoye vremya [Baltic times])
Bolshaya Volga [Big Volga] (Samara)
Chas pik [Rush hour] (St. Petersburg)
Delo [Business]
Deloviye lyudi [Business People]

Delovoy mir [Business World]

Demokraticheskaya Rossiya [Democratic Russia]

Dyen' [Day] (after it was banned it was published under the name
    Zavtra [Tomorrow])

Express khronika

Iskusstvo kino [Film art]

ITAR-TASS

Izvestiya

Izvestiya TsK KPSS

Kalinigradskaya pravda

Knizhnoye obozreniye [Book review]

Kommersant [Merchant]

Kommersant-daily

Kommunist

Komsomolets Uzbekistana

Komsomolskaya pravda

Kontinent (formerly Paris, now Moscow)

Krasnaya zvezda [Red star]

Kuranty [Chimes]

Literaturnaya gazeta

Literaturnaya Rossiya

Megapolis express

Molodaya gvardiya [Young guard]

Moskovskiye Novosti [Moscow news]

Moskovskaya pravda

Moskovsky Komsomolets

Moskva

Nash sovremennik [Our contemporary]

Nedelya [Week]

Nevskoye vremya [Neva times] (St. Petersburg)

Nezavisimaya gazeta [Independent newspaper]

Nizhegorodskaya pravda (Nizhny Novgorod)

Novaya yezhednevnaya gazeta [New daily newspaper]

Novoye Russkoye slovo [New Russian Word] (New York)

Novoye vremya [New times]

Novy mir [New world]

Novy vzglyad [New view]

Obshchaya gazeta [General newspaper]

Obshchestvenniye nauki i sovremennost [The social sciences and the
    contemporary world]

Ogonyok [Little flame]

Oktyabr

Panorama (Los Angeles)

Poisk [Search]
Polis
Pravda
Rabochaya tribuna [Workers' tribune]
Rossiya
Rossiyskaya gazeta
Rossiyskiye vesti [Russian news]
Russkaya mysl [Russian thought] (Paris)
Ryech [Speech] (Cherepovetz)
Segodnya [Today]
Selskaya zhizn [Country living]
Semya [Family]
Sintaksis (Paris)
Smena [New Generation] (St. Petersburg)
Sobesednik [Interlocutor]
Sovershenno sekretno [Top secret]
Sovetskaya kultura
Sovetskaya molodezh [Soviet youth]
Sovetskaya Rossiya
Sovetskaya Sibir' [Soviet Siberia]
Srochno v nomer [Stop the presses]
Stolitsa [Capital]
Strana i mir [Country and world] (Munich)
Sudarushka
Teatr
Teatralnaya zhizn' [Theater life]
Trud [Labor]
22 (Jerusalem)
Vechernyaya Moskva [Evening Moscow]
Vek [Century]
Vek XX i mir [20th Century and the World]
Voprosy literatury [Problems of literature]
Vremya i my [Time and us] (New York)
Yevreisky mir [Jewish world] (New York)
Yunost' [Youth]
Zhurnalist
Znamya [Banner]

INDEX